What America's highest leaders had to say about
Jessica Buchanan's dramatic kidnapping and rescue . . .

"Jessica Buchanan was selflessly serving her fellow human beings when she was taken hostage by criminals and pirates who showed no regard for her health and well-being. The United States will not tolerate the abduction of our people, and will spare no effort to secure the safety of our citizens and to bring their captors to justice."

—PRESIDENT BARACK OBAMA

"This successful hostage rescue, undertaken in a hostile environment, is a testament to the superb skills of courageous service members who risked their lives to save others. I applaud their efforts. . . . This mission demonstrates our military's commitment to the safety of our fellow citizens wherever they may be around the world."

—LEON PANETTA, UNITED STATES SECRETARY OF DEFENSE

"Last night's mission, boldly conducted by some of our nation's most courageous, competent, and committed special operations forces, exemplifies United States Africa Command's mission to protect Americans and American interests in Africa. We should remember that Ms. Buchanan . . . [was] working to protect the people of Somalia when violently kidnapped."

—GENERAL CARTER F. HAM, COMMANDING GENERAL,
U.S. AFRICA COMMAND

IMPOSSIBLE ODDS

The Kidnapping of Jessica Buchanan
and Her Dramatic Rescue by SEAL Team Six

JESSICA BUCHANAN AND ERIK LANDEMALM

WITH ANTHONY FLACCO

ATRIA PAPERBACK

NEW YORK   LONDON   TORONTO   SYDNEY   NEW DELHI

To our son, August.

*Before you even existed, you helped us survive
the most trying time in our lives.*

ATRIA PAPERBACK
A Division of Simon & Schuster, Inc.
1230 Avenue of the Americas
New York, NY 10020

First Atria Paperback edition August 2014

ATRIA PAPERBACK and colophon are trademarks of Simon & Schuster, Inc.

For information about special discounts for bulk purchases, please contact
Simon & Schuster Special Sales at 1–866–506–1949 or business@simonandschuster.com.

The Simon & Schuster Speakers Bureau can bring authors to your live event. For more
information or to book an event, contact the Simon & Schuster Speakers Bureau at
1–866–248–3049 or visit our website at www.simonspeakers.com.

Designed by Kyoko Watanabe

Manufactured in the United States of America

10 9 8 7 6 5 4 3 2 1

The Library of Congress has cataloged the hardcover edition as follows:

Buchanan, Jessica.
    Impossible odds : the kidnapping of Jessica Buchanan and her dramatic
rescue by SEAL Team Six / Jessica Buchanan & Erik Landemalm with Anthony
Flacco. — 1st Atria Books hardcover ed.
        p.   cm.
Includes bibliographical references and index.
    1. Buchanan, Jessica—Kidnapping, 2011–2012.   2. Kidnapping victims—
Somalia.   3. Kidnapping—Somalia.   4. Rescues—Somalia.   5. United
States—Armed Forces—Search and rescue operations—Somalia.   I. Landemalm,
Erik.   II. Flacco, Anthony.   III. Title.
    HV6604.S58B83 2013
    364.154092—dc23   2013000485

ISBN 978-1-4767-2516-1
ISBN 978-1-4767-2518-5 (pbk)
ISBN 978-1-4767-2519-2 (ebook)

Contents

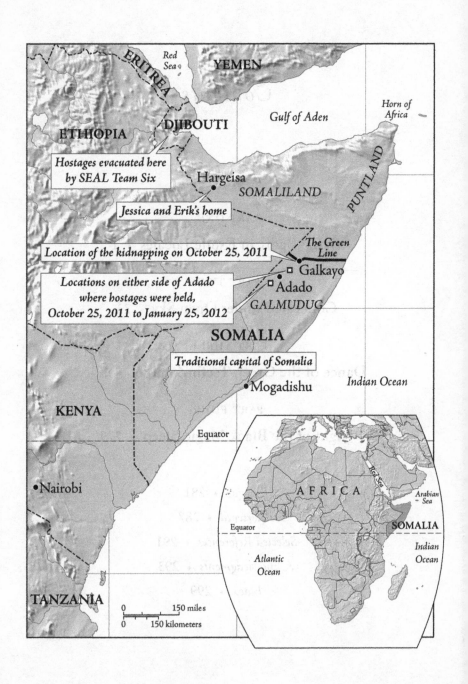

Part One

———

DYING BADLY IN
EXOTIC LOCALES

CHAPTER ONE

Jessica:

Erik tells me for the umpteenth time, "I just don't like it, Jess."

"And I still agree," I tell him. "I've just got no choice."

"Oh, come on. There's always a choice. You can get around it."

"I've canceled three times already and I *can't* get around it, at least not by complaining about security anymore. I'm not sick, so what do I tell them?"

This stops him for a minute, but I can see it does nothing to make him feel better. The sense of danger has gotten to us. It's no help that neither of us has been sleeping well. We acknowledge that much; the question is what to do about it. I know it's not the best time to leave our home in the city of Hargeisa, Somalia, and make the journey 480 miles southeast. My NGO (nongovernmental organization) keeps a field office there, next to a dangerous border called the Green Line separating territories partially controlled by the Islamists from those still controlled by the official Somali government. The Green Line is invisible, known best by the people it divides, never included on official maps of Somalia. I've had my eye on the violence down there for a long time. It isn't something I actively fear; I watch it the way a farmer keeps an eye on the horizon.

3

Our destination is only a short distance from territories controlled by the Islamist group Al-Shabaab, which rules major parts of southern Somalia and imposes Sharia law with terror tactics. Local unrest is potentially explosive, rolling across the region in waves, but I've never been the soldier of fortune type. I started my life in Kenya as a grade school teacher a few years ago and ended up here in Somalia, developing classroom materials for a Danish NGO and working throughout eastern Africa. Our mission is to instruct local people how to avoid the rampant war munitions and land mines that have created a generation of amputees here.

But I realize doing charitable work is no protection from local violence. Criminals are indifferent to social work, and to those who traffic in hate I am a Westerner, which is bad—an American, which is worse, and both my appearance and my occupation are equally repellent in my status as *infidel.* To me this morning's destination feels too close to their home territory, where many of their people are violently opposed to the presence of Westerners in their region. No matter how modestly a Western woman dresses or covers her hair, those who traffic in hate don't see a gesture of cultural cooperation. They see an example of Westerners wearing disguises aimed at lulling the faithful into accepting foreign sacrilege in their homeland. And while bigotry exists all over the world, this is a region where people can really lose their heads over it, generally between the chin and the shoulders.

My continuing concern is getting caught in the crossfire of any one of the countless acts of clan warfare or random hooliganism that plague southern Somalia and keep it in a state of general anarchy. For potential robbers, Westerners may represent a chance at fast money. This is a part of the world where hardly anyone has any, with an average per capita income of $600 USD. Many people have far less. But then that's why we never wander the region without good cause and we always travel with security.

The sticking point is simple: My NGO thinks this is an important staff training session, while on top of my concerns over civil unrest, my husband Erik's concerns are stronger still. He has worked in the local political arena here for the last six years, and his sense of the local mindset is good.

My NGO's plan is for me to fly from Hargeisa to North Galkayo where, for safety, the excursion from North to South is to be made in a three-car caravan. The security caravan is our standard mode of travel, and I'm not at all surprised to be using it now. But what my colleagues have neglected to tell me is that there is a kidnapping threat for expats in the area, and that our destination is situated about five hundred meters from a known pirate den. My sense of dread is strong, even without factoring that into my decision.

Nevertheless, I love my job in spite of these moments of concern. The very fact that it is unsafe is what maintains my concern for the children who have no choice but to live there. Every time I think of quitting, I consider the lives we're saving with this mine awareness program and the mutilations we can prevent in the future with this work.

I realize Erik's back is to the wall with his concern for me. Most of the time he is a big teddy bear who embraces the role of taking care of me, and I can see he's trying hard to do that now. But six months earlier, a busload of passengers—including women and children—was bombed on the same road we'll be using, innocently caught up in someone else's dispute. He reminds me, now; it's only been six months. I have to resist his objections. I tell him (and myself) that in the months since the attack on that bus, the roads between North and South Galkayo have remained calm. I add the helpful fact that earlier today, my NGO's security advisor cleared me for safe travel in that region. After all, if we don't rely on their information we can't do the work.

Shortly before my scheduled departure Erik reluctantly gives in and turns to me with a heavy sigh. "Look, Jess," he tells me, "you know I want you to do the best work you can, to feel right about it. I don't know, maybe I'm being too protective . . ."

I beam back at him. "So you won't be upset with me if I go?"

"I wouldn't go that far," he replies, then laughs and adds, "Of course I can't be upset with you. I get that you need to do this. Just listen, *please*: Don't trust anyone's judgment but your own. Don't trust anything but your own intelligence. Stay aware and listen to your gut feelings."

He takes a deep breath. "So just go get it done and get back here safely and let's move past all this, okay?" He opens his arms for a hug. I throw my arms around him, grateful for his style of loving support. Of course I'm also instantly concerned that this now means the trip is really going to happen.

But neither of us wants to argue; we're secretly nurturing a hopeful glow that after more than two years of marriage and recent efforts to have a baby, I might be pregnant. I'm only a few days late in my cycle, but hopes are high for both of us. I know how much he prefers for us to stay close and cocoon at home, to focus on willing this child into our lives. But part of Erik's loving nature is that he really does want to give me the space I need, so even though it goes completely against the grain for him to relent on this, he somehow manages to send me off with a smile.

My colleague Poul Thisted and I bring along a few small work bags holding computers and training materials, plus one small personal bag apiece. That's about it. He's already left, so I grab a UN flight of several hours to the town of Galkayo. We spend the night at the NGO guesthouse just to the north side of the Green Line, in the safer zone. From there I send Erik two text messages that will always stick in my memory.

If I get kidnapped on this trip, will you come and get me?

He responds, *Nah, of course I will come but nothing will happen!! Make sure it doesn't, ok? Love you too much to even think about that, so make sure you will be super safe.*

"Safe" is a word whose meaning varies in our part of Somalia. I'm continually reminded of that after we arrive at our southern office and the training session plays out. Outbursts of urban violence can be heard all around the building. The gunfire becomes so bad outside the compound, people avoid sitting outside on the veranda for fear of a random bullet strike.

I spend the whole trip eager to be out of there and back home, feeling like time is just dragging along. Of course I do this still unaware of the very long and hard way time can truly drag. So far in life I have experienced time, at its worst, as a form of slow boredom—never as a form of torture.

Once we finish the training session and we're ready to be on our way back to the safer northern zone, I send Erik the second of those two text messages. Sadly, this one is to let him know I'm cramping and it looks like I was wrong about the pregnancy.

Started period :(Guess there's next month. Love you and miss you so much.

I assure myself that we'll just have to keep trying. I'm only thirty-two years old. There's plenty of time—*we have all the time we need.*

Before Erik has a chance to respond, our convoy arrives to whisk us away from the south office and back to our guesthouse on the north side of the Green Line. The distance isn't far, maybe twenty minutes of driving time. It's going to be a relief to get out of there.

And so at 3:00 p.m. on October 25, I toss my small bag in the Land Cruiser and get into the backseat while Poul climbs into the passenger seat in front of me. Abdirizak, our locally hired security manager, climbs into the backseat behind the driver. I've already noticed this driver is new, but I don't know anything about him. Ordinarily, I'd ask for an explanation, but Poul appears to be in a hurry to get going and doesn't show any concern over the driver. I sit there balanced between relative safety or mortal danger and decide I've spoken too much of my concern.

After spending the entire training session eager to be anywhere but there, it feels wrong to second-guess things now. I remain quiet about this unfamiliar driver while the caravan pulls away with us.

It's a routine ride—for about ten minutes.

◆ ◆ ◆

The attack begins as if an umpire has just blown a starting whistle. A large car roars up beside us and careens to a stop, splashing mud all over our windows. Men with AK-47s encircle our car, pounding on the doors, shouting over each other in Somali. Their behavior is ferocious.

My heart goes straight to my throat. Adrenaline sends a jolt of fear from head to toe. The terror feels like heat, like we are suddenly being roasted alive inside this car.

The men scream in hyped-up fury; there are many distinct dialects in Somali, some unintelligible among the various speakers. I can't understand any of it except by trying to read gestures and tones of voice. None of the messages are good.

My brain is seizing up from trying to process this. I hear a little version of my own voice in the back of my skull chanting: *This is really bad this is really bad this is really bad,* and for some reason I can't get myself to stop.

Two Somali men outfitted in Special Protection Unit (SPU) uniforms yank open the doors. They may or may not be real SPU members, in this zone of dubious authority. Whatever they are, the men close behind them have gun barrels trained on us.

I know nothing in this moment except to show no reaction, avoid doing anything that looks aggressive, but also not to cower. Hold still. With or without training, every mouse knows to freeze in the presence of vipers.

The attackers leap into the passenger compartment. One pulls open the rear door and grabs Abdirizak, our useless "security manager," from behind the driver's seat. The attacker looks somewhere between thirty and forty years old. His face is a tarmac of acne scars, punctuated by the crazed eyes of somebody who has had plenty of *khat* leaves to chew that day. The stuff is a stimulant in low doses and a mind-bender at higher doses over time. It's a national scourge because those higher quantities are eventually sought by all regular users.

The attacker will later tell me his name is Ali, though he doesn't just yet, and he is bigger than the average Somali male, maybe 1.8 meters—around six feet in height. His amped behavior is completely intimidating. I turn to our Abdirizak for a little assistance, but that's really grasping at straws, because I can't help but notice good old Abdirizak really could look a lot more surprised. Predictably, he does nothing at all to defend us, and in the next instant the crazy-eyed Ali drags him through his seatbelt and out of the car.

Ali makes a show of beating Abdirizak to the ground to establish superiority, but he doesn't appear to inflict any damage. It's mostly an assault of stark male voices bellowing at the top of their lungs. They behave more like brothers in arms who just happen to be on opposite sides of the fence on this day. Maybe they'll go for a beer tomorrow.

And with that, everything slips into slow motion.

Crazy-eyed Ali climbs in next to me with his AK-47 pointed at my head. The moment plays out in a language of images—he is close enough that I can see the weapon's ammo cartridge, glimpse the bullets, notice there are plenty of them. The beat-up gun is probably older than I am. I imagine it's been used to kill plenty of people.

My body constricts, moving on its own with the expectation of being shot. The other attacker scrambles through the rear hatch, and our last line of hope for escape collapses when our "this-is-my-first-day" driver reveals who he is really working for. He speeds away with us like a furious drunk, slamming us around in the passenger compartment while Ali screams the first English word to us I have heard so far:

"Mobile!" (meaning our cell phones) and then, "Thuraya!" (satellite cell phones). He and his cohort wave their gun barrels in our faces as if there's a chance we haven't noticed who's in charge.

The fact that they immediately rob us actually calms me, a bit. *Maybe they're just going to carjack us. Maybe they'll push us out, take the vehicles, the cash, and drive away!* A rash of carjackings has recently occurred in nearby Kenya where victims were simply driven to distant locations and pushed out, but left otherwise unharmed and allowed to walk back home. So if we're simply being robbed and carjacked, then walking home suddenly sounds like a great way to finish off the day.

And in that fashion my name is changed to "Alice" and I am plunged through the looking glass. Here inside the mirror world, the notion of a gunpoint robbery passes for positive thinking.

The vehicle plunges out into the wilderness, slamming over rough roads. There is no way to avoid wondering whether an impact with a pothole will cause one of these slaughter weapons to go off. I still have no idea who has attacked us, but the way they're bouncing us around, it might not matter. All we need is for one hard bump to meet one careless trigger finger, and there we are: dead or maimed in the middle of this horror show. For all I know the only upshot to that would be Mr. Crazy Eyes giggling over our corpses and exclaiming the Somali equivalent of "oops . . ."

As soon as Ali takes our phones, he decides Poul should sit in the back next to me while he climbs into the passenger seat—just Ali and the driver with Poul and me behind them, plus one creepy-looking little guy who jumps into the very back and starts going through our belongings.

For a moment, I lock eyes with Poul and silently mouth the words, "What's happening?"

He answers in a soft, grim voice, "We're being kidnapped." The words are so quiet I can barely hear them, but they feel like they were shot out of a nail gun.

The men scream at Poul to shut up and force him to turn around. We don't need to speak their language to understand their commands for silence. They keep whipping out cell phones to call distant cohorts, shouting at the top of their voices.

Still, even here in these first few moments, it seems apparent to me that their level of hysteria far exceeds the need. After all, they pulled off their first phase without a hitch. They have us in a clean capture and they escaped without a struggle. No one is in pursuit, as far as I can tell. But from their behavior, you'd think the guns were being held to their heads, not ours.

This hysteria is surely fueled by their *khat* use, amplifying their emotions. But they have us, and that's the truth of it. The result is that every skill and ability I possess has been pulled away. Nothing else I know is of any use, in this moment. Nothing I can do in my working life is relevant here. The person I am to my loved ones, my husband, my friends, doesn't mean anything. My colleague and I are objects of pursuit, nothing more.

The glaring difference between Poul's situation and my own is both simple and deadly. Poul is a sixty-year-old Danish male and I'm a thirty-two-year-old American female. The proverbial elephant is not only in the middle of the room, it's high on *khat* leaves and waving automatic weapons. Homophobia is dominant there, so Poul has little reason to fear gang rape. But I do. And while the news media here did carry that story of mobs protesting outside the Danish Embassy after the uproar over cartoon images of the Prophet Mohammed, in most neighborhoods there is generally not the same danger in being Danish as in being American.

As the only female here, my local experience curses me with the knowledge of what has happened to many other women, Somali or otherwise, taken by these roving gangs of criminals. The horrible irony of my recent attempts to get pregnant with Erik is not lost on me.

All that remains of me as I know myself, in this moment, is this little voice chanting *this is really bad this is really bad*. The thought is just too awful, that I might die with my joking text message to Erik about getting "kidnapped" now playing out in earnest. Regardless of what I think I can accept, the attackers continue screaming orders and arguments back and forth, always seeming to be in conflict over something or other.

"Money!" Ali now bellows, waving at us to give him ours. For some odd reason, Poul responds to their demand by claiming not to have any. I wonder what he intends to say if they search us and find it. Fortunately, they let it go for the moment. Ali gestures to our few pieces of jewelry and shouts something in Somali that we can tell is a command to part with our bling. I start to remove my chunky necklace of costume jewelry, but he sneers and shakes his head. They only want the good stuff. My rattling hippie junk is of no interest.

I'm worried about losing my wedding band and a diamond of my mom's that was given to me after her passing. I am somehow able to make my shaking hand still enough to palm the diamond down into my bag, and then offer Ali a less precious ring.

At first it seems to work. But my heart sinks when he confiscates my bag and keeps it at his side. He'll obviously go through it at some point and catch on to my ruse, leaving me in the same dangerous position Poul just assumed. I can only hope when he finds the diamond it might make him happy enough to forget about my attempt to deceive him.

Beyond that I can't move. All I can do is struggle to recall anything useful from our pitifully brief hostage training session, which was taken from a larger program called HEIST, for Hostile Environment Individual Safety Training. I rack my brains for every scrap of information given to us, wishing I had memorized it all.

The HEIST instructors impressed on us the importance of hiding our anger and avoiding any unnecessary conflict. They stressed that attackers will likely be in such an excitable state, they may be provoked into killing even if they don't plan to. The trainers urged everyone to memorize a reliable phone number of someone who would be the right person to receive a "proof of life" phone call. Their reasoning was grimly practical—the only way to aid your own survival in a kidnapping is to have a line to a potential ransom source. Your chance for life is your captor's hope for money.

Coming up with a phone contact is the easy part. There's no chance I'd forget Erik's number. But I also can't help but recall the instructor's warning that a "proof of life" call only matters if a kidnapping is done for money.

If we are being taken by ideologues who are out to make a political or religious statement, then there is nothing to be done for us. In that case, our only purpose here will be to endure a gruesome public execution.

Ideological attackers in this region will almost certainly be forces of Al-Shabaab. I try not to obsess over how they would use our torture and death to spread their message, but I've seen the same internet videos of doomed hostages as everyone else. The kindest end brought to those victims was the cessation of pain and terror with a single gunshot. If this is a death squad, that's the best we can hope for, here in this twisted mirror world where oblivion translates as mercy. I think any American adult living abroad knows of journalist Daniel Pearl, snatched from the streets and butchered alive in horrifying close-up video. Too many other horror shows have taken place since then, and so far there's nothing to indicate this isn't going to be another one.

Meanwhile the car slams its way along the primitive roadways.

My head and shoulders keep colliding with the door frame. I silently push myself, *Think! Think!* I recall the main point of HEIST is to focus on surviving the first twenty-four hours. After that, survival percentages surge upward. If we can get through the first day, we might have a shot at entering that small golden ratio of people who actually come out of these things alive.

Some do come out alive, I silently tell myself. *The numbers are small, but they do exist.* Of course at this point we aren't through the first hour yet, let alone the first day, so the twenty-four-hour tip is of no immediate help.

Ali wants everything Poul is carrying. He even demands the ballpoint pen in Poul's front pocket. For some reason Poul refuses. I wonder, *What is he doing? Is it a male thing?* He's an old hand at the humanitarian expat life, and in his world you stand up to the man. Squawk back to authority.

I try to ignore their little spat so it won't seem as if we're acting in concert by refusing to cooperate, but out of the corner of my eye I see Ali rip the pen out of Poul's pocket. He makes it a point to stare back at Poul as if daring him to do anything about it while he carefully dismantles the pen into its various pieces, then tosses them out the window. I can feel reality being twisted through some kind of terrible grinder. We're up against schoolyard bullies carrying the weapons of mass murderers. I haven't realized until this moment, when I see Poul's tough-guy routine fail, that I've been hoping it would actually work.

Still no word on what their intentions may be. We don't know who these people are and we can't tell where they are taking us. The horror show proceeds to that point and pauses, as far as any information about what is actually going on here. After that, things happen but nothing changes. Time drips, while the sickly awareness of how toxic and deadly the situation is builds up in my blood.

Hours move along at a slow crawl, and still nothing gives away their intentions. All Poul and I can do is exchange troubled glances. After a while I stop looking. It only makes things worse.

We stop several times and are forced to change into different vehicles. Somewhere during our ride in the third one, the sound of a certain voice inside the car finally registers on me. It's so high and thin it could be female. I turn around to see instead a young boy who appears to be about eight or nine years old. He's dressed like the others, in a billowing shirt over those loose trousers that are the alternative to saronglike *macawiis*. This child copies the older men's fashion of wearing his traditional shawl around his head like a turban. The obvious joke about him being a miniature kidnapper doesn't work at all. The sight of him is twisted and wrong.

I wonder, *Is he the son of one of these men? My God, is this kid here to learn a trade? The strangeness of this amps me up tighter. My muscles feel as if they're about to start snapping my bones. The feeling doesn't wear off.*

The afternoon bleeds into evening while we go through a process of making a series of stops, one impoverished-looking location after another. The kidnappers go through elaborate changes in personnel and vehicles for reasons that I can't fathom, and that Poul and I aren't allowed to discuss. Whatever is happening, there are certainly a lot of people involved in this operation.

I have to wonder. *All this for us?*

Every time we change cars or drivers, armed enforcers hop in carrying huge chains of ammunition around their shoulders. I can only guess that these personnel changes have something to do with various clan members guaranteeing safe passage from one contested territory to the next. Here again, this implies a large amount of preorganization. It demonstrates complex maneuvering on somebody's part.

But these guys behave like morons. They must be acting out a plan controlled by somebody smarter. Needless to say, my attempt to rationalize this as a simple carjacking and robbery hasn't survived the evening. This isn't just some local gang.

I've worked in the region long enough to understand our kidnapping presents dangers far beyond whatever intentions drive these men. A greater risk is that if we are spotted by a larger group, we could be kidnapped a second time—maybe by unorganized opportunists and thugs, or perhaps by people convinced they represent the will of their God. If that occurs—and it suddenly feels like it easily could—this lunatic game will become even more deadly.

But by this point in the night I've been convinced the scope of the operation makes it clear—at least to me, since I can't discuss it with anybody—that either we are in the hands of the same people who control the Somali pirates at sea and who have moved their ransom schemes onto land, or this is an Al-Shabaab operation.

I remember breakfast this morning. It was normal.

In this fashion, "likely to die" meets "certain to die" and finds us trapped between them. We continue late into the night, rattling along over roads of inconsistent quality. I'm feeling all the little places where the bruising is beginning set in. Eventually the kidnappers seem to get some invisible clue among themselves and pull our latest vehicle to a stop.

This time it's different. There's nothing here. And now Ali demands that we both get out. Until that moment, sleepy boredom was just beginning to fill me. Now it instantly gives way to a cold rush of fear. It's a bad one, like freezing and boiling at the same time.

"Walk!" Ali shouts, pointing out into the open scrub land. Then, just in case we haven't heard, he shouts again, "Walk!"

With that, he stomps off and disappears. Ali is not coming on our "walk" with us. But I have to believe he really has left us. We appear to be in the middle of nowhere, but he moves off like someone who knows his destination. Anyone would recognize his movements as the intention to be gone.

His job has apparently just been to lead the muscle attackers in grabbing and delivering us here to this place that looks like every other. With that done, his part must be complete. So he's likely off now to collect his fee from whoever is behind this. I hate to lose a translator, but he doesn't seem like the conversational type.

After that, everything is shouted in Somali. There isn't even an occasional English word to clarify a meaning. It doesn't really matter. The language difference doesn't shield us from knowing what they want of us from one moment to the next.

And now rough shouts and the waving of gun barrels make the message all too clear—they repeat Ali's order for us to start walking away from the vehicle. *So he wasn't just being melodramatic about his exit; they actually want us to head out into the scrub desert.*

I can't keep quiet anymore. Somebody here has to understand me, understand my intentions if not my words. "Why?" I cry out, trying to look each man in the eyes. "Why go there? There's nothing out there!" Now I'm crying, but no tears are allowed. Everybody out here has a broken heart; what they don't have is money.

To me, this new development has all the earmarks of a prelude to an execution. My stomach is a ball of ice. I refuse to go, clinging to my spot while the men scream orders. Every one of them appears loaded on *khat*. Their eyes are completely bloodshot and they're hyped to frantic levels.

I feel desperate to stall them for no more reason than the sheer terror of the moment. I point at the small suitcase they took from me and try to get them to understand, "There is a little black bag inside and I need to bring it with me. Medicine!" I cry, pointing at the bag. "It has my medicine!" I have to regulate my thyroid levels with regular medication. Without it, the wheels tend to come off as far as the rest of my physical system goes: deep fatigue, rising inflammation, obviously a long-term problem and none of this is related to the moment, but I'm grasping at shadows.

I stare into unblinking faces. "Medicine! I need my medicine!"

With Ali gone, I don't know if anybody here will even bother to try to understand me, but I repeat over and over, "I need my medicine!" while I point at the large bag, scraping for any way to convey the information. Finally somebody seems to catch on and I'm allowed to go remove my small powder bag. There is absolutely nothing I will actually need if we're about to be put to death. But I'll grab at anything to slow this down. So the bag, sure, the little bag, got to have the little bag.

I am still too petrified to obey their commands. The moment hangs like a pendulum at the tip of its arc. Then I see movement in the corner of one eye. Poul slips over to me and gently takes my arm. "It's all right, Jessica," he quietly lies. "It'll be all right. Come on. We have to do what they tell us."

"Poul, no!" I whisper. "We can't go out there! They'll kill us!"

Why doesn't he see that? We cannot go out there. We can't go.

"Jessica, listen . . . no matter what they have in mind, unless we cooperate we'll have ourselves a fatal confrontation, right here."

I look around at the other men. Several have their rifles trained on us. *They will slaughter us as easily as blowing away a mountain goat.* The truth of this registers with a part of the brain that's been around for a long time. There is no hope in this moment except to perhaps earn another few minutes of life.

I check Poul to see if he's come up with any great ideas in the past couple of seconds, then look around one last time at the useless "safety" of the vehicle . . . and give up. Now the only control I have over anything here is to attempt to keep from dissolving into hysterics, if for no other reason than to avoid letting my life end that way.

So we walk off into the wilderness. "I'm too young to die," I blurt out to Poul. He gives me a blank look and keeps on walking. I know by panicking this way I must seem weak, but there is nothing I can do about how I feel. I keep my mouth shut from that point on, while my obsessive inner voice switches from reminding me how bad this is, to: *I'm too young to die, I'm too young to die,* repeated in a loop.

The men fall in behind us. My God, there are a couple of dozen, at least. And those are heavy machine guns carried by some of them. A few of the men also have those long belts of ammunition I've been seeing all day, slung over their shoulders. The caliber of the bullets is very large.

I want to scream out at them. *You think you need enough artillery to stage a military assault, just for me and Poul? What's the matter with you?*

What do they think we're going to do? Do they really believe we might make some sort of hero play? I don't even know karate.

I have to think. Clear my head. Have we done something terrible without knowing it, some cultural mistake? Do they think we've got something to do with their enemies, whoever their enemies happen to be?

Because otherwise, what possible purpose could it serve to use up this much manpower on the two of us? Why would anybody commit these sorts of weapons for two unarmed humanitarian aid workers?

Right there, the thought occurs: Heavy weapons only make sense if they are there for protection. But what would other attackers want that these men have? Well, there are the guns, the ammunition, and of course, there's always Poul and me.

The heavy weapons aren't there to keep us from running away. They're there to keep us from being stolen. This thing is closing in around us like a cave-in.

They move us farther into the scrub desert and keep us walking out there for a long time. The night air is quickly cooling off. I'm shivering steadily now and can't stop. We are walking in the middle of the group and all moving quickly. I guess that's good, since it helps to generate a little body heat. Poul is close by, but we are forbidden to speak.

The darkness is heavy, no moon, no ambient light. The sky is crystal clear and the stars are brilliant, comforting in their familiarity. Nothing else about this situation or these people is familiar in the least.

We stumble between the low thorn bushes. I'm not wearing boots or sneakers, but at least my heavy sandals are tough enough to stand up to the terrain. Still I keep scraping the tops of my feet on low-hanging branches.

A river of small noises follows along with us. People recognize it from war movies. Soldiers call it battle rattle: the sounds of dozens of guns and ammunition belts being carried by dozens of men. Even if they aren't talking, these men are putting out that low undercurrent of metallic noises. I suddenly hate the fact that my taste for clunky large necklaces and bracelets too cheap for kidnappers to bother stealing means that I now make similar sounds. I'm harmonizing along with their battle rattle and for some reason I am angry about it. There's nothing to be done with the anger, so it just adds to the curdling sourness out here.

I can't keep myself from crying in fear, but I do my best to keep it quiet. Some of the men talk in low voices, but most of them just march along. They seem particularly grim. I wonder if they know something to be grim about.

The young boy appears close to me, walking along and toting his AK-47 like a toy. I've heard him called Abdilahi by some of the men. It sounds familiar enough; the name "Abdi" is used on its own and as a prefix to longer names by many men in the region.

Abdilahi jumps over next to me and snorts in derision. He gets close enough for me to see him pointing his rifle at me. He makes a few shooting noises, and this amuses him to the point of laughter. I don't know what to do in response, so I simply turn away and avoid anything that would invite interaction. Even for his tender years, Abdilahi is far gone in both his *khat* use symptoms and his child soldier mentality. The wild eyes, the speeded appearance, the unformed brain of an adolescent *khat* addict are all over him. Abdilahi is what your brain looks like on drugs.

Fortunately, something else grabs his fleeting attention, and he fades off into the dark. It's good to have him go, but it doesn't stop my obsessive inner voice from continuing to spout my fears in variations of *This is really bad* and *I'm too young to die.*

There is sharp pain pulsing in both my feet from the ground obstacles, but there is also an odd form of reassurance to that. I'm gasping at life like a fish on the beach, and pain at least is evidence of being alive. This isn't a hallucination in Hell; I'm still alive so far.

Finally, we reach some random place that looks no different from anywhere else out there, but either the men have decided this is our destination or else they simply agree we've gone far enough. Far enough for what?

This is it . . .

A life that ends this way expires in a daze of confusion. There is some small measure of comfort in this confusion, some shielding of awareness. The mind searches for a reason, any reason at all, to believe what is happening somehow isn't real. For me, denial doesn't help. The machine guns around us are all too real. These men are the spitting image of those familiar terrorists on internet videos—standing in the background with scarves and sleeping sheets wrapped around their faces while the captives get slaughtered like livestock.

Straining my eyes in the darkness, I see that some of these men's weapons seem like long-bladed knives whipping by while we stumble along. There's no way to tell whether the long thin shapes are gun barrels or blades. I don't want to think they're about to execute us by beheading, but I'm scrambling for any other explanation for all this. I am on a terrain of fear I've never known.

When beheading is the goal, a modicum of respect is granted if a single swing of a long blade is used, assuring instant death. But special contempt is expressed by sawing through the throat with a long cooking blade, assuring a fully conscious experience for the victim.

I know nothing else to do but scream to God in absolute vocal silence. I silently scream with all of my heart and soul, knowing full well I will not be able to scream once they slice in hard across my throat. *God almighty! To endure this piece of Hell . . .*

My blood inches through me like frozen slush. If there's a personal terror more extreme, I hope to never feel it. All I can do now is to keep silently telling myself I'm too young to die. A few times I whisper the words. For the rest I just repeat it internally, as if it's a protective mantra: *too young to die, too young to die, too young to die.* I whisper prayers for mercy, for strength.

I can't imagine never seeing Erik again. It seems completely unreal for our future to be stolen from us in this way.

And then the attackers order us to get down onto our knees and turn our backs to them.

CHAPTER TWO

Within hours of the kidnapping, President Barack Obama received a security briefing letting him know a thirty-two-year-old American humanitarian aid worker named Jessica Buchanan had been snatched off a roadway in southern Somalia, along with a sixty-year-old male Danish colleague. The NGO had informed the American Embassy in Nairobi about the incident, which triggered the case with the FBI and notice to the White House. Apparently the emerging philosophy in that region was to ask, "Why not start kidnapping Americans right along with everyone else? Equal opportunity misery for everybody."

Still, the fact that it had actually been done electrified underground news lines. The early information was sketchy, but from the opening details it was clear this case represented a whole new threat level in Somalia. There was no provocation to the attack; this woman had been in the region teaching children for several years and also worked for a Danish NGO instructing local people how to avoid deadly war munitions. Her work was nonpolitical and nonreligious. As a statement of utter defiance of American authority, the kidnappers could hardly have picked a worse victim. The actions were the international equivalent of

23

hard fighting words, along with a high-stakes gambler's bet that this American president might rattle a saber or two but would ultimately do nothing to stop the criminals behind the operation.

The takeaway for the president was that the Somali pirates had graduated from seizing merchant ships on the high seas and were now seizing innocent people on land. Moreover, they were willing to capture American civilians—even those in their country peacefully working on behalf of the local population. As the president's experts were also aware, the percentage of survivors in such cases was very low. These two captives were reportedly surrounded by dozens of heavily armed men. These were impossible odds.

◆ ◆ ◆

Approximately one hour after the kidnapping, Jessica's husband, Erik, still had no indication of trouble. He was about to head off to a workout over in the small city of Garowe, about a hundred miles north of where Jess was working, when the call came in from Dan Hardy, the regional security advisor for Jess's NGO. His voice sounded so upset it caused Erik's adrenaline to spike before he caught any details. He quickly got the main message that his wife, Jessica, had been kidnapped. It hit him like a haymaker to the face.

Dan Hardy went on with details, but Erik couldn't seem to take it in. His head jammed on the thought, *After everything we talked about and everything we feared, it's actually happened?* It simply couldn't be true. But Hardy went on to explain that unknown forces had somehow waylaid the caravan, probably using overwhelming numbers. The NGO was already forming a Crisis Management Team and they felt certain she had survived the initial assault. Nobody could say where she was. They assumed she was still alive at this hour but couldn't confirm it.

Erik found himself standing on the roof veranda trying to get a better cell signal and shouting, "What are you saying, Dan? What are you saying?" But there was nowhere to turn for more information. There was nothing to do but wait to be contacted, hope to be contacted, pray to be contacted with word that Jessica was alive.

Dan Hardy told him all they could do was keep quiet and say nothing at all, publicly, do nothing to give these kidnappers any information that might be turned against the families. Beyond that, every other thought ended in a question mark.

He felt the specter of death throw his love for Jessica into strong relief, along with a dark wave of guilt over allowing her to talk him out of his position against the trip. This news threw him up against the cold truth that simply fearing the worst doesn't protect you from it. He now had to face the terrible fact that he had willingly kissed her good-bye.

Erik hung up and immediately began a call to Jessica's father, John Buchanan, who lived in Virginia. He cringed at the thought of dumping this news on a single, isolated man who had been living alone since his wife's passing and would absorb this news on his own. John had married his high school sweetheart. After both experienced a spiritual rebirth, they raised their family in a Christian household. It was strict, but not overbearing, and the family was supported across the years by John's skills as an expert woodworker carving period furniture.

John taught his spiritual message by example while independently earning his way with his own handiwork, loving his wife and family. Then came a vicious strain of flu, just fifteen months ago. She fell sick fast and hard. The end came for her within three days.

While it would be natural for Jessica's dad to reach out to his closest friends and relatives for support, it was vital to close down as much public information as possible, as fast as it could be done. Erik expected the commercial media in the United States to find Jess's father.

He was so shaken he placed the call before thinking up a clear strategy for revealing this dreadful information. As soon as John Buchanan got on the line he decided there was no reason to withhold anything.

"John, it's Erik . . . John, I don't know how to say this, but I have some very difficult news. Dan Hardy, the security advisor over at Jess's NGO, just called . . . John, they believe Jess and one of her colleagues were kidnapped this afternoon."

There was a pause, then John's quiet voice: "God in Heaven. Not Jess . . ."

"John, I, I want you to know, there's no reason to believe she isn't still alive." His fingers were damp and his hand was shaking. It was hard to keep a grip on the phone.

"Is there a reason to doubt it?"

"No, no! They were clear about that part. But you know she's so smart and resourceful, and she's received special training for things like this."

"Do they know why she was taken? Or where she is?"

"They know more than they're willing to tell me, for security reasons, but the security advisor thinks it was done for money, not to make an anti-American statement or anything like that."

"What can I do besides pray for her? Is there anything you need?"

Erik thought about the famed Somali gossip lines running through every level of their society, as old as the people there, an invisible network linking families, friends, and cohorts all across eastern Africa. He considered the fact that each and every one of those kidnappers also had family and friends. Any one of them could be a source of information passed on about Jess to somehow use against her or against her negotiators.

"I think we should all keep in mind that her kidnappers might try to get personal information on her, to force ransom negotiations in one way or another, and we shouldn't help them."

"So we need to keep this quiet?"

"Please. Completely. You can never tell where something could leak out. Her NGO is putting together a Crisis Management Team, and as soon as I have a number for them, I'll put you in touch."

Erik could hear the concern in her father's tone, but the older man kept his voice strong. "I'm so glad you're there for her, Erik. Please, if there's anything I can do . . ."

"Just keep up good thoughts, John. We've got no reason to think this was done to make a public statement of some kind."

Of course he didn't know that for certain. And he couldn't tell if his words sounded as hollow to her father as they did to him. If so, he noted that John Buchanan was the kinder of them for not mentioning it.

There was little more to say but to exchange awkward assurances. After he hung up, he found the call most notable for what John Buchanan didn't say: *You promised to take care of my daughter!* Erik wouldn't have blamed an anguished father for jumping to that thought, but he heard nothing but concern in her father's voice. It eased the guilt but didn't make it go away. The older man's generosity of spirit made him feel as if he had swallowed a lump of iron.

Shortly after he hung up on that call, his cell phone rang again.

"Hello?"

"Is this Erik Landemalm?"

"Yes, who is—"

"Agent Matt Espenshade with the FBI Legal Attaché Office in Nairobi. But please call me Matt. Anyway, we're responsible for investigating major crimes against Americans here."

". . . Yes. Uh, hello, Matt."

"I just want to check in with you, let you know we're on this."

"Holy . . . I mean, who called you? I *just* found out myself!"

"Yes. Now while we wait to be contacted with their ransom demand, is there anything special you need from us?"

"Is there going to be a ransom demand?"

"If there's a crime against an innocent American citizen, there will be an FBI foreign office responsible for that region. It's our job to oversee live investigations. That's why you're hearing from me and not someone from the Agency. The CIA goes after political players, military players. We step in when American citizens get snared in local crime."

"I'm serious; is there going to be a ransom demand?"

"Of course that's what we hope for."

"But will there be one?"

"Well, these things tend to resolve one of two ways: ransom or rescue."

"Then you mean one of three ways, yes?"

"Let's think positive."

Erik felt the wiggle room in that reply, and his stomach sank. "Okay." He exhaled a deep breath. "Well, I'm amazed you guys responded so fast, that's all. And that's great. It's great. But listen, first of all you need to understand that Jess isn't some idiot backpacker, taking risks out there for nothing. This is her life's work. She didn't even want to go near the Green Line, but she felt pushed to do it. And now this has happened."

"We know about her background. I'm working on this along with my full staff. I want you to know that when we open a case, it *will not end* until she is back with you. Now, what can we do for you at this point? Have you been in touch with her family?"

"I've spoken with her father, but I don't know how he and Jess's family will hold up. Can someone from FBI contact them to assure them you're on this case?"

"We've already sent a car over there with colleagues of mine who are trained to take care of situations like this."

"Oh. Wow. Thanks. I appreciate . . ."

It hit him then. He felt a sudden rush of dread. He had no proof this guy calling himself "Matt" was an FBI agent at all. What if he was a snoop from the media?

Far worse, what if this "Matt" person was from the kidnapper's organization, using a ruse to extract information? And there was Erik, chatting away as if he actually knew the guy. The dread surged so abruptly he nearly got sick to his stomach.

He asked the person calling himself "Matt" for a callback number so he could verify his identity, then hung up and called back through the American Embassy. There was a long wait for a pickup, but he soon breathed a sigh of relief when the guy calling himself "Matt" got back on the line.

So Matt Espenshade was really with the FBI team handling this, and there was a small group of very good agents working together to gather intelligence on these kidnappers. With that much reassurance in place, it felt good to have a safe source of information.

The unreal knowledge that the U.S. government was now actively tracking the pack of thugs who had taken Jess captive offered some immediate consolation, but with a little more time and thought he was left with the conclusion that he had no idea what the FBI could actually do about any of this.

But he also realized his state of overload was so severe, he didn't know what to make of anything. He only knew he had to stay firmly in a functional mode or he would lose control of his emotions and do something rash. He could already feel the rising urge to personally rush down to the spot where Jess had been taken and start tracking her down.

Matt went on, "Now, Erik, listen to me—you can't do anything *proactive* here."

"What do you mean?"

"You can't try to insert yourself into this. Even the best-trained professionals find it extremely difficult to get these things to play out right. If we get family members involved, you can slow the process. Anything you do can be counterproductive to our goal of getting her back. Or you'll get yourself captured and just ramp up the danger to everybody."

"Matt, I did counter-special ops in the military. I've got friends who'll join me down here. It's my responsibility to get her out. I'm her husband—and what if something happened to the soldiers who get sent in after her? I know Jess couldn't live with that, and neither could I."

"It's no better for you and your friends to die. You have to listen to me, Erik. Do nothing. I know it's the last thing you want to hear. But do nothing. . . . Tell me you understand me, here."

"I can't believe I'm hearing this! Matt, I need to get her out of there!"

"And I realize the helpless feeling is the worst part. It's in your DNA to charge in and get her, especially if you have resources in the area. Not only that, I have to admit this part doesn't get better over time. I know it sounds completely backward for you to stand down, Erik. It would to me. But you *cannot* insert yourself into this."

Erik felt the jaws of a vise tightening on his throat. "Matt, I just, I just want to tell you, I hope to God you guys really will get on this. We need the U.S. government behind us. How am I supposed to rely on the local authorities to rescue her? I know the ways of this region. They can't even keep order in the streets. We both know the local authorities could be involved, themselves! How can you ask me to do nothing?"

"Okay, here's how I can ask: What you do is, ask yourself how it would be for Jessica—out there alone and surrounded by hostiles—if she heard you attempted a rescue and got yourself killed? What is she supposed to do then? Can you even imagine her despair?"

The question sucked all the air out of the room. The call was quickly over.

Within hours, the couple's immediate family members began a series of calls back and forth among their own group, burning up the long-distance lines to help pull each other back from panic. They asked the same questions of one another without arriving at any answers. They learned hardly anything, but gained some measure of relief in being able to speak among themselves.

Erik was especially grateful for the company of the other family members, even if just by phone, to keep him from buckling under the combination of primal fear and forced paralysis. He felt certain he couldn't have kept the secret alone. So he got to work at closing down her social media sites. If they forced her to turn over the passwords, they could get all sorts of information and then use it to somehow strengthen their position. He knew of instances in which family members had been individually contacted by kidnappers and played off against one another to jack up the price.

Erik greatly regretted in those hours that he knew so much about the sorts of medieval torments the male criminals of that broken culture might inflict upon his wife. Against that toxic knowledge he could only apply his own insights. In addition to avoiding the media, he also determined to keep it secret in their home region and avoid discussing anything in the presence of his Somali staff. The strength of the fabled gossip lines in that country was not to be doubted, and even the most innocent-sounding information about Jessica might fan the flames in unpredictable ways.

Unfortunately his efforts didn't do much to slow down the flow of information. Within hours, a number of his colleagues from the local population began stopping by to express their concern over Jess's disappearance. He was touched by their show of sympathy, but it was a jolt to see how efforts to restrict information did nothing. He smiled and thanked them on auto-pilot, eager to regain his privacy.

A new fear hit—the telephone. Had he already managed to make things worse for Jess simply by using the phone? For all he knew, the kidnappers might have tapped his line to track the family's strategy and siphon the same information he'd been pulling down from the internet. When desperation is everywhere, great profits can be made by eavesdropping. In Somalia, freelance spying is a cash-and-carry business.

He had to wonder—how much of a bribe would you have to pay somebody at their phone carrier's office to pull that off? Maybe twelve hundred dollars? Two years' wages. After all, how many people who work at a phone company in a developed country would refuse to grant unauthorized access to a single phone line in return for two years' wages?

Just take a break for a coffee and let us put a tap on this line, then forget you ever saw us.

If they'd already hacked his phone, then he had been helping them just by talking to their families or the FBI. He resolved to make it a point to deal with the authorities in person whenever it involved sensitive information.

So he was left with the long wait for a ransom call and the knowledge that if Jessica was carried too far south of the Green Line, she was unlikely to return alive. In spite of the fact that nobody could see the Green Line and it held no official status, it was one of the most important borders on the African Horn. With the economy of that region broken, desperation lurked amid civil chaos. The kidnapping itself was a crime of opportunity. Erik's and Jessica's good intentions had somehow exposed her vulnerability and desperate people had seized upon that.

Paranoia became the order of the day.

CHAPTER THREE

OCTOBER 1993

Jessica Buchanan was fourteen years old and living in rural Ohio in October of 1993 when the "Blackhawk Down" ambush of two American Special Forces choppers took place in Mogadishu, Somalia. The helicopter crews had thought themselves protected because they were in the country to guarantee aid shipments to the people. Instead, Delta Team Master Sergeant Randy Shughart was pinned down there and used up his ammo to provide as much covering fire as he could for team members who were too badly wounded to defend themselves. Shughart died without knowing he would be awarded the Medal of Honor.

In the following days, the Western world blanched at the searing images of dead American soldiers dragged through the streets, bodies violated by screaming mobs of young Somali men. It's natural to imagine the emotional effect on the American people because the dead men were their own, but as it happened, there were other places around the world where private citizens were also appalled and greatly concerned.

One of those places was in Sweden, in the household of Johan

Landemalm and his wife, Lena, their young daughter, Linnea, and their seventeen-year-old son, Erik. The household took sharp note of that story because Erik was already considering a life in international aid work. Thus Somalia's surprise failure of money-and-food diplomacy was of special concern to him.

Erik had the same view shared by many people of the region, namely a personal appreciation for negotiated positions, instead of the confront-and-conquer mentality. He loved the image of well-negotiated agreements forming paper bridges to carry opposing sides away from the sort of warlike contests that get sponsored by whichever hothead is in charge.

His concern was a natural product of his upbringing. Erik's parents were not only vocal supporters of beleaguered people throughout their own country, they also held sympathies that extended to any group of nonwarlike people. They amplified Erik's concern by observing that the tragedy went much deeper than a loss of American soldiers; the ambush spoke out loudly against the rule of sanity and reason. The rule of mob violence called into serious question an entire system for capping the wells of passion in international conduct.

His background supported that worldview. Swedes have survived on the concept of neutrality, and have long kept a wary eye on international politics, living as they do in a small country vulnerable to European warfare.

Unlike other passing news stories, this one got to Erik. He was otherwise consumed with his junior year of high school, in days filled with his passion for soccer and for spending time with a wide circle of friends, so remote disasters seldom had much impact on his life. This one was different. The Somali massacre made his dream seem naïve, and he hated the feeling that it was merely some callow, boyish fantasy to think he might one day actually work to help boost the process of peaceful reason among nations.

In spite of the distances and cultural differences separating

Erik's family in Sweden and Jessica's in America, his parents were just as concerned about instilling a strong moral code in their children as Jessica's folks were. His father worked as a specialist machinist in the nuclear industry and his mother taught special education programs for adults. While the driving motive in Erik's life wasn't a matter of spirituality, as it was for Jessica's Christian family, it was strongly propelled by the desperate straits of so many of the world's people. His parents lived out the reality of their social concern, which was to *do something* with one's time in this world, in this life, and make things better for others.

They didn't need to force lectures on him; he witnessed their daily commitment to standing against unfair social forces in favor of the health and dignity of the individual. He observed that in his household, such sentiments were not matters of table talk but of practical and proper survival.

In this fashion, as early as 1993, the lives of both Jessica and Erik were already charting a course to intersect. The forces at work had begun to weave the invisible net that would ensnare them, first as individuals and later as a couple.

◆　◆　◆

During the same hours of 1993 when the chopper crews in Somalia were slowly being overpowered and gunned down, there were twenty-four young boys back in the United States who would grow up to be future players in that African struggle. They had no way to know anything yet about the unique fighting group every one of them would eventually strive with all his determination to join. They also couldn't know, though they would one day find out in person, that this particular battle corps is so elite, the candidate must first be a Navy SEAL just to attempt to get through the training—and even then, three out of four of those superb warrior-athletes fail to qualify.

The group has had numerous military names during its long rise from the murky history of the early "frogmen" swimmers, to the black operations of the Underwater Demolition Teams whose only calling card was to render their targets dead, to the latest appellation as the U.S. Naval Special Warfare Development Group—or DEVGRU, for those who prefer names ugly and short. But the group is better known to the general public as the near-mythical warriors of "SEAL Team Six." Their complex training supports a brilliantly simple task: to be the very last thing their opponents see, if they are ever seen at all.

◆ ◆ ◆

While the battle of Mogadishu flared in Somalia and those two dozen young boys peacefully slept in the United States, a young Harvard Law School graduate was building a new life as a married man. Young Barack Obama settled with wife Michelle into their new home in the liberal middle-class neighborhood of Hyde Park in Chicago. Having married a former staffer for Mayor Richard M. Daley, Obama was a Chicago newbie eager to make friends.

His personal ambition had already displayed itself at Harvard, but no doubt he would have been astounded to learn he would one day sit as chief executive in the White House and—as a part of the covert side of his daily duties—approve a plan to send SEAL Team Six into Somalia. Their lethal mission: to attempt a night-raid rescue of American citizen Jessica Buchanan and her colleague Poul Thisted from their desperate criminal captors. Complication: The target subjects were known by photo evidence to carry the highly lethal Russian AK-47 automatic rifles and rocket-propelled grenade launchers.

But in the Chicago of 1993, the young future U.S. president was still far from the apparatus of power. He learned about the fates of the stranded American fighters down in far-away Africa through the same channels and from the same helpless standpoint as any other observer.

❖ ❖ ❖

At best, the story of downed Blackhawk choppers registered indirectly on Jessica. Her perch in life was that of a fourteen-year-old living at a distance from the city, safe from much of its danger.

She lived close enough to feel its urban influence, but the city was there as a resource and never represented a trap. And while she and her teenaged girlfriends didn't deliberately follow international news, sometimes pieces of it filtered into her line of sight for other reasons. In this manner the Africa connection for Jessica began with her awareness of child soldiers in Africa and the Middle East: girls and boys kidnapped by brute force and used as cannon fodder in local wars. Her sister, Amy, and brother, Stephen, had been raised with the same Christian values and weren't immune to news of a foreign tragedy, but it was Jessica who found the plight of many children in Africa a source of torment that wouldn't go away.

She found to her surprise that the phenomenon somehow struck her at the core of her being. It was as if her bones resonated with the desperation of the families ripped apart by it. Nothing in her life up to that point prepared her to stare into such a pit of misery, and her own natural empathy staggered in the attempt to visualize what such lives could be like. News photos left her sputtering in disbelief. She waxed so indignant people at school began to notice and comment about it. Oddly enough, nobody seemed to object.

Thus, instead of causing some sort of social backlash with her concern for faraway children, she found that as the daughter of an independent furniture craftsman she was expected to behave like a latter-day hippie. Her schoolmates just rolled their eyes and smiled. In this way the stereotype protected her by establishing a handy identity. It freed her to explore her social concerns on a number of topics without whipping up a backlash amid the hyper–image consciousness of other teenaged girls.

Whenever she studied Africa, the media obliged her curiosity with a fountain of stories covering the full range of human misery, but the worst always ended with the child victims. She came to realize no end to child warfare was in sight. Too many attempts to snuff it out succeeded only for the cameras, without lasting effect. It was as if the purveyors of child labor and child soldiers followed the cockroach rule and for every one you saw, a hundred more hid deep in the walls.

She kept active enough to maintain friendships outside of cultural interests, and the good news in that year was Jessica was also having the much happier experience of feeling her self-consciousness about her height go away. Until then, the growth spurt that left her standing nearly six feet tall early in the sixth grade had caused her to fear a forced career in the circus.

But now, at fourteen, something very interesting indeed seemed to be happening to everybody around her. Instead of mocking her for her gawky dimensions as they had in the past, they suddenly perceived her as fashionably tall and model-thin.

The change in perception brought her first real chance to test her personal limits as an emerging young woman just prior to a school dance. Jessica had mixed emotions about going, and while her father drove her to the event, she talked with him about a book she had just finished reading. It was a true story about a girl who lived a life of great social service and made a real difference before her own untimely death. Jessica was as moved and stirred by the story as any idealistic teenager is capable of being. She confessed to feeling troubled because she couldn't see any life path that made room for her as she wanted to live, in the middle of the world's struggle to humanize itself.

She had no idea how to visualize her own future. A conventional domestic lifestyle had no attraction to her at all; neither did a life in the business world. She liked the idea of being a teacher, but she hated the thought of the conventional life that went along with teaching, if she remained in her own familiar society.

The dance that evening soon faded in her memory, but the conversation with her father stayed with her. John Buchanan didn't expect his daughter to go into his business, he just encouraged her to ignore the world's baser temptations and choose a life of service. For him, the details of her life choices were not as important as the attitude she brought to the world and the honorable state of mind she maintained there.

Her mother, Marilyn, was determined to keep Jessica from feeling as if she needed to live just down the road and encouraged her to follow any honorable dream that appealed to her. A dilemma over her future arrived soon afterward with the local newspaper's call for teenaged girls to appear as models in print and television ads.

Jessica showed up at a large open audition with a few of her school friends. They attended as a group of bored local girls looking for something to do, but the "adventure" turned out to mostly involve waiting. Once each girl got in front of the casting board her moment in the sun was brief. The board members knew in a glance if they were looking at workable talent. Most of the girls in the room passed by without causing anyone to blink.

Then it was Jessica's turn. She watched their eyes light up when she strolled in at five feet, eleven inches tall. She quickly discovered she was what they were looking for. In this uniquely attractive teenager they saw a thin body to drape with couture garments and a face whose lines and angles would mold themselves to countless combinations of color and shade.

At first, their enthusiasm for her swept her up on a warm wave of social approval. It felt appealing and frightening at the same time. But once they began to send her out on auditions, the real nature of that world blossomed in front of her. These were environments where she received automatic approval just for entering the room looking as she did. It was bizarre to recall the catcalls she had drawn over her awkward height since the age of twelve. Now there was this surreal experience of walking into the modeling world to see coiffed strangers light up at the sight of her and hurry over to greet her.

Everyone seemed to assume the attention delighted her. She could tell plenty of other young women loved everything about it. Many of them found the payoff worth the stress and sacrifice.

But Jessica discovered that the prospect of receiving automatic success via the DNA lottery was about as satisfying as trying to quell real hunger with cotton candy. New faces beamed back at her, but their gazes stopped at the pores of her skin. She imagined herself in a line of work based on promoting the material world's fascination with consumer goods. That image was bleak. Rather than picturing a set of exciting opportunities, she felt herself repelled by the odor of slow death in a pretty box.

A wordless message settled in: Her emerging identity didn't matter in those places. For them, this semihippie, with her childish dreams of doing something for the downtrodden of the world, was of no consequence until she helped them sell something. Those sensibilities prevented her from finding any satisfaction in the prospect of a career as a clotheshorse.

She knew many other women would consider her arrogant and ungrateful for failing to appreciate easy offers of legitimate modeling work. But their approval wasn't enough to justify that life to her, and neither could their disapproval be allowed to steer her off course on something that felt so vital. Her life up to that point was spent watching her mother's and father's charitable service to all sorts of organizations, leaving Jessica immune to the sneers of those who saw such service as a foolish waste of time.

The delayed outcome of that ride to the dance with her father finally arrived when she realized that the world's easy benefits, such as they were, had little attraction to her. She listened to people obsess over their houses and their cars and it felt like listening to alcoholics obsess over their choice of drinks.

Even if it were presented to her on a platter and tied with a bow, a life lived for the camera wouldn't stem her growing desire to get involved on a direct personal level and do something in the humanitarian field, to work with real people, hand to hand. She quit the audition process in its early stages and never went back.

At that point Erik and Jessica had developed a connection. Neither one could feel it at the time, but it was already pulling them onto the same ground.

CHAPTER FOUR

Jessica:

It was June 2006 when I first stepped off the plane in Nairobi, ready to experiment with living another life in Africa. After spending my late teens and early twenties abstractly concerned about the dreadful phenomenon of child combat soldiers, I'd become convinced much of the deprivation on that continent would be eliminated only through education. My field of study was in general education for children, but my concern was the neglected girls of Africa. I had already cut my teeth on teacher training in America and Guatemala, and at the age of twenty-seven I felt fully charged for the task, having finished clearing away the mistakes of my early life. My three-year marriage to my high school sweetheart had collapsed into an abusive slog that ended with him abandoning our relationship altogether. For me, getting married had felt like a natural and expected life step, something I was supposed to do. Once inside the marriage it quickly became apparent that in getting married both of us had done what we thought we were supposed to do, but neither one had thought through what our lives were supposed to actually be like together.

I guess the trauma of the failed marriage left me numb to

thoughts of spiritual life for some time afterward. In spite of my Christian upbringing, I wasn't in Africa to do missionary work. I needed to make changes in the world that I could see and feel, among people I could deal with and come to know. Any thoughts I had at that time about my spiritual condition were pushed to the back of my mind. It all just felt like a realm I couldn't understand.

Of course the divorce felt something like death at the time, but it didn't take long before I saw it as an emancipation. The goofy nickname "Africa Jess" had been bestowed on me by college acquaintances in their attempt to help explain my obsessions, but it also represented their unspoken recognition of a force that has driven me from an early age. By the time I was ready to actually make the trip, "Africa Jess" felt like a built-in part of me. Why I cared about children in Africa was an irritating question I could never answer well. So there I was, standing in a foreign airport, knowing my individual efforts would be a drop in the bucket but no less determined to get started.

The air was pleasantly warm and made the transition to this new climate feel easy. It was neither the location nor season for any of Africa's famed desert heat or jungle steam. The arrival was sweet.

I was met by my friend Susan, who had originally hailed from Texas and was there to pick me up with a middle-aged expat named Larry. They were cheerful companions, and I was glad to have no romantic encumbrances to inhibit this journey. At this point in my life the only romance interesting to me was the one I planned to have with this new adventure.

After my husband left I'd avoided the dating scene and taken a couple of years to finish classwork for my teaching degree. The phrase "throwing out the baby with the bathwater" can sometimes have a positive meaning. When my ex threw away our marriage as if it was worthless, his betrayal freed me from the guilty shackles binding me to a conventional life that had come to feel no more authentic to me than it must have felt to him. The bathwater may have evaporated, but the baby had just stepped onto the tarmac in Nairobi, Kenya.

Soon afterward the airport was behind me, and I found myself jolting along in Larry's beat-up Land Rover while he cheerfully narrated our passing surroundings. "Yup," he said, grinning, "nice to have new people arriving. After being here for the last twenty years, it helps me see this place with fresh eyes! Look out across there—termite stacks as tall as a man! Yucca plants as tall as a tree! Got anything like that at home? Ha!"

In every direction were striking and strange reminders of how far I'd ventured. It was odd to still be under the same sky, in a place so alien. We plunged down the road passing those giant yucca plants and termite stacks, along with massive anthills the size of guard towers.

Larry drove us past a particularly dilapidated neighborhood. I later learned it's one of the poorest in Nairobi. Video journalists like to use it for backdrops to their stand-up pieces. It makes whatever they say sound important. It's so bad, the sight of it glues people's eyes to the screen.

Nothing prepares a person for a sight like that, pornographically degraded "housing" sprawled for acres in hand-built shanties of scavenged boards and plastic sheeting. This was no refugee camp, but a permanent residential district. Public sanitation was nil; the place itself was a sewer. The shock of that sight hit me like smacking my head into an overhead branch.

Susan and I had originally intended to go on this trip with a group from her master's degree program, but they canceled due to security concerns—a theme I didn't yet appreciate. We had already been making preparations and raising funds, so we decided that just because the group canceled didn't mean we had to.

We bought ourselves a ride on a tiny puddle jumper that looked as if it should have been retired back when my mother was a girl, both deciding that things like absurdly obsolete aircraft were just going to be part of life here. We took off for the Republic of South Sudan for my first bout with volunteer work in Africa, and I felt confident I could handle anything, with her along. She'd already been coming down to Africa to volunteer for several years.

Giving in completely to the idea of flying in such a tiny old plane made the turbulent flight fairly easy to tolerate, and we landed ready to volunteer at an orphanage called Shekinah Fellowship Children's Village, run by a man named Sam Childers. What I knew on that day, as opposed to what I assumed, was that the Childers organization specialized in reclaiming child soldiers who had been kidnapped and pressed into combat—boys and girls who were stolen from their families while the families themselves were often executed by the kidnappers. The working goal of the place, stripped of slogans, was to provide the orphans with some semblance of a chance for a productive life. Education was paramount. Without some form of practical education, few of them could avoid becoming criminals, with drastically shortened life expectancies.

I didn't doubt this was the time and place to begin the life I'd dreamed of leading for so long. Walking away from that chattering prop plane and into these new surroundings, I saw most of all that this was the time for me to attempt to become the person I hoped, but had not proved, I could be. The question was whether I could grapple with the harsh ways of this world, deal with them honorably, and keep my heart intact. I'd already met too many jaded expats and had no desire to become one myself. If the end result of a life of humanitarian work was a personal outlook of bored detachment and ironic disdain, it seemed like a waste of time and a poor excuse for an adventure.

So I was in an optimistic state of mind when I got my starry-eyed self to South Sudan, ready to let the healing begin. The Shekinah Fellowship Children's Village sat on donated land near the Ugandan border. Susan had been in touch with the organization through an instructor from her school, and we knew they needed help. Our plan was to stay down the road at night and work in the orphanage during the day. A nearby church compound housed young soldiers training to be army chaplains, and they kindly took us in.

It seemed like the way to go. People might question the methods Sam Childers used, but nobody doubted his determination. He was born in America in 1961 and experienced years of youthful drug addiction while he wasted time with outlaw behavior. After a religious epiphany, he learned about the destructive work of a quasimilitary criminal gang with the dubious name of the Lord's Resistance Army. Childers was outraged by the group's sadistic policy of kidnapping children and drafting them into combat units, sometimes forcing these young people to shoot their own families before the LRA took them away.

I couldn't help but resonate with the revulsion Childers expressed for the LRA tactics against children. Somehow, this man managed to carve out a place in the wilderness under the constant threat of torture and death by his LRA opponents. My admiration for his courage was probably the thing most responsible for bringing me to that place.

I was running on momentum and brushed aside my initial observations of the squalor of the "Children's Village," but it was startling. I knew funding had to be a constant problem, yet the grounds had a look of sloppy indifference completely out of step with the mission of the orphanage. A smattering of small, rough-hewn huts or cabins were scattered around, but there was no sign of a medical center or of schooling of any kind. There appeared to be no resources for teaching and few for amusement. The orphanage's land grant of two hundred acres was large enough that no security walls were required, and the lightly forested terrain kept visibility local, giving a pleasant pastoral quality to the environment, if you ignored the people living in it. The orphanage residents sat or played in the dry air amid the dust that seemed to cover everything.

We asked if we could meet Childers, but were told he had been back in America for some time, doing public relations. I had to wonder if the apparently lax condition of things around there was because in his absence the overall system had unspooled. I tried to imagine a child being "rehabilitated" there and couldn't get a picture to come into focus.

Still, we had just arrived, and it would have been a bad idea to start walking around questioning why things looked so bleak. The orphanage was everything I expected it to be: an isolated place in a clear state of need. The children there struck me as reasonably open and friendly, given their backgrounds, but I think somehow my unconscious mind was already taking note of things I wouldn't allow myself to openly consider. The message "you should have known better" began to tug at the edge of my awareness.

A desperate atmosphere pervaded the entire place. Nobody seemed to have enough of anything. But the younger kids were willing to engage with us after some initial hesitation, and I began to pass out the art supplies.

It was a measure of my failure to appreciate the level of desperation there that I soon noticed the glitter had all disappeared. It took a while to realize the kids apparently thought it was candy and ate it. Their desire for some sort of a treat was strong enough that they ignored the metallic taste of the stuff for the joy of eating something shiny.

It hadn't even occurred to me to look out for that. And the message in it was clear: There was a huge disconnect between my enthusiasm to be of service and the lethal gravity of the situation in that place.

I tried to sense the staff's compassion or the humanitarian concern that seemed inseparable from a job such as theirs, but if those attitudes existed there I somehow missed them. I was completely unprepared for the level of fatalistic acceptance in that place.

Most of the young residents were escaped child soldiers or orphans created in raids by the LRA. This terrorist/criminal group is widely known for the kind of savagery that forms a working definition of raw psychosis, or as some would put it, of evil on a biblical scale. Those children were subjected to horrors that surpass all understanding, including being drugged into near oblivion and then, with a gun to their heads, forced to kill their own family members so there would be nobody to look for them. It was a systematic method of terrorizing an entire population. The dark purpose was to effectively stigmatize the captured children among their own communities and ruin their family base, traumatizing them so thoroughly that they never wanted to go home again. Shackles weren't needed; the kids had nowhere left to go.

I knew of few places other than that orphanage that were making any serious attempt to reacquire and rehabilitate children who'd seen every source of hope snatched away. For most of these very young people, their grim situation was amplified by a drug regimen forced on them and sustained until addiction took over and drove them on its own. Getting away from the drugs was only the first step of their long recovery, if there was to be one at all.

After an awkward and confusing first day, we joined some of the student chaplains in their hut back at the compound during the single hour of electrical power provided for the night. They were fans of the TV series 24 and made it plain this was how the hour of electricity would be spent. It was so odd to see that very American program in this place, when the locations on the screen were as foreign to this audience as another planet.

I'll never know what sort of headway Susan and I might have made at the orphanage. That night, in the stillness and darkness of that isolated place, automatic weapons fire abruptly broke out all around us. Chaos exploded and bullets flew everywhere in the darkness. The explosions of gunfire were so loud the sound itself was painful. The armed men of the compound grabbed their weapons and began returning fire, creating an instant war zone.

Instinct took over. Susan and I pressed our bodies flat against the ground and crawled through the darkness to a hut farther away from the shooting. We lay there in stark terror while gunfire and screaming went on all around us. Somebody whispered that the attackers were from the Lord's Resistance Army.

This meant we were under attack from fighters who were known to torture and kill their victims. The gunfire raged around us while the defending soldiers put up a stiff fight. We were unable to move. There was nothing to do but wait and hope the defenders were up to the job. If the LRA soldiers overran the place and took prisoners, they would undoubtedly consider women like Susan and me interlopers in their struggle. After all, we were there to aid an organization whose mission was to draw fighters away from their "army." They would almost certainly want to set a public example in the way they killed us.

I am alive only because the attackers were either driven back or stole what they were after and departed. We escaped the gunfire by lying low, and learned many of the children ran off into the wilderness to escape being kidnapped again. At that time there was no way of knowing how many would be reacquired by the LRA or killed trying to run, or how many might live to return. The aftermath of the adrenaline overdose left me nauseated and shaky.

Welcome to Africa, Great and Heroic Saviors. What now?

It later turned out that the attackers didn't seem committed to killing or torturing, but just fired into the air to scare people away and then raided the compound's supplies—the local version of grocery shopping. They were successful in that no bodies were left behind, so they would have every reason to repeat the raid at will. It seemed plain that our capture was only a matter of time—after all, we were just two schoolteachers with no combat training and no weapons. My first attempt at volunteer work in Africa turned out to be sadly brief.

Susan was able to contact the pilot of our puddle jumper and arranged for us to evacuate the next morning. It was completely disorienting to be retreating so soon, but our mission was to attempt to nurture and educate orphaned kids, not engage in combat with gangs of marauders. Even trained soldiers hate to go up against fighters who are drugged into fearlessness.

We gladly climbed into the tiny plane, whose size and condition didn't trouble me nearly as much this time. It rattled and coughed its way into the air, carrying us away from the Lord's Resistance Army and a problem just a tad larger than we expected. I didn't see anything in the Childers orphanage that justified attempting to return to that place, and I had to ask myself what sort of help I would be providing to the orphans if I did. The departure was sudden and painful but the message in it was clear. Wherever my future happened to lie in Africa, it sure wasn't there in South Sudan. But I had seen enough to know it was somewhere there in Africa. I could already feel the roots taking hold.

CHAPTER FIVE

It wasn't Erik's stint as a conscript sergeant in the Swedish military back in the day that landed him in Africa in 2006. Although his military unit dealt with antisabotage and counterintelligence, teaching him things he still used in Africa, all that had no bearing on his decision to go. He had studied international law and politics for years and was fascinated with the twists and turns of legal arguments, but those things alone never would have taken him so far from home. His commitment to work in places like Kenya and Somalia was cemented by his work at the Swedish Migration Board in the position of asylum officer in the four years just before his move to Africa.

The job kept him face to face with asylum applicants from the Horn of Africa region, one after another. Many showed up desperate to pour out their stories of repression in their far-off homeland, often describing a list of lethal dangers menacing them if they were forced to return.

He ran across a few fakers from time to time, knowing every public resource will have its problems of abuse. But he didn't believe the average human being could convincingly fake such stories when the audience is someone who listens to them every day. A person develops the unhappy skill of spotting liars by listening to so many tales of organized state psychosis. Erik soon came to believe that the daily experience of working in this atmosphere will either teach you something important and vital about the human experience or turn your heart to stone.

The trade-off for the knowledge of such terrible things was that the job changed him forever. He found that a few simple but powerful messages had become riveted into his worldview, chiefly the conviction that any level of fraud within the system paled against the sheer human misery facing many of those people. More than anything else, it's his memories of them that brought him to such a faraway place—not just their stories, but the sense of truth they radiated while they spoke.

He met with asylum seekers two days each week, listening to a litany of horror stories. His division was sometimes able to prevent people from being returned to troubled regions, but after years of listening to stories of misery, the root problems behind them became his prime concern.

His friends tolerated that in him and accepted his aversion to sugarcoating the truth, but it wasn't always appreciated around the office. The impact of those years as an asylum officer had left him impatient with bureaucracy and hungry to get involved on a more direct and local level.

By the time he arrived in Africa, he was emotionally finished with life in Sweden, comfortable as it was, and with the familiarities of his homeland. That plodding line of asylum applicants, combined with the safe predictability of life, driving him to seek the unpredictability that was the essence of his new position at a major Swedish NGO, working in the semiautonomous state of Puntland in northeast Somalia. After a long series of interviews he convinced their hiring committee he was a good fit as their new legal and human rights program manager. This was a position formerly filled by an experienced man in his fifties, so Erik felt a healthy level of anxiety about doing a worthy job. It required negotiating with governmental heads throughout the region, and it could put him across from them in tense negotiations over human rights reforms in the judiciary sector, or make it necessary to poke around in the worst prisons imaginable and stare into the faces of the walking cadavers held there.

It was the right time in his life to make this journey. A few months earlier, his fiancée back home had called off their planned wedding. He wasn't happy about it but had to admit she might have done right by both of them—trooping around Africa was never going to be her cup of tea.

This made it a lot easier to put himself through all the necessary steps before making the journey to Africa. Once his life there actually began, he was relieved to be without the sort of strong emotional ties that would have put up distractions in the new job.

As for family back at home, they weren't thrilled with his choice of assignment, but nobody seriously questioned his motives. He was grateful for that. Instead they promised to visit as soon as possible and see his new hometown of Nairobi, Kenya, for themselves.

He was struck by how good it felt to be alone, in terms of not causing anyone at home to worry. It seemed obvious that it would be completely unreasonable to expect to find a woman who could understand what he was doing and accept his need to be in that place.

When it came to personal time, it was all too clear that work like his was destined to be an individual sport.

CHAPTER SIX

Jessica:

My truncated stay at the Childers orphanage in South Sudan was like being awakened by a plunge into freezing water. My senses had never been so overwhelmed. The experience didn't change my overall goals, but it completely realigned my approach. I pulled back to work out a new strategy designed to actually allow me to be of service while also avoiding a pointless death there.

I had done a summer teaching gig in Honduras, but nothing there prepared me for the normalized psychosis in Africa. The stark impact of every one of those boys and girls was enough to stop me in my tracks. Their expressions, the very flesh of their faces, had been carved by conflict. They were already old hands at drug addiction, sexual sadism, the uses of wartime weaponry, and the receiving or inflicting of savage outbursts of violence. They were "child" soldiers only in the counting of their years.

The impact on my neophyte self was profound. Humbling, to say the least. We even had to flee the area before it was known whether any of the children had been kidnapped again by the LRA fighters, or if any were still in hiding. The shock left me cowed into silence, not by fear, but by the vague sense of having been rebuked by circumstance for showing up unprepared. What did I think I was doing?

While our rickety plane sputtered into the air, I considered the miseries visited upon those children and the fact that we were so powerless to give meaningful help. I was barely out of rifle range and already anger was bringing back my natural stubbornness.

If you grew up as a nice girl or you know someone who did, then you realize that nice girls the world over are mostly sweet, good-natured, nonconfrontational, and quietly cooperative in most things. People like having nice girls around because their rough edges have been filed down and sanded smooth.

But if you are one of the nice girls in question, there is only one weapon of social resistance available to you, and it is the trait of quiet resolve. Yes, some people call it stubbornness. I've never been the loud and rowdy type, and I don't believe anyone thinks of me as confrontational. But I can plant my feet and root them to the ground.

That's how one does the nice girl thing without resorting to life as a wimp. Our failure at the orphanage really turned up the heat on what I continue to call quiet resolve, in spite of those who might describe me as being stubborn enough to teach the skill to mules. It wasn't the dangers of Africa that appealed to me—I've never had a death wish and I'm not an adrenaline junkie. But in the plight of those innocent ones, I saw a place where I could make a badly needed contribution as a teacher, doing this wonderful thing that is essentially the same all over the world, but doing it in a part of the world foreign to me. There was more to learn than to teach, and I loved that.

Susan went on to other pursuits, so I returned to the United States to complete my last semester of college, secure my teaching degree, and then come back down and try it again. A semester later, with my teaching certificate secured, I applied for a job at the Rosslyn Academy in Nairobi, Kenya. Nairobi is a metropolis with modern infrastructure, and Rosslyn Academy is a Christian school, meaning my troublesome status as a single working woman wasn't considered a cultural threat. I was glad to take the job in a place where I could begin to get a close-up look at the realities of daily life, but from a position of relative safety, protected from random gunfire and the feuding of clan hotheads.

I would be living in a city, after all. If the new job turned out to be unfulfilling, why, a person could always move out to someplace less developed. For the time being, Nairobi sounded just right. I wasn't hired to act as a missionary. All the academy asked me to do was handle the core classroom duties with several subjects and teach their fourth-graders in the hope of eventually helping them qualify for productive and legal means of attaining self-sufficiency. I was moved by their humble goal, a variation on the same thing most parents want for their children.

So I happily packed for the return to Africa and pushed the sound of gunfire and the memory of my own screams in South Sudan to the back of my mind. That brief preamble to my Africa journey turned out to be an experience of self-discovery. The first revelation highlighted my vulnerability in remote places. The second was that I only felt more determined because of it.

It was my great fortune in life to come from parents who understood the notion that people can find themselves called to all sorts of things. Mom and Dad understood my return to that continent, with Dad even lamenting that he couldn't come along. For all those reasons, I felt ready for anything when the day arrived for me to step off the plane in Kenya for Africa redux.

CHAPTER SEVEN

Erik met Jessica for the first time in late September 2007. He was two days away from his thirty-first birthday and by that point he had spent nearly two years in Somalia, with frequent travels around Kenya and Zimbabwe for work and recreation. In spite of the difficulties and frustrations of local political work—three steps forward and two steps back—he could look back on his time in Africa and actually see a measure of progress on the ground.

In spite of his satisfaction at work, things were definitely dry in the romance department. He'd gotten a stern lesson in all the ways job satisfaction can be limited. While the years rolled on, it began to dawn on him that career advancement can't stand in for a trustworthy and loving partner.

Workaholic habits and the occasional date with female expats did nothing to relieve the creeping sense of aloneness that had begun to haunt him. It seemed clear this was a time in his life when there was no real choice other than to go it alone—at least until he got back to Sweden someday. It left him with a torn feeling of living an incomplete life, dancing to the music but singing off key.

He had just returned to Nairobi from a week in Zambia. That evening, he went to a small party at a friend's house. Nothing really clicked there, so he and another single guy went to Gypsy's, a local nightclub that was popular with the expats in the area. The place was a bit of a dive, but in a comfortable way: cheap eats and drinks, plus a casual atmosphere that was civil most of the time.

Erik found the crowd at Gypsy's that night to be the usual mix of foreign aid workers, British military on leave, foreign tourists chasing Kenyan nightlife, and local Kenyan party people, plus a few prostitutes following the money. People were on the dance floor, but that looked like a lot of work to him. The evening was doing nothing for the restlessness that put him there. After one beer he decided to call it quits.

The place was far too noisy to make a phone call, so he leaned back against the wall and sent a text to his friend to let him know he didn't plan to stick around. He happened to glance up while he was typing away, and over on the other side of the room a young woman on the dance floor locked eyes with him. She was a pretty European-looking woman, a tall one, and she had obviously been doing a lot of dancing; her long hair was plastered down from the exertion. When their eyes met, she smiled and reached out one hand to playfully crook her finger at him.

He laughed to cover up the fact that he didn't know what she was doing. But he figured it must be some sort of joke and the cool thing to do was to nod, give a knowing laugh, and drop out of the moment.

He went back to texting and hit Send, but that was as far as discipline could take him—he had to look again just to see what was going on with the tall, sweaty dancer. Surely by now she would be casting her attention in some other direction.

Their eyes locked again.

This time she laughed and swirled her whole arm in a sweeping gesture, "commanding" him to cross the room to her. This was a new one for him. It seemed clear she wanted a dance partner. Unfortunately, Erik had spent thirty-one years learning to accept himself as a guy who will never tear up a dance floor unless somebody tosses him a crowbar and a hammer.

But there wasn't any reason not to go over and find out if the tall dancer with the pretty face was serious about wanting to talk or dance or whatever. She seemed to radiate a playful sense of humor, and he was already curious to see what that might be about.

◆ ◆ ◆

Jessica:

It had been a tough evening so far. I was out to dinner with two friends from Nairobi, "chaperoning" them on a fix-up blind date. The guy, Evan, was an American artist who had done aid work in South Sudan, and Jen was a fellow teacher at the Rosslyn Academy. She was a lot of fun to hang around with, a real wild child when she was away from campus, and Evan seemed like a perfect fit for her unconventional personality.

After the first five minutes it was clear my inspiration to put these two together was a disaster. Honestly, it was like they secretly planned out how badly they would fit together, finding themselves in agreement over almost nothing, with personality styles that caused each one to dissolve into dull indifference. There was no disguising their lack of chemistry; you could almost hear the air leaking out of the balloon.

We decided to all go dancing. They wouldn't have to deal with each other if they stayed on the dance floor with other partners and the music was too loud for conversation. We made our way over to Gypsy's, where Jen and I liked to stop in on weekends and sometimes dance until three or four in the morning. We avoided the heavy drinking some expats fell into to disguise their feelings of being out of place, but a night of dancing was a great way to blow off steam.

As soon as we got there Jen and Evan both found other dance partners and disappeared onto the crowded dance floor. I danced for a while with a few random partners, but didn't see anyone interesting and would have gone home except that I was their ride. Having instigated this shipwreck, I felt obligated to see it through.

I looked around for my two friends, but didn't see them anywhere at the moment. *Ten minutes*, I figured. *Then I'll find those two and tell them we either leave now or they can hire a ride.* There is a limit to how much responsibility you can take for somebody else's bad date.

That's when I looked across the room and noticed a very nice-looking guy about my age casually leaning against the wall and thumb-typing a text. He was clean-cut, short hair almost military style, strong looking, and he didn't seem to be there with anyone. I caught his eye and made a little come-hither gesture, inviting him to dance.

He just gave this awkward little laugh and went back to his texting. *Okay*, I thought, *if he's going to laugh off an invitation like that, he better be married or gay.*

I could see his left hand, and there was no wedding ring. *Okay, he better be gay.*

I don't normally go after men in public and wouldn't have been so playful and bold if boredom hadn't gotten the best of me. So I stared at him until he looked up again. This time I used my whole arm to make a large "come here" gesture I knew he couldn't miss.

He paused a moment, then gave me a modest little smile and headed my way to inform me either that (a) he was gay, so quit it already, or (b) his girlfriend was in the restroom and again, quit it already.

He stepped up and introduced himself, but the music was so loud I could barely hear him. "Hi, I'm Orik."

"What?"

"I'm Orik."

"Orik?"

"No, Orik."

"Okay, Orik. I need relief from these grabby drunk guys. You want to dance?"

"What?"

"Dance?" I waved my arms and wiggled to the music.

"Oh, dance. Okay." He smiled but didn't exactly look thrilled. It made me wonder if I just wasn't his type.

We got into dancing without trying to engage in more conversation. I jumped right in, working my whole body to the rhythm, but I noticed this guy Orik just sort of rocked to the beat without really letting loose. We weren't out there for very long when it struck me that I might have misunderstood his lack of enthusiasm for getting on the dance floor. He wasn't what anyone would call a gifted mover.

Pretty soon I just pulled him off the floor, and we found a table far enough from the noise that we could sit and talk. *Ten minutes of conversation,* I told myself. *Maybe fifteen, tops. Then I will go grab Jen and Evan and tell the failed lovebirds their party's over.* We made some idle chat for a while and established the essentials. Orik was from Sweden and spoke fluent English with just a mild Swedish accent.

My friends still weren't in sight, but suddenly that didn't seem like such a bad thing. Orik was attractive, charming, well built, and sober. He was attentive in getting us set up at the table and making me comfortable. He was charming to our waitress but not flirtatious. *Wow,* I thought, *he just transformed from a dud on the dance floor to a knight in shining armor, all by force of his personality.*

I tried to recall anything I could about Sweden, to help drive the conversation. It was embarrassing to realize I had studied Africa all my life and practically ignored Europe. Fortunately, Orik didn't seem interested in giving me a pop quiz on all things Swedish. Instead he sketched a picture of himself and his life: dealing with legal issues for an international NGO, traveling the region to promote human rights and democracy. Even in those early moments it was clear that he spoke with passion and commitment about his dedication to his work, his purpose for being in Africa.

"You like to travel?" Orik asked. "I just got back from a week of meetings down in Zambia. While we were there I got to take time to visit Victoria Falls. What an amazing place!"

Uh-oh . . . Victoria Falls is one of the status locations for big-time vacationers. It seemed as if Orik might push things too far and start bragging. I've never found a blowhard attractive. The expat community attracts some very individual personalities, and some of them are all too eager to let everybody know how unique they are. But those types didn't seem strong to me, just loud.

On the other hand, it seems natural for the males of most species to try to court a little bit. I think a courteous female lets a man puff out his chest once in a while. It's true in the jungle and true here at the watering hole—a man is mostly following genetic orders when he does that. Boring sometimes, but no real threat. I figured he had his DNA and I had mine.

Orik kept going. "I know you have Niagara Falls in America but this is just as impressive, maybe more! Yesterday morning I got to take one of these small microflights over these amazing falls, and then on the way back we saw elephants crossing the Zambezi River just below us. It was unbelievable. Nothing but fantastic!"

I got it, then. He wasn't bragging. He was sharing something important that happened to him. Not only that, it only happened to him because he got himself down to Africa and did the work that took him to that spot in the first place. He was telling me about a source of true joy in his life.

We had come across each other at a time when I felt a personal emptiness, romantically, but I also believed my current situation had no room for love. Up until then I was even managing to take pride in my sacrifice of that. The problem, of course, was the inescapable drive for intimate companionship. As much as I liked my local friends, even cherished some of them, there was always that wall of lighthearted conversation we didn't cross. There were definite lines of closeness we didn't traverse, either. Or maybe I should say there was a line of closeness out there somewhere, and I hadn't crossed it yet.

But right then time was sliding by. Orik was such good company, I found myself waiting for him to say or do something to break the spell. It never happened. If somebody had given him a dossier on me and prepped him before going to the club that night, he couldn't have done a better job of saying so many of the things I didn't even know I was waiting to hear.

Still, on that first night after a random encounter, it was going to take a lot more than that to pry me out of my shell. When Orik asked for my phone number I told him I didn't feel comfortable giving it out yet. Instead of arguing, he said he understood.

"Let me give you mine," he said with an easy smile. He took out a slip of paper and jotted down something, then handed it to me. Over his phone number he'd written the name:

"Erik Landemalm."

What? I thought. *His name is Erik? I've been calling him "Orik" all evening and he never said a word! Is he too polite to mention it? Or did the combination of loud music and our different accents blur the distinction? Or does he think I'm an idiot? If he does, he sure isn't showing it.*

We talked a little more, private small talk that doesn't mean anything more than the feeling of closeness it allows. Soon afterward my friend Evan decided to be responsible for his own ride home. Now we only had two other cats to herd; Jen had run into a man her age and hit it off with her new acquaintance as strongly as I'd been struck by mine. (Proof: They were inseparable after that night and later got married.)

When the four of us left the club and began to make our way

back to my old car, Jen realized she'd left something behind, and she and her new friend went back to get it, leaving me to wait outside alone with Erik-not-Orik.

Well, I thought, *if there's a rude awakening coming with this guy, it's probably going to show up while we're alone out here.* But his attention had been caught by a fellow in a wheelchair who was begging on the street. Erik walked over without hesitation and gave the man several hundred Kenyan shillings. The amount is only worth a few U.S. dollars, but those dollars had real buying power to secure him several good meals. Erik seemed spontaneous about it, very offhand, and didn't try to come back for some sort of approval from me. It really looked like more of a knee-jerk reaction on his part. Something he just did as part of who he was.

That simple gesture did more to impress me than anything so far. Some people will use displays of charity as an excuse to show off, but his gesture was so underplayed it convinced me his actions were heartfelt. Just as his story about Victoria Falls revealed itself not as bragging, but instead an attempt to share a meaningful experience, his gesture of kindness to a stranger was a clear sign of his character.

So we stood waiting by my car. He insisted on staying with me until my friend returned. My resistance was fading fast. There were no rude awakenings from the spell of the evening, just more of this sweet masculine energy from a guy so appealing the only thing I felt uncomfortable about was how quickly my defenses were disappearing.

Jen returned with her new guy, and the four of us arranged a double date for the next night. Erik and I gently kissed goodnight, Jen hopped in the car, and I drove away feeling an unexpected mix of anxiety and exhilaration.

Our second date went beautifully, as did the next one and the next. Things just kept right on being good. I wasn't sure what to think, but by this point I was eager to see how far this thing might actually go.

The oddest thing was that the more he told me about his background, the farther apart it appeared we ought to be. After all, I'm from a Christian household in rural Ohio, and he came from a small social democracy in the middle of Scandinavia. But instead of presenting major obstacles, the differences turned out to be mostly cosmetic. We were each raised by tolerant families. Our households shared a strong emphasis on the moral content of our lives. The fact that my parents had a religious backdrop for their teachings while his focused on ethics and personal honor seemed to be two sides of the same coin.

We had each seen relationships dissolve out from under us because of our commitment to our work, and while both of us might sometimes give the appearance of being loners in the romance department, it turned out that we shared a strong sense of the value of a healthy family. We acknowledged the challenge and difficulties faced by anybody who might dare to love us. But neither one of us actually expected to go through life as a single entity. We had both just figured such things lay in the future, out of necessity.

Everything about Erik Landemalm seemed so right and fit so well that I sailed through those first two weeks on a romantic high. He gave the distinct impression that he was returning my strong interest, and we began a pattern of seeing each other as often as our work schedules would permit.

It went on that way for those first two weeks, and the feeling of it all was like running in total darkness down a smooth, steep hill. It was scary and exhilarating at the same time. This probably made it especially rough for Erik when I broke the news that after carefully thinking it over, I decided we really should stop seeing each other.

It was a head-fake, okay? I didn't know it at the time, but of course that's what it was. It was all just too good. My emotions were too strong, the impact was overwhelming, and my last deep entanglement with a man hadn't exactly been a stellar experience. I began to feel overwhelmed by the prospect of finding out I was wrong about this guy. I found myself wondering if it could be possible for such a fine and true and powerful thing to actually be taking place at that point in my life.

So of course I told him we had to break up. It makes perfect sense that an exciting new person can't let you down if you run away before he gets the chance to disappoint. Thus the backward logic of self-doubt caused me to make one of the worst decisions of my life.

I had no idea, until later, that what I really wanted him to do was prove my fears wrong. The cruelest thing he could have done at that time would have been to let me have my way.

By that point I was getting to know him well enough that I should have realized it wouldn't be so easy to discourage him. He's gentle and his manner is calm, but he's a force to be reckoned with. This is a man who spends his life dealing with terribly difficult situations that sometimes also involve difficult people, some of whom have few qualms about killing opponents and no particular reason to do anything he asks, except for the strength of his personality and determination. Without realizing it, I put myself up against that particular form of strength, the same one that had caused his parents to start referring to him as "the little diplomat" back when he was five years old.

I learned he could argue a strong point without raising his voice. He could quietly reason his way through any objection I raised. He was determined to give us the chance to see if we were genuinely right for one another. And he wasn't at all like guys who refuse to take a hint. Instead he introduced me to another part of himself that I didn't even know I was hoping to see. He began to lay out his feelings. He revealed them freely in spite of his masculine persona, and so much of what he expressed rang all the right notes. Before long, his combination of a poetic sense of romance and dogged persistence won me over. If I had known him better at that point I would have expected nothing else.

This began a period of a year and a half of dating, and we became inseparable whenever Erik wasn't out in the field somewhere. A few months after we met he was transferred to the city of Hargeisa, capital of the unrecognized State of Somaliland in northern Somalia, and we were reduced to spending only five or six days a month together. On most weekends he would fly down to Kenya to be with me, since his job paid better than mine. We struggled with all the usual joys and frustrations of a long-distance relationship and found the absence only increased our desire to be together. Christmas came, and we traveled back to the United States so my family could meet Erik, and his first trip to my home country spanned the gamut from New York City and Philadelphia, which we toured together first, to a trip to the heartland of Ohio to meet the folks.

Here was where the cultural differences between our homes really came to the fore. Erik had never seen giant roadside billboards advertising faith in Jesus. We both got nervous about whether he would fit in with my straitlaced family. "No talking about religion," I warned. "Also, nothing about politics."

"Right." He smiled. We arrived at my family home, introduced everyone all around, then spent a lovely evening at dinner where the conversation was lively and pleasant. I could see my family coming around to my view of him, and I was overjoyed by that. After dinner we retired to the living room, where I lay on the sofa and took a little nap to sleep off some jet lag while the others kept on talking. I lay down with my head on my mom's lap and drifted off, just as I had done when I was a little girl. It was beautiful.

I woke up to hear him debating religion with my mom. *What?* It should have been a disaster—he was inviting bursts of exasperation, storms of outrage, indignation! But again I failed to realize how much time he spends with people who don't agree with whatever he is trying to tell them. Somehow, he was able to have the "forbidden" conversations with my folks and endear himself to them in the same moment. By the time we left I knew my family understood why I was in love with this man.

In October 2008, he asked me to marry him and I accepted. We were married on the beach in Kenya on March 28, 2009, and I finished up my obligation to complete the spring and summer term at the Rosslyn Academy. On August 15 I moved from Nairobi, Kenya, to Hargeisa, a distance of almost nine hundred miles, to join Erik full-time and truly begin our married life together.

We'd made it past the many obstacles to a successful relationship that can sprout up between two people with backgrounds that appear to be so different. It was a marriage designed to be an adventure for both of us, living and working in Africa together.

The way ahead was all clear for smooth sailing . . .

Part Two

———

CONCEALED UNDER
OPEN SKY

CHAPTER EIGHT

By the time Jessica Buchanan was kidnapped in Somalia on October 25, 2011, the twenty-four boys back in America who had been so young during the 1993 attack on the downed American aid support choppers in Mogadishu had since grown to manhood. Now they were between the ages of twenty-three and thirty-five, and each one had become determined to qualify for the elite U.S. Navy unit called DEVGRU. After enlisting in the U.S. Navy and undergoing their essential basic training, every one of them endured the challenges of BUDS (Basic Underwater Demolition/SEAL) training, where the happy goal is to become "drownproofed" via what amounts to repeated semidrowning, while also learning dozens of ways to deliver explosive death and demolition. This was only the starting point.

Once qualification was over and the candidates were sworn in, three-fourths of the qualified Navy SEALS who tried to also qualify for DEVGRU dropped out. Those super-warriors were overcome by the challenges, regardless of their peak physical condition and being in the prime of their lives. This happened because of the intensity of the training. Long study and practice went into developing a program specifically designed to seek out and expose any individual's weakest points.

If the same ordeals were imposed on captured terrorists who were known to be guilty of killing innocent civilians, the officers in charge would get thrown in the brig. Still, no matter how many Herculean physical challenges are presented to a DEVGRU candidate, the brutal training is primarily mental. It reveals each soldier's principal foe to be himself. His mortal fears and deepest survival instinct emerge time after time as the essential demons he must overcome.

Each DEVGRU member must reach beyond mere proficiency at dealing death. He must become two fighters combined: one who is trained to a state of robotic muscle memory in specific dark skills, and a second who is fluidly adaptive, using an array of standard SEAL tactics. Only when he can live and work from within this state of mind will he be trusted to pursue black operations in every form of hostile environment.

Therefore the minority candidate who passes into DEVGRU becomes a member of the "Tier One" Special Mission Unit. He will be assigned to reconnaissance or assault, but his greatest specialty will always be to remain lethal in spite of rapidly changing conditions. From the day he is accepted into that elite tribe, he embodies what is delicately called "preemptive and proactive counterterrorist operations." Or as it might be more bluntly described: *Hunt them down and kill them wherever they are—and if possible, blow up something.*

Each one of that small percentage who makes it through six months of well-intended but malicious torture emerges as a true human predator. If removing you from this world becomes his mission, your only hope of escaping a DEVGRU SEAL is to find a hiding place that isn't on land, on the sea, or in the air.

◆ ◆ ◆

On the day Jessica was kidnapped, Barack Obama had long since made his move from Chicago to the American White House.

As the president of the United States, he had the services of the DEVGRU warriors at his disposal. By the time he received notice about the kidnapping, the most alarming aspect was the possibility that this was an organized act by Al-Shabaab, southern Somalia's Islamist governing force with known ties to Al Qaeda, which is in constant conflict with Somalia's internationally recognized transitional government. If they had taken her, the U.S. president and the rest of the world might soon witness a viral internet video showing the execution of a female American aid worker, while an anonymous voice-over delivered a lecture to all the Godless Ones and a stream of Arabic writing played across the screen.

Still there was no hard information to act on and no line of communication, thus nowhere to aim a DEVGRU team even if the president felt inclined to deploy them. So the report of the kidnapped American and her Danish colleague went into watch-and-wait status at the White House. Jessica Buchanan's case took its place among a massive collection of other situations also standing by on the watch-and-wait status. Erik realized, coming from his line of work, that every one of them was a matter of great concern to somebody.

By far the largest conundrum facing the president was the provisional Somali government's difficulty enforcing authority. While the northeast portion of Somalia, called Puntland, had achieved a semiautonomous status and managed to get a basic infrastructure going, the rule of street violence still reigned supreme throughout southern Somalia. Without a reliable structure to protect and guarantee shipping and commerce, there was no way for the population to rebuild a functioning economy.

Therefore desperation gripped a once proud and independent collection of clans and subclans, reducing many of their young men to the lunacy of sailing motorboats out to sea and attacking large ships and tankers with the intention of hijacking them for ransom. Every nonswimming teenager with a head-buzz of *khat* and a borrowed AK-47 who dared to ship out on such a mission was undoubtedly powered by the story of a neighbor or a cousin who made only one of the lethally dangerous raids and yet *earned enough to live on for years!*

Of course the odds against any individual pirate finding personal success were about the same as the odds against hitting a jackpot at a roulette wheel. The compelling part was powerful, however, because it was better than the prospect of remaining on land and slowly rotting to death. The courage of despair drove them into small boats to sail far from shore and stage attacks so one-sided and absurd they would be comical if not for their deadly consequences.

And once in a while a comedy of errors ended up with a bamboozled shipping company breaking down and paying out millions of dollars to get back its vessels, their crews, their cargo. When such a massive payout actually went through, it landed as a giant pile of cash in a region where men of working age would fight to the death over a fistful of *khat* leaves. Word traveled at light speed: *The casino is open, boys.*

Soon after the era of big ransoms began, hidden alcoves dotting the Horn of Africa played host to a variety of boats, ships, and tankers lying at anchor and awaiting ransom payouts. Captured crews were often held below decks in medieval conditions for months at a time. Many were killed in the initial attacks and others succumbed in captivity.

In the minds of their attackers, the victims' collective guilt was simple; no matter what country a captive hailed from, it had to be a place with more opportunity than anything available in Somalia. After all, the captured crews came from places capable of building and steaming seagoing vessels across international waters, while the Somalis watched them sail by from the beaches of a stagnating homeland. The desperate attackers couldn't concern themselves with the laws of other nations; they endured existence every day with no law greater than that imposed by whoever had the weapons and the cohorts to use them.

But by this time in late 2011, the beleaguered insurance companies and shipping companies were finally starting to follow the lead of the crews themselves, who had begun to arm up and fight back. The prospect of a military-level private shooting war between pirates and the entire shipping industry attracted various governments, and those governments sent military forces to get things "stabilized."

The whole world knew about the piracy case of the tanker *Maersk Alabama*, in which three Navy SEAL sharpshooters saved the imprisoned ship captain. Those SEALs spent a full day lying in wait with their weapons trained on the pirate boat, waiting for the kill command. When the order came down, they instantly fired their sniper rifles, with their own vessel bobbing at a different rate from the pirates' boat, having no room for error if the captive was to survive. The snipers took out all three pirates in a single shot while sparing the kidnapped victim. Captain Richard Phillips was freed unharmed from the close quarters of that little boat, while the dead bodies of the three armed pirates slumped around him.

Details of DEVGRU training are not available to explain this feat of timing and marksmanship, but the results testify to its deadly effect. SEAL Team Six founder Richard Marcinko has said that his budget for ammunition for his men's training was greater than that of the entire Marine Corps. The comment might be dismissed as braggadocio if not for undeniable results produced under intense and deadly pressure.

Consequently, by the time Jessica Buchanan was being marched into a pitch-black desert to her own mock execution two years later, the same people at the White House who took note of her disappearance had reason to wonder if it might be time for another visit to the region from the men you don't see coming.

The Somali attackers knew they had reason to fear such a thing. They kept their eyes on the international press. Even in a land of nearly nothing, anyone who can mug a tourist can get his hands on a smartphone with satellite and internet capabilities. Then he will engage in that great irony so unique to the twenty-first century: sleeping on straw, dining on garbage, and surfing the internet's endless images of everything a heart can desire.

Even if the websites are entirely religious or politically based, there are those darn ads, those pop-ups, those little typos that cause unpredictable sites to appear. In this fashion even a faithful man of religion with no desire to see the internet's baser temptations may find his bitterness steadily increasing while he encounters products, so many products, every single thing he might dream of, and more—much more than he ever imagined. A fountain of temptation squirts into his eyes through hypnotic imagery, while the sexuality employed to sell, sell, sell it all fills him with rage because it affects him so strongly.

The battery on that device will die, of course. When it does, he might not have a way to charge it, but he knows how to get another one. Pandora's box has been opened. Every viral eyeful of the world's temptations amplifies his frustration. With time comes the attitude: *Why not snatch one of those rich bastards? Grab them! Make them get money from their rich bastard friends and rich bastard relatives. What, you make thirty thousand USD a year? Pay up, rich bastard.*

You can become a kidnapper and play the long odds, or you can bend over and take it from the whole world. Three choices greet you: Scrape out a life in a legal way, chew *khat* and wait for the deliverance of death, or take a desperate gamble.

The warships successfully protected merchant shipping in the region by beating down most of the piracy, for a while. The world's ship commanders and company chairmen and concerned stockholders all breathed a bit easier every time another group of desperados went down in a firefight or were captured and sentenced to long prison terms.

However, on land in Somalia the desperation didn't change at all, simply because pirates were sometimes gunned off the water. The desperation simply reversed and ran back toward the shore. Its progress was invisible, and the people on land were unaware of its danger.

Thus the men who once fired away at giant steel tankers from tiny boats out on the high seas now prowled Somalia's inland regions. They crossed into neighboring countries carrying the same hungers that first put them out to sea.

Terrible forces were in play, as dangerous and random in their violence as lightning strikes. For anyone in range of this storm, victimhood was a matter of timing and location.

CHAPTER NINE

Jessica:

Our executions were about to proceed, and there was nothing we could do. We were forced onto our knees somewhere in the wilderness of the Somali scrub desert region, and the terror of those moments was made more awful by the waiting. I remembered it, then, not with my thoughts but with my body itself—the old feeling of being rendered helpless in some game of childhood cruelties. The memory was in the survival instinct's sharp sting: that feel of wrongness over being held captive.

I discovered a special form of living hell in that combination of helplessness and terror to be endured while waiting for execution. No doubt the horror of this moment is known to all condemned people. They would surely recognize that sensation of sharp nausea, the loss of fine motor control, the difficulty with balance when smaller support muscles spasm and misfire.

Any victim taken by force is subjected to a complicated group of insults to his or her humanity. Your freedom, well-being, mental state, physical state—they all suddenly mean next to nothing.

I knew so little in those dripping minutes, but it was more than enough to leave me stranded in the compliance mode, legs trembling. I knew these men despised female emotion. It's a common trait in the culture. A woman's emotional plea is regarded as an unfair and dishonest attempt to manipulate circumstances in the female's favor. It is looked at as being done without regard to consequences for the male. The emotions themselves are therefore an affront to him: a honeyed attack. So short of jamming my fist in my mouth, I did everything to tamp down my rocketing emotions. I could see nothing there in the darkness, down on my knees, facing the ground. I could sense nearby men surrounding me, some of them standing still, some pacing the ground, all with guns. But I couldn't see any details at all.

When the human body moves beyond the "fight or flight" response, the best thing our ancient instincts can do is prepare for grievous injury; pull the blood supply away from extremities and toward the major organs, and throw out one last grab for survival. I felt the massive adrenaline surge contract my muscles so hard they began to seize up.

In most cases these symptoms would immediately be lost to permanent silence with the coming of the end. But the moment hung suspended. Nothing happened. More nothing happened. Enough time went by for stabbing knee pains to set in, throbbing with my pulse.

My back muscles started to twitch. I tried to pray for help and found that my fear was so intense it dissolved my thoughts into a formless plea for strength. So I focused on controlling my breathing: *Stop gasping, take deliberate breaths.*

And then one of the men yelled out, "Sleep!" They pushed us to the ground. "Sleep! Sleep! Sleep!"

Sleep? Just like that? You can keep your head for now. Just sleep.

I hated the instinctive gratitude that washed over me, but in that moment the word "sleep" was wonderful. It was a reprieve, and it came across as something close to mercy. It meant for the time being we had permission to exist, to keep breathing. The knife blades and rifle bullets weren't going to be coming for us on this night.

But of course, neither were they going away. So there was no real sleeping to be done that night, more of a fitful dozing that alternated consciousness with dreams. When daylight came and I was still alive to see it, I cheered up a bit in spite of the groggy and surreal hangover left by the lack of rest.

With the coming of a new day they marched us to a new spot. I began to wonder if I would be spitting in the eyes of fate by daring to think about getting out of there. Poul indicated he was trying to mentally record anything he could that might be useful against these guys if we survived. While it wasn't a plan, it was a piece of one; I began gathering any information I could. There was no way to know what might be useful, so I just tried to observe everything and commit as much to memory as possible. Our main focus was on the kidnappers themselves, since the temporary locations they ducked us in and out of didn't really make much difference. They kept us outdoors the whole time.

The region was sparsely populated. The only other people we saw were glimpses of wandering nomads, always passing. They seemed not to see us, detached from the doings of outsiders, as they have been for centuries.

I began to put forth a timid question or two in spite of the belligerence exuded by the men. The first problem was to determine who their "leader" was. Poul broached the topic, and together we tested the situation, using pidgin and pantomime to ask if we might be permitted to place a call to our NGO. We weren't going to be allowed to make phone calls, but it was important to see who would make the decision. I tried to convey the idea that our people would surely be worried about us, but that was a difficult idea to mime.

Finally they appeared to get the message. Our suggestion was rejected out of hand. But I noticed the decision seemed to be a group sentiment, not a response made on anyone's order. One of the men barked something indicating that before we communicated with the outside world, everybody had to wait for permission from the "Chairman." Whoever this was, he hadn't arrived yet.

Now we had that much—not only was there an identifiable leader, but he went by the businesslike title of the Chairman, instead of a clerical title of any kind. If someone referred to a mullah, that Muslim title would indicate Al-Shabaab, in this region. Thus the difference in title was no small distinction. A secular title was good news. Very good news.

Someone brought me a scarf to make sure I stayed covered, and I was provided with a can of tuna, a packet of sugary cookies, and a small bottle of water. Funny how the mind works to shield us from grave danger; I felt concerned about how I was supposed to eat tuna with my filthy fingers after hours of being pushed in and out of cars, stumbling hands to the ground, and sleeping in the dirt. The answer in that moment was a wrapped tampon in my small black bag. I took off the wrapper and used the applicator as an eating utensil, then tucked it back in the bag to keep handy. At least I could do something about dirty fingers. That small victory in hygiene somehow made it easier to tolerate the fact that I could do so little about the odds of getting my head blown off.

◆ ◆ ◆

There were about twenty Somali men milling around our latest stopping place. Their number included that same boy I'd noticed during the initial attack because of his high voice. My first assumption was that he must be the son of one of these men. But it quickly became evident that nobody was watching over him; he looked completely wasted on *khat*, and he fidgeted away the drug's stimulant effect by constantly running his mouth and throwing out macho poses with his AK-47.

Here you go, Jessica, my own thoughts taunted me—*a child soldier. Help the poor thing.* Although I came to Africa on a wave of concern about the plight of child soldiers, I hadn't asked myself what I would do if I was taken prisoner by them. My first lesson in this boy's case was simple: The term "child soldier" was a misnomer. This boy's childhood was long gone. He had a *khat* user's black holes where his eyes ought to have been. I had no doubt he was capable of forgetting why we were kidnapped in the first place and killing us for his own amusement. Even if he could control his impulses, he and all the other armed men were so offhanded in the handling of their weapons that even now with the terror ride over, my experience of the fear of accidental death through lunatic carelessness was at least as bad as the fear of execution.

I asked for permission to use the "toilet," and upon receiving a grunt of affirmation, tried to ask if there was any toilet paper. Nobody had any idea what I meant. I knew the cultural custom was to use a small bottle of water and one's bare fingers, but as a Westerner the idea was highly unattractive. I wound up tearing the cardboard liner of the cookie package into strips. After that there was nothing more to do but pick a bush. Within the coming days I would end up ripping my thin scarf into narrow strips for personal use, one strip at a time.

Fortunately, the men all appeared to be ignoring me for the moment, so I selected a bush for its remote location and walked over to it shaking with nerves, trying to watch from the corner of my eyes for any men who had followed me. This began a daily grind of petty humiliations over my need for personal privacy and the general lack of it.

At the bush I looked out and saw a nearby road that ran away, tantalizingly away. I won't deny it occurred to me to run, an instinctive impulse. But in the next moment I also realized any escape attempt on my part would only leave Poul to their revenge. As for me, out there in the middle of nowhere without identification or even money for bribes, there was no such thing as a lone escape. Any such attempt would fail. A minute later I turned my back on the road, the beautiful road, and resumed my place among the squabbling Somali kidnappers. I could only hope Poul would feel the same loyalty if the idea of bolting occurred to him.

The skies opened up, and a chilling rain began to pour, quickly soaking us. We weren't given any form of shelter, and were left to a single sleeping mat. They made me lie down on half of the mat and pull the other half up over me, but that made little difference. I was already drenched and freezing. This new element of discomfort plunged me into that place where the distinction between the mind and the body blurs. I discovered the odd fact that shivering from the cold somehow made the shivering from fear feel much worse. I curled into a ball and felt my muscles tightening like weighted ropes.

Although I couldn't talk with Poul, I knew he wasn't being treated any better than I was. My emotions were running the gamut. Even though I was grateful to have someone for company in this thing because enduring it alone would be worse, I also wanted to slap him and scream. He had repeatedly met my concerns over this trip with casual dismissals, as did some of my colleagues. In those moments I felt a strong sense of betrayal.

It felt as if my life as a "good girl" had sent me down the wrong path, leaving me eager to cooperate instead of eager to use common sense. I racked my brain to answer why I went along with this moronic plan to stick our toes over the Green Line and put ourselves in grabbing range of people who either saw us as nothing more than an economic opportunity worth killing over or regarded our very existence as an affront to their ideas of the Deity.

Had my willingness to replace my judgment with his been some sort of father figure thing? Not only was Poul of my father's generation, but throughout most of my lifetime he had lived in

Africa. He and his wife had raised their child there without major mishaps or deadly cultural conflicts. I guess when it came down to it, I had simply decided he knew Africa's people better than I did.

But Poul's career had largely played out at a time when the hegemony of Western culture and ingrained fear of American military might have restrained the hands of many would-be attackers. In more recent years, the psychological barriers had become walls filled with holes.

The view of my new world was clear from the low vantage point of a kidnap victim on that soaking mat. What we had failed to realize in taking this trip was the simple but vital fact that although our organization had been providing for these communities for years, not only had that not been sufficient to prevent this; it had attracted it to us.

Once the rain finally subsided, I lifted the mat to have a look around, only to see the barrel of a Kalishnikov pointed at my face. "Sleep!" the gunman yelled again.

Okay, got it. He wasn't talking about actually sleeping, he just wanted me to lie down and stay down. He gestured with the barrel to indicate I should get back under the mat, whether it was raining or not. I lay back down and remained that way for the next hour or so, too frightened to move.

My body and brain only allowed me to stay in a condition of abject terror for a fairly short time, then the level dropped down to a persistent, low-grade animal fear. I guess our instincts carry ancestral knowledge that if you're still alive after the initial confrontation, you need to relax enough to work on your chances of survival.

So the fear eventually gave way to an extremely prickly form of boredom, and I dared to lift the mat a second time. There was immediate yelling and gesturing with gun barrels to communicate that I was to remain in that spot. Their meaning was clear enough, but fear or no fear, I was shivering from the damp chill. I asked for a blanket or for another scarf.

Oddly enough, one of the men actually gave me his jacket. It helped a bit, which was fortunate, since we ended up "sleeping" there for hours. He didn't have to do it. That was something. It was a human spark. If there's one you can find another. Or at least you can try.

When I was allowed to rise again much later, a man named Abdi introduced himself. It's a common name in that region, and there was no way of knowing what an important figure Abdi was going to become, or to glimpse the depth of psycopathy he was able to display. But at least Abdi spoke some basic English, and I was grateful to finally meet a kidnapper I could communicate with in ideas beyond the simplicity of rough orders and frightened obedience. He looked to be somewhere between thirty-eight and forty-five, with a full beard. When Abdi raised his hands to gesture above his head, as he often did, his shirt lifted up to reveal a bullet scar on the right side of his stomach. So there he was: jagged bullet scar, volatile temper, red eyes, Abdi was a player.

Abdi grinned, devoid of humor and full of malice. He assured me they were not going to kill us—but they wanted money, big money, too. When he spoke, he showed teeth stained mossy green from chewing khat leaves. My problem with him was that it wasn't clear if he was actually in charge of our destiny. He might be speaking for genuine authority, but he might not. When these men were full of khat, they all loved to strut and preen.

He could just be some guy who speaks a little English and likes to brag. I had to let it go. After all, whatever Abdi's level of authority might be, we had been told to wait for a verdict from the "Chairman," and Abdi wasn't him.

◆ ◆ ◆

Nature has its own way of setting priorities. In spite of all the shock delivered by these terrifying events on that first day, for me the biggest surprise didn't come from my captors. It came from the fact that the cramps that caused me to text Erik early that morning and tell him we weren't pregnant had abruptly ceased.

Boy, the news was really pouring in. Not only had I been kidnapped by belligerent quasimilitia thugs, it now appeared I might actually be pregnant after all.

I decided to assume I was, as if I needed further motive to look for a way to escape alive. Therefore my waiting game took on layers, as you can imagine: worried boredom, smothered resentment, badly concealed outrage.

The only way to wash was to use the same bottled drinking water we had to conserve. The feeling of being hungry to get clean grew while the hours melted into the following day. I was glad to at least have my little bag with my thyroid medicine and a few small hygiene items. The medicine was important enough in keeping my thyroid levels balanced that if I went even a short time without it, I could feel the gears in my system begin to grind. I knew I'd be in trouble if they kept it.

The kidnappers rotated crews once more, and a fresh bunch showed up. It seemed like a lucky break that up to twenty-six of our captors were around us at any given time; I rationalized that I might be safer from rape if the men had to answer to one another for their behavior. Once several catnaps and numerous trips to the bush for a makeshift toilet passed without a physical attack, I was able to relax a bit.

There appeared to be some measure of discipline among them that restrained the worst of their savagery, even as ragtag and drug-addled as they were. I found when I had to pass by them to visit the bushes, they more or less ignored me. Abdi's initial prediction that we were to be protected for our cash value appeared to be genuine, at least for the time being.

Whoever controlled this operation, the Chairman or whoever else it might be, was obviously using a regular supply of reliably fresh and therefore effective *khat* leaves each and every day. Addiction bonded the men better than actual loyalty. A happy side effect may have been that common to any form of heavy stimulant use: temporary physical impotence.

CHAPTER TEN

Jessica:

The second day melted into a third day. Our kidnappers subjected us to a routine of daylight hours spent under a scruffy stand of old acacia trees surrounded by giant termite mounds. The whole night was spent under open sky. It was a strange pattern. The men showed such extraordinary concern over concealing us during daylight hours that it was obvious they were afraid of aerial surveillance. At night, however, we were force-walked out into open fields to throw down our sleeping mats and sleep away from the trees. It was as if the men's fear of being seen from overhead didn't apply to nighttime. Perhaps they had never heard of infrared cameras. I wasn't about to bring the subject up.

That second night they walked us out into the desert again, just as they had done the night before, and once again there was the sour fear of an apparent execution. After an hour or so of stumbling around out there, they ordered us to the ground.

This time, instead of putting us on our knees for another ghoulish performance, they just yelled once again for us to "sleep!" There seemed to be no reason for the protracted night hike. I wondered, did these guys actually think the U.S. government would send drones to spy on us? And did they actually think that could happen this fast?

Still, the shouted order to "sleep!" soon became recognizable as a more general form of command and control. The kidnappers kept moving us on foot every couple of hours, then stopping again and commanding us to "sleep!" whenever we halted. It felt crazed and pointless and did nothing to convince me they had any idea what they were doing. The only logic to it was that same concern about secondary kidnapping by roving gangs. On top of the heavy weaponry our captors flaunted, they seemed to be taking no chances of letting word get out about our location.

It appeared that when it came down to rank, among this group, the rank below Abdi was held by the "Colonel," and above him was the Chairman. But I wondered, was the Chairman actually the one in charge? It was clear we had no chance of getting out of there unless we could deal with someone who had decision-making power. The most authority the guards seemed to have was the power to grant us permission to make a toilet run to the bushes.

If the Chairman was really running the show, he was likely to be the money man behind this. This would be true whether he used his personal funds or someone else's invested money. It was puzzling; I didn't think the Chairman gave off the air of the complete alpha dog.

But if not him, *who* was making all these decisions?

Somebody had a substantial vested interest here, and these squabbling, prancing morons didn't seem like they could organize a decent picnic. Did they even know who pulled their strings?

I had to wonder: *Did I just happen to get picked up along with Poul, or was my kidnapping also intentional?* Because even though I only recognized a few words of their dialect, I kept hearing the term "*Amer-ee-cahn*" over and over while the men pointed toward me. Some appeared to be nervous and unhappy at the sight of me.

Great. So if I'm a fly in the ointment for them, the question is: Are they afraid an American will draw the ire of the U.S. military?

And will they feel safer if they just kill me or sell me off to other criminals, or worse yet, to Al-Shabaab?

For an instant I also wondered whether I might get released just so they could reduce their risk. But that thought felt like the empty hope it was. I let it go.

They kept us silent, as if afraid we might come up with an escape plan if allowed to communicate. They were probably right about that, but even with the clarity of hindsight I can't imagine how we would have pulled it off. I think the forced silence was mainly directed at us as another mechanism of control by domination. They knew we hated being isolated, so of course that's what they did. This kept us sealed off from the outside and from one another as the two victims.

We remained at our next stopover point for several days, a spot the men called the "Banda place." It was essentially a large thatched roof mounted on tall poles. We were permitted under the roof's shelter in the daytime. That was notable because it was the only time we weren't kept under the scraggly tree branches during daylight hours.

Here, too, they marched us down near an abandoned goat pen and once again made us sleep out in the open air. I could never see any point to it, but they were adamant. No matter how the day was going otherwise, as soon as darkness fell they wanted us clear of all structures, whether natural or human, and out under the open sky.

Abdi was the camp sergeant, I guess. He acted as the point man in the rare moments when something needed to get done. Nevertheless, his green teeth revealed a man who loved his *khat* leaves at least as much as the other enthusiasts. Thus the even-handed logic necessary for competent command was a slippery concept for him. He could chew through an entire kilo of the tender shoots in a single day. Protocol itself was all the more tiresome to a hyperventilated brain.

As long as Abdi had plenty to chew, he loved to talk. Listening wasn't Abdi's strong suit, but under the stimulant effect of a cheek full of *khat*, he could run his mouth nonstop while keeping his hands busy puffing on cigarettes and sucking down quantities of Coca-Cola.

Communication, it turned out, wasn't always desirable. Abdi's command of English allowed him to make the depths of his lunacy clear. They revealed a cauldron of rage.

His face was pocked by acne and his voice perpetually hoarse from shouting from within his constant state of tension. His mood swings were like nothing I had ever seen, cycling from chattiness to confrontational anger. He appeared to suffer from a massive bipolar disorder. I quickly came to regret being able to understand him, and instead longed for the pleasantly meaningless babble of an unfamiliar language.

He enjoyed discussing philosophy for as long as the *khat* supply held out, and when he got wound up tightly enough he felt compelled to offer words of wisdom. Sometimes he liked to riddle us with philosophical questions and then stare through us while we tried to answer. His eyes were completely empty, focused on some unseen faraway point while the imagination raged under the stimulant effect after chewing so long and so hard. It's the common link between *khat* users: eyes empty of warmth but present in a vaguely malicious anger.

In their laughter there was even a specific sound to the *khat* high with these men. *Khat* laughter: a frequent, nearly constant chuckling, done with an inflection to the sound that effectively portrays sneering and mockery. If it's coming from you, a nasal-sounding cackle will start up when your brain waves hit a certain frequency. You will then maintain that frequency until the *khat* runs out, or exhaustion claims you and you have to flop over and sleep like the dead—and then get up and do it again.

The cackling is a constant declaration of cleverness and an expression of the *khat*-generated sensation of "victory" over anyone else, everyone else, over all of it. An attacker can beat that *khat* user down with a billy club, and he'll still go right on cackling over how many opportunities to inflict further damage the attacker missed, thus proving the *khat* user to be the more clever of the two.

One moment Abdi would be on the phone screaming orders about the daily delivery of *khat* leaves for all the men to chew, demanding more cigarettes to help fill his boredom, or haranguing someone on the other end to refill our supplies of canned tuna and biscuits. With the next intake of breath, Abdi could become curiously peaceful. In his calmer state he reverted to his philosopher role, with a series of questions he liked to pose to us. One of his favorites was, "Which are the four directions of the earth?" After the first few fruitless arguments about the correct answer, we learned to respond the same way each time.

"Well, Abdi, there are four directions: north, south, east, and west."

He would then nod in approval, his worldview validated once more, and perhaps yank another leaf or two from a leftover stem. It's amusing now, but wasn't then, that Abdi wanted nothing to do with the concept of secondary directions: southeast, northwest, and so forth. And the finer distinctions such as north-northeast, south-southwest? Forget about it. He seemed to find the very notions tiresome and nonsensical. In his world, there were four directions. Abdi didn't need any foreigners coming around to muck up his sense of cosmic order.

Early one morning, he offered up his most noteworthy moral precept, one I would often hear him repeat. "Jesses and Poul?" he began. For some reason he insisted on pronouncing my name

"Jesses." Since he was the one who spoke English, the other men copied it.

"Yes, Abdi?" we responded with the exaggerated politeness that worked best in speaking to these men.

Abdi gave a smile of triumph and flashed his mossy greens. He pronounced the words with a knowing nod. "Every dog has its day."

Sometimes Poul felt the need to counter with a question of his own, but I was happy to agree. "Yes, Abdi, you're right. Every dog has its day," to which I silently added, *And we can only hope yours is coming soon.*

Abdi, it seemed, considered us his long-overdue payoff after his years of poverty. Even though my compassion for his people had brought me to this country, I had to differ with his rationale. In my eyes, when it came to matters of karma, Abdi was stacking up a mountain of consequences. I would have gladly handed him the bill. No matter how hard his life was, regardless of what he'd endured, he crossed the line when he made his rage the problem of people who were only available for capture because they were there to help ease his people's misery.

By the end of the third day, I began to menstruate, so that was that. My reaction came in waves of disappointment and relief. As much as Erik and I wanted a child, under these explosive conditions I was in no position to be ushering in a new life. I was relieved to have packed tampons in my small bag, just in case.

But I opened the bag to find that the guards had gone through everything and taken my jewelry. They also took my tampons, for reasons I couldn't fathom. So I had to be inventive and tore my tank top into strips to use as sanitary pads. When I ran out of the strips, I then tore strips from the scarf they gave me. The combination of using dirty pieces of cloth and being prevented from washing regularly only heightened my anxiety over the unsanitary condition they were keeping us in and our fear of what it was doing to our bodies.

Still, now that events had caught up with the story, it was a bit less painful to think of having already told Erik I wasn't pregnant. It left me in the slightly better position of only going hungry for one instead of two. My task remained that of surviving through any combination of ways that might get me back to Erik, back to the joyful experience of starting our family.

So I prayed for protection and for strength. Beyond those silent requests, I could only hope Abdi was right in ways he couldn't begin to imagine: that every dog would indeed have its day.

CHAPTER ELEVEN

From the time Erik first got back to the their house in Hargeisa after Jessica's abduction, their dog, Smulan, seemed to realize Jessica was in jeopardy. The dog had a special bond with both of them, instinctively grateful after being rescued from the streets, matted and starved—Smulan means "crumble" in Swedish, in reference to the dog's initial appearance. Now upon Erik's return, Smulan's usual independent behavior changed to that of a worried dog, scurrying around close at his side.

Or maybe it was just his reaction to Erik's condition. One of the security guards kept at the house by the NGO had been a fan of Jessica's ever since her arrival there. He took one look at Erik and hugged him, angry tears in his eyes, and repeated over and over, "Sister Jess! F***ing Hawiye!" He spat out the name of the main clan ruling the area where Jess was said to be held.

His distress appeared genuine to Erik, but here again was a third party who knew details that were supposed to be kept quiet. The man was informing Erik of the name of the principal clan with members suspected to be behind the crime, something shared with Erik by the FBI in confidence. It made him wonder if he should go ask the dog if he had any details he might want to share.

In public, it was dangerously inflammatory for Erik to hold a

101

specific clan responsible for capturing a female aid worker who was only doing politically neutral work. It carried the prospect of inserting ancient tribal rivalries and disputes into this situation and rendering it into something complex beyond sorting.

The flow of information to the public remained difficult to control, and not all of it was bad. Erik was contacted by people of Christian, Muslim, and Hindu backgrounds. Nonbelievers expressed their concern, while everyone else spoke of praying for Jessica and for her safety. Some mentioned actively forming prayer groups on her behalf as well. Given Erik's fear that Jessica would fall into the hands of Al-Shabaab, it was a beautiful and compelling indication of the difference between people who live their faith and murderers who hide behind it.

By the fourth day, he began to feel his anger getting to him. Every ring of the phone could have been news about Jess, leading to a spike of disappointment when the caller ID indicated something else.

In spite of the news blackout, calls came from people offering to "help," but they clearly just wanted to inject themselves into the case. In truth there was no way anyone could offer genuine help until Erik found out whether they would get the chance to negotiate her return.

It sometimes helped him to write out his thoughts, so from the beginning he began writing to Jessica each day. It was a process he decided to keep up from then on, in a combination of journaling and love letters. It felt better to have some feeling of communication with her, at least a private place to put the torrent of emotions.

Jess, for some reason it feels good to cry and write to you. I imagine that you can see what I write and that you are doing the same thing, maybe not on paper but in your head. I just love you so much. You have to come back to me so I can show you all the wonderful things in life that we stupidly put on hold . . .

His imagination was his worst enemy during those early days

and nights, as it is for anyone who waits in fear and concern for word of a disappeared loved one. He tried not to picture the terrible things he already knew about the fates of some of the region's captives, as if merely thinking the thoughts might somehow give them power to manifest for Jessica. He had never been a superstitious person, but the possibility of somehow causing a negative outcome with nothing more than the wrong thoughts suddenly felt real to him.

He wondered if that was a form of guilt for letting her take the trip. The weight of anything he might do *or fail to do* to gain her freedom suddenly loomed in every direction. There was no escaping the images of all the terrible possibilities that lay ahead for Jessica and everyone who existed along the chain of love for her. And as terrible as Erik knew it was for all of them, he was especially concerned for John Buchanan after the fairly recent loss of his wife. She had been the love of his life from the time they were childhood sweethearts. How could he possibly endure the loss of his daughter Jessica now?

Erik looked around to see how others handled this terrible stress. In dealing with John it was clear that the depth of his spiritual faith held him up like a better set of bones. John Buchanan reeled from the blow, but right away his internal gyroscope ramped up and began to spin. It appeared to Erik that the man was stabilized by the internal workings of his faith.

Seeing this quality in Jessica's father made John Buchanan precious to Erik in a way he hadn't felt or thought about until then. He realized he was now an intimate witness to the active spiritual life of this family. He felt convinced that anyone with an open heart would be touched to see John remain rational, strong, and purposeful, in spite of the terrible potential loss confronting him.

It made no difference that Erik had grown up so differently from Jessica and her family; those differences affected only the language used to interpret living. He saw that this man had raised the girl with whom Erik had cast his lot in this life. John Buchanan had helped mold the essence of Jessica's personality into something so fine Erik could no longer picture living without it. He was surprised to find that he was not only willing to take on Jessica's fear or pain, he would have gladly taken her father's as well. To Erik, John lived out the phrase "grace under pressure" while all of them hung by the hands of the clock.

The persistence of misery was fierce. Erik was unable to turn off the thoughts of Jessica's torture, rape, murder—any of the most vile possibilities. It still felt like a betrayal of her to even consider such things, but his personal knowledge of the region tormented him. Moments after he forced himself to quit a negative thought pattern and switch to something positive, the terrible thoughts were already back. They returned and intruded, seeping in like poison gas, finding every crack in the house.

◆ ◆ ◆

Jessica:

Our fifth day in captivity started out like the others during our stay at the "Banda place." We were rousted off the dew-soaked sleeping mats and got up shivering. I was so thirsty I might as well have had a mouthful of dirt. They moved us back under overhead cover to spend the daylight hours.

The survival instinct was my substitute for a cup of coffee. The challenge of getting to a toilet bush and back while out in the open in front of a dozen men lifted the morning fog right out of me. I took the last scrap of thin cardboard from the cookie package and headed for a bush that was close enough so that nobody got nervous about an escape attempt, but also hidden enough that I could pretend there was a little dignity left to the situation. The pretense itself was worth something.

I got back to the Banda structure without trouble from any of the thugs, who mostly looked strung out, as if they had been up all night and were ready to quit their shift. But there was nothing else to start the day, not even any water. The small bottle given to us once each day was far too little. They were also holding back on getting me antibiotics from any decent source for the inevitable urinary tract infection burning away inside me as a result of our medieval sanitary conditions. This was on top of the strain to our kidneys already caused by depriving us of water and forcing us into dehydration. Poul was just as concerned about water and got assertive with one of the guards, pantomiming the need for water and persisting when the guard hollered to silence him.

But a moment later Poul grew angry and began shouting back at the man. It happened quickly—the voices hit just the right pitch, things ignited, and the guard leaped toward Poul. He cocked his AK-47, pulled the trigger, and held it down while the firing mechanism went *click* on the empty chamber.

It was only a second later that I realized I should have been looking at Poul's dead body and expecting to join him. But no, it was only a joke. A power play. A little reminder that Poul's macho display had been recognized but slapped to the ground.

Good morning, then. Pretty sure I'm awake now.

Abdilahi, the young boy I'd been seeing around since the beginning, happened to walk close to me. I noticed for the first time that he was wearing one of the Mine Risk Education bracelets my NGO gives out to all the kids after they attend our classes on avoiding war munitions. I had to swallow hard to keep from gasping out loud while the thought hit me: *This boy was one of our students?*

I might have trained the teacher who taught this boy's class. The visual materials I helped create to effectively convey information to people whether they are literate or not were most likely used in his class. This was one of the kids we were fighting to protect. I forced myself to look away from him. *Thank God I haven't been teaching locally, because if this kid recognized me, he might feel the need to impress the elders by revealing that. Who can tell what sort of resentment they have toward my NGO in spite of our work?*

A few seconds of casually observing him confirmed his exaggerated macho posturing as an obvious bid for authentication from the adult males. This was a kid who could cut your throat for pocket change.

I couldn't take my attention off him. He was a bomb with an invisible fuse. Swaggering, grinning, compensating for his youth with loud behavior and an aggressive voice, he seldom spoke in a normal tone. I searched for anything about his behavior to give a clue to how and why he happened to be in this place, a pubescent boy swaggering around with a deadly weapon and chewing through the daily *khat* ration of a grown addict. I didn't get his story, but he effectively communicated his mindset when he took off the Mine Risk Education bracelet and used it to fasten a front bipod to the barrel of a machine gun.

Well, I thought, so *much for winning hearts and minds.* More than anything so far, that little detail made everything I hoped to accomplish in Africa just seem ridiculous. If we were truly dealing with people who could take our help with one hand and do this to us with the other, then what was the point of my presence there? I reached out for my usual internal assurance that the work was worthwhile even if many local people didn't acknowledge it. Our work could be called infidel propaganda and every other hateful thing a person could dream up, but surely some of these men had relatives we had saved from the land mines and other unexploded munitions littering the region. The fact that every one of them had at least one relative with one or more limbs blown off was a virtual certainty. *Surely,* I thought, *no matter what they think of Americans or Westerners in general, everybody can agree on the desirability of keeping one's arms and legs?* Then I remembered the Islamist punishment for theft. So maybe not.

When I was able to exchange a few words with Poul about it, I whispered to him, "Poul, that boy's bracelet—"

"Yeah. I know. I saw it."

"It's from our—"

"I know."

"But he must have—"

"I *know*, Jess."

"I feel like I'm losing my mind."

"Welcome to the club. Listen. We have to establish some ground rules."

"For what?"

"To keep up our spirits. You know, places we will not allow ourselves to go, not with each other and not with ourselves."

Ground rules to guide our thinking? This was one my dad would understand. So there in plain sight of these armed men and their constant shouting spats we whispered our way through the resolution until we fleshed out the general idea: *You can acknowledge feeling fear and loneliness. You can get mad, bored, resentful, anything at all. But despair is the one big no-no. Despair isn't just a mood or a state of mind, it's a disease and it can kill you by making you give up. Despair is a killer as sure as the Black Plague.*

We agreed not to allow hopelessness into our conversation, and neither would we permit it in our thinking. We resolved not to indulge in a single moment of it, because while it couldn't be of any positive use, it could surely start either of us down a path to disaster.

So. Good, then. No despair. It's a fine idea, to be sure. But we all recognize how easy it is to say that, yes?

I was still longing for the fundamental dignity of feeling reasonably clean; the filth covering us only added to the demoralization we were trying to combat. When at last they relented and allowed us a bucket of washing water, though, I was pushed into the next concern: how to wash myself and maintain a reasonable level of modesty.

It was a matter of common sense—there were a couple of dozen males milling around the Banda place, most were loaded on *khat*, and they all appeared capable of rape if the notion struck them. I couldn't leave the camp, so what to do? Bathe with my clothing on?

The best solution I could come up with was to take my small share of the bathing water and carry the little bucket over to a deep depression in the earth that allowed me to stay down out of sight from ground level, if I squatted low enough. So with the men close by in all directions, I undressed down in that hole and ran water over myself as well as I could, spending more energy in watching out for any male who showed too much interest than I did in the bathing itself. When I finally ran out of water and was ready to climb back out, I felt as if was a notch or two cleaner, but the anxiety of the experience made the payoff of getting clean hardly worth the effort or the risk.

Next a new man arrived on the scene and came over to introduce himself. He was an older man who walked with a slight bend to his spine, and when he opened his mouth to speak it was obvious his top teeth were missing. But he spoke passable English and told us his name was Jabreel.

Jabreel identified himself as a "neutral translator" from Mogadishu. The strangest thing about Jabreel was that he immediately began to ingratiate himself with us; it was unlike anything we'd experienced in this place. Then there was the idea of a "neutral translator" and whatever that might actually mean.

"These men—pirates! Crazy! Stupid crazy! They want $45 million U.S. for you!"

"What?" I cried out. "Forty-five million? Do they even know how much that is?"

"No! Stupid crazy! That's why I say they crazy! Unreasonable!"

"Jabreel, please listen. Listen: This is not possible. Impossible, Jabreel. We are aid workers. None of us have money. No money, Jabreel!"

"They say NGO pay for you."

It's odd how pidgin English comes naturally, almost without thinking, when someone speaks it to you. I guess it's just the desire to communicate without cluttering speech with too many qualifiers.

"Jabreel, you say crazy? You're right: crazy! Not $45 million for us, not 45 million Somali shillings! Nobody pay so much for two aid workers. We only have family! Private money. Small family money, Jabreel."

"Yes, yes! I tell them: You make crazy demands, you get nothing. But they only pirates! No brains!"

"Okay, Jabreel. Please, now. Please listen. If you want money—"

"Not me. Not for me. I not pirate. I have NGO here. Very important! I only want to help! I tell them the most they get maybe $900,000. Less than one million. Not like big ships full of oil." He snorted at the idea of big ships full of oil.

At last, here was someone who seemed to have a reasonable appreciation for the realities of the situation. I couldn't evaluate his inflated claims about himself or how they applied to the task of negotiating ransom demands. At least his sense of money was better than the drug-fueled fantasies entertained by the others.

After darkness fell, the Chairman himself finally arrived, and the camp got active. He looked to be in his late thirties or early forties, balding, with thin facial hair and a mustache. He addressed the men in a quiet, hoarse voice. Jabreel took his orders from the Chairman along with the others, and when the Chairman decided the time was right he muttered something to Jabreel, who simply said to us, "Phone call."

Phone call! At last, it was time for our "proof of life" call, basic to every ransom scheme. I think my adrenaline spiked even higher at that than it did at Poul's mock execution, because that little episode was quickly over and done with, before fear could set in. But the prospect of a phone call indicated some sort of action, at least. Action meant a chance to get this thing worked out and get ourselves out of there. I felt like E.T. about to phone home.

At that point, five days seemed like an eternity to wait in the company of these wasted marauders before letting people know we were alive, but I knew that kidnap victims at sea have waited far longer. Some spent months in the hold of a captured ship before anyone at home was contacted. Some were never heard from at all.

Therefore, under the realities of our new situation, this was what "luck" felt like. "Luck" was now the chance to bathe in a hole without getting raped and then make a call home, so a fortune could be demanded for your return. "Luck" was meeting a man who claimed to understand that $45 million was too much but who thought $900,000 sounded about right. Here in this place on the other side of the looking glass, we were having ourselves a lucky day.

He and the other men piled us into a silver Helux Surf, a typical type of SUV there, and drove for a few minutes until they were able to locate a decent cell signal. They gave us cell phones and indicated it was time to make our first contact with home. I immediately tried Erik's number in Hargeisa, but it was disconnected—which was very strange under the circumstances. I explained to Jabreel that Erik must be in Nairobi and something was wrong with that number. Next I tried my father's number in the United States and to my utter consternation that one also had a recorded message: disconnected! *Could it just be the network? Are we getting a bad signal out here?* I knew better than that, since I'd seen the men place other calls without a problem, but once again I found myself grasping at straws.

The strangeness of the moment was amplified another notch

when Jabreel announced that he had a number to call "for" us. I watched him dial, and the country code looked like Kenya. With the phone on its speaker setting, I heard a man answer and identify himself as "Mohammed."

"*Mohammed?*" That made no sense at all to me. I had no idea who this Mohammed was or who he actually worked for. In my confusion I wondered if he was using a fake name and if he might actually be our NGO's security manager. Then he identified himself as the assistant to Daniel Hardy, our regional security advisor. I knew Hardy well enough that it would have been consoling to hear his voice. I had no idea why we weren't speaking to him instead of this stranger, leaving me to wonder if something was wrong on their end as well.

Finally something happened that was recognizable from the world of sanity. Mohammed announced he had a few security questions to ask me by way of confirming my identity. I knew the office kept questionnaires we all filled out for just such emergencies, containing preset personal questions.

Mohammed asked me the name of my first dog. I told him it was Sadie and added we got her in Indiana. He liked that answer and asked a second question, then a third. I was only too happy to play the game until he was satisfied, if that was what it took to get a message to Erik and my family assuring them I was unharmed.

But at that point Jabreel snatched the phone away and began challenging Mohammed himself. He didn't know Mohammed either, and he sounded suspicious. Jabreel paused and asked me if Mohammed worked for the NGO, so we both lied agreeably and answered, oh, yes, he worked in Nairobi and was a colleague. Even though it wasn't true, there was no reason not to vouch for him. If Jabreel didn't know him then he wasn't on Jabreel's side, and if he wasn't on Jabreel's side we had to consider him on ours.

There was no more communication than that. What a disappointment. Although I was glad to send a proof-of-life message back home, even by a circuitous route, I had no explanation for not being able to connect using the phone numbers for Erik or for my dad. What was that about? There was nothing else to cling to but the voice of a man we vouched for but actually didn't know, who claimed to work for our company. But being in communication with *somebody* was at least something to cling to. It was a bit more than just another straw to grasp at—maybe something closer to a good-sized stick.

Throughout the short phone conversation the Chairman stood back with Abdi, staring at us with bleary red eyes. With the call finished, the Chairman barked an order, and we were herded back into the cars and driven back to the Banda place. There they force-walked us back out into the open field and placed us down on the ground again and onto the damp sleeping mat, ending that day the same way the four preceding days had ended, with the waving of a gun barrel and the shouted command, "Sleep!"

CHAPTER TWELVE

They were several days into Jessica's kidnapping, and the phone conversations between Matt and Erik were becoming contentious. Erik knew Matt was on their side, but it fell to Matt to be the messenger of misery in keeping Erik's expectations in line with those of the experts on the Crisis Management Team.

"Matt, I still feel ashamed for not going in to get her. I think my contacts could track her down, and I know trained men who will go with me! I'm telling you, I think we could locate her."

"Erik, I promised you we would put all our resources into this. I've kept that promise so far and I'm going to keep it until we have Jess back here with you."

"I trust you, Matt, but do you know where she is? I need to know."

"I can't say."

"What? *Matt . . .*"

"I can't tell you, Erik."

"What? Why?"

"She needs you here. We can't risk having you attempt to go get her yourself."

"Wouldn't you, if you were in my shoes?"

"I might. Plenty of guys would want to. But if I did, it would be a stupid mistake. I would be letting my feelings get the best of me and cause me to make some macho dash to get her. Even an assault by the best-trained men in the country is full of risks."

Erik sat on the edge of his bed and gave a heavy sigh. "All right. All right. I want to do this however it's best. So—what options do we have?"

"There are three conditions that have to be met before we can go in for Jess: one, if we believe her to be in immediate lethal danger; two, if her health fails; and three, if negotiations have completely stalled."

"Okay, but since you convinced me about the risks of an assault I don't want anybody authorizing a raid without telling me, you understand? She's my wife, Matt. And if there's just one guy with a gun to her head when your men get there, it won't matter how many soldiers you send."

"My point exactly, and that's the same reason I need you to promise you won't try to go cowboy on us."

"I won't. I promise you, Matt. Just please, if you believe Al-Shabaab holds her or will be in a position to get her, tell me you'll go after her then. Because if that's the case, a raid is the only hope we've got."

"The decision to go has to come from the highest level, Erik. But I can assure you we have the best guys anyone could ever ask for, and if anyone can do it, it will be them."

"I just need to know I won't be sitting here in a week's time, looking at my computer screen and seeing video of Jess being killed."

"Erik, we need to focus on what we can do. And you need to be there for Jess's family, for your family in Sweden. And when she comes out she's going to need you more than ever before. This is not the time to let emotions take over."

"I know. I know, but you have to understand, I promised her if something happened—"

"*Anything* you do that increases her jeopardy—you won't be doing it for her. You'll be doing it for you."

Erik found that the truth of that was like a gorilla blocking the doorway. There was no way to ignore it.

"Damn it, Matt."

"It's a rough road. You have to hold steady."

"What about an exchange?"

"Of what?"

"Prisoners. I'll go in. They can swap her for me."

"No we can't."

"What difference does it make to them? They just want money, yes? If it comes to a point where Jess is sick and we can do an exchange, I want to do it."

"We're not even going to talk about it. Desperation won't help. Give us a chance to get things working."

"It's been six days."

"Right. And these situations never get resolved quickly. They take time."

"How much? That could mean anything."

"That's right. And the answer is, nobody knows. But it seldom takes less than a matter of months, Erik. *Months.*"

That night, alone in their apartment, Erik felt one of those particularly dark waves of emotion pulling him down. The doubts he had been holding back about his responsibility for Jess's predicament ran through him like vandals, in spite of the fact that he knew there had been no stopping her from going on that trip once she agreed to go. It was, as she said, the work she had come here to do.

But this—this ordeal of waiting. It was not improved at all by the cultural experience he'd gained there over the past six years. The hot zone of southern Somalia is a place an entire young male population is confronted with virtually no opportunity. In some parts of that country, crime openly rules the streets. That didn't mean these criminals knew what they were doing. Successful ransom kidnappings have always been notoriously tricky. A kidnapping that didn't go wrong was far more rare than the ones that fell apart and got people killed.

All Erik could do was write his daily letters in hopes she would live to read them. He wondered if some element of magical thinking was involved, as if he might convey some unknown power to her, generated by holding the thought of her as close as possible. He concluded science couldn't prove any such thing was possible, but neither could it prove that it wasn't.

I'll understand if when you return you feel resentment and even want to never see me again. If so, I will do whatever you feel is right for you, but I will always be there for you. My love for you is without conditions, any rules . . . I will always be there for you even though I don't know where you are now and it breaks my heart completely. I don't know what to do, I just don't know what to do . . . I've talked with Dan, I've talked with [the] FBI, with all kinds of people . . . everyone says that we should be hopeful and I am, I know you are strong, but I'm just so afraid for everything that can happen. . . .

You need to come back here. I can't live a life without you, I just can't. There's nothing the kidnappers can do that can make me stop loving you, there's nothing they can do that can lessen my love for you.

He found himself repeating the same things, over and over. As if it was a sacred duty. He wrote as if the idea of stopping the imaginary conversation was a form of giving up.

✦ ✦ ✦

Jessica:

There was a bad argument going on between Abdi and Jabreel, and while I didn't understand them word for word, the conflict was obviously over money. Nobody in the upper echelon of this

gang seemed to believe that I really wasn't worth the many millions of dollars they wanted for my return. In Poul's case, they
appeared to accept that there wasn't any golden treasure there; at
least I never got a sense of their concern over it. The mere fact of
my American citizenship was enough to convince these men there
had to be barrels of money involved. I wondered if part of the
reason America is so resented around the world is the result of
the Western entertainment world's false rendition of our culture.
These guys were essentially demanding that we make Santa Claus
appear and spill out his big toy bag, just for them.

The day after that fiasco of a proof-of-life call, which we had
no way of confirming, things deteriorated around the Banda place.
There was a lot of verbal aggression coming from Abdi against
Jabreel. Jabreel was older, smaller, crooked, and toothless, but he
stood up to Abdi and was giving it right back to him. We couldn't
get the details, but I also couldn't avoid the mud-sucking feeling
that their dispute was all about us.

Poul and I were being allowed to sit together that afternoon,
close enough to risk quietly rehashing our "phone home" event and
trying to make sense of it. Meanwhile, Abdi started shouting with
forceful anger at Jabreel. Jabreel kept insisting on something right
back at Abdi, and he wasn't backing down to the younger and fitter
man. That sent Abdi into such a fit of anger that he threw a full
roundhouse punch to Jabreel's belly. The older man doubled to the
ground.

Fortunately Dahir, one of the drivers, hurried over and pulled
Abdi off him, leaving Jabreel to hobble away, crying out in pain and
outrage. This was completely unexpected even in that bizarre environment, and whatever the details of their argument happened to
be, there was no way it could be good news for us. Jabreel was our
point man, and yet he had just lost a major notch in his standing
with these men.

Before long he limped over to us and whispered, "I cannot stay here! You see. You can see. He say less than one million not enough for you. Maybe eighteen million."

"Eighteen million! They can't be serious!"

Jabreel nodded. "Too much *khat* for them. They want everything."

"Oh, my God. Please tell me these guys aren't insane on *top* of being morons!"

"All evidence to the contrary," Poul muttered.

Jabreel spoke with real urgency. "I think Abdi kill me now. I must go."

"Jabreel," I protested, "don't go! You're important to us! Very important!"

"Abdi thinks I will keep the money. Because I speak English, he says I work for your people against Abdi. Against the men."

"No, Jabreel! We'll talk to him. We'll tell them you never did anything to interfere."

"He will say you lie."

I felt myself starting to cry and hated the feeling. We might as well have been perched on a high cliff in a huge storm, with Jabreel our only lifeline. When I tried to speak, my words got trapped between sobs I couldn't control.

"Jabreel, nobody else here can speak with us. Please! Please don't go!"

I remember Poul appealing to him, assuring him he was of great value to us. But we also knew it would be a fatal mistake to offer him a side bribe of any sort. If he reported it, we would fall into a sinkhole.

Jabreel just stared at me for a long time before he looked back and forth at both of us and nodded. He quietly said, "I stay for you for longer, but I am now afraid for my life in this place."

"Yes, Jabreel," I agreed in solemn tones, nodding. I made it a point to acknowledge him out loud in front of the others with an obvious display of respect and gratitude, just in case any of the horde were taking note.

What I did not allow myself to do was grab him by the ears and scream up into his nostrils hard enough to vibrate the nose hairs, "*You're afraid for your life? You're afraid for your freaking life? Welcome to the* cluuub!"

But at least he hadn't left us, even though he was now thoroughly plugged in on our shared afraid-for-your-life thing. It was great to have common ground. If we were going to get more communication with home, we needed someone capable of navigating the language with the others and a clear sense of what we were experiencing here. Jabreel appeared to have a reasonable grip on reality so far. At least he wasn't screaming about cashing us in for tens of millions, amounts so huge and fanciful the numbers didn't matter.

Two days after the proof-of-life call we sat stranded beneath the cover of the Banda place roof, which for some reason they'd decided to put us under for the day. The air was dry, disturbed by a warm dusty wind. It was hot, not at the level of the open desert's kill-you-in-a-day heat, rather just hot and dry enough to gradually suck the water out of your body. Since the Chairman's goons refused to give us enough to drink, the inside of my mouth came to feel like a realistic sand carving of itself, devoid of all moisture. The nagging sensation of thirst combined with the feeling of having a thick layer of dust covering every inch of my skin.

The two acted together to weave a blanket of misery. I'm no princess and I can rough it when I have to, but this feeling of being filthy and unable to do anything about it was something I could have happily gone a lifetime without knowing. It had a surprisingly oppressive effect on morale. I couldn't help but react to my strong sense that when a person gives in and accepts that level of filth, some line is crossed into territory where further difficulty, perhaps lethal difficulty, is guaranteed.

We appealed for some water to wash our clothing, and a resentful young man brought a ridiculously small container of it. The same guard who pulled the machine-gun prank on Poul, who we later learned was called Fizel (or Failsel or Faisal; Somali names have multiple spellings), waited nearby until we moistened the clothing and rubbed in some soap before he sauntered in and kicked over the little container of remaining water. Boy, was he proud of himself for that. He looked like he could flap his wings and crow.

We had to stretch out the soapy garments to dry as they were. By the time we put the crusty laundry items back on it was hard to tell if the whole endeavor got us any cleaner or if it just gave us something to do. Still, it was better than sitting idle and getting stuck thinking about all the things that could go wrong with this picture.

Jabreel's continued presence there paid off that same afternoon when he hurried over to us and announced we were going away to make another international phone call. I was ready to go in a heartbeat, eager to do anything to move this train along. I dared to wonder if this meant some sort of deal was in the making? My optimism ran too far in the other direction, and I found myself wondering if Erik and I might still be able to meet our friends in Zanzibar as we had arranged. Sure, our little vacation for four. Maybe it wasn't too late. Why not? Why not?

I kept right on grasping at straws while they drove us out into the middle of nowhere, but I couldn't tell if their purpose had anything to do with getting good reception or if they thought they would somehow fool potential aerial surveillance by moving us around that way. They continued to be aware of the sky and watched for aerial traffic.

Sure. The U.S. government knows all about this and they're tracking us as we speak.

I only found one explanation for this odd mix of carelessness and paranoia. Although these men understood how to use a cell phone and knew how to drive and do basic maintenance on vehicles, they were also unschooled in Western popular culture and they had major holes in their knowledge. For example, they knew about airplanes and international travel, but it was likely the closest any of these men had been to an airplane was to drive by the local Galkayo airport.

Holes in their knowledge. It was the only place in the region where major air traffic could land, but the city was too poor to have landing lights. Planes operated in or out of there only during daylight hours.

Holes in their knowledge. These men who had learned how to seek out phone signals by going to higher ground and who knew about airplanes capable of seeing us from above also had an important blank in their knowledge of flight—they had concluded from observation that planes did not operate at night. Pilots are only human, and see in the dark no better than they do. But they appeared not to have heard of infrared night vision cameras, or unmanned drones that can stay aloft for many hours, day or night, and even see you clearly in the darkest of night and under thick cloud cover.

I filed away that piece of speculation with a mental note to watch them during this phone-home excursion for any sign they might know about night vision, or that someone had alerted them about it. But I never saw any indication of that, and the pattern of marching us out into the open for sleeping was repeated every night. Whatever their purpose, they were consistent.

Jabreel dialed the phone this time. He handed it to me once the connection went through. I heard a woman's voice on the other end, but didn't recognize her. She sounded British or possibly South African when she spoke my name. She claimed to know me, or know about me anyway. I asked who I was speaking to, but she only replied that she worked for something called "Mine Action."

The name didn't sound familiar to me. I felt a strange mix of hope and skepticism. She went on to assure me "everyone" was working around the clock to secure our release. I had no idea what that actually meant.

And I wasn't sure I heard the next part right at all—she asked what I would want to have in a care package if they were to put one together for me. She meant it as a gesture of consolation, but all I heard was, "Get ready to spend serious time in captivity." The idea of a care package was even more upsetting than being provided with replacement clothing; they both implied a much longer stay. I was already counting the minutes before my sanity broke.

Jabreel put Poul on the line and had him give a rehearsed speech about how the military must not try to stage an attack on us. Poul also had a few other locations he had been instructed to pass along as "no attack" zones, if we were to ever be returned alive. With that Poul lost patience with the idea of speaking to yet another stranger instead of any of our known people. He told her to get off the line and keep it clear for our people to reach us.

But that was it. No more calls, no explanation for the "disconnected" numbers of Erik and my family. They packed us into the SUV again and drove us back to the Banda place. The loss of the optimism I felt when this trip began was as abrupt and hard as a belly flop.

Jabreel told us of the men's concern about surveillance satellites and high-flying planes with tracking capability. They seemed to think we also had these things at our disposal. At least that would justify the constant paranoia about keeping us under cover in the daylight, even if it failed to explain why they didn't fear night vision when they made us sleep out in the open.

I tried to play it as casual as I could and rolled my eyes at the idea of anyone coming for us. "We're just aid workers," I assured them. "Nobody would use such things to look for us. Our government doesn't know we exist."

After nightfall, a caravan of four SUVs pulled into the camp.

Poul and I were loaded into the back of one with a guard on each side of us. There were three men in the front seat and four more in the rear, along with a stack of supplies. My anxiety began to spike, partly because I couldn't see Jabreel anywhere in the caravan but mostly out of intuition. Whatever was happening with these men, they were plainly jumpy and paranoid over something or other, and I had a sick feeling it had to do with us. More specifically, I feared it might have to do specifically with me—not as a woman, the way I initially feared, but as an American.

Maybe they hadn't bargained for an American captive after all. The men kept jabbering to one another and glancing over in my direction. I couldn't understand them, but once again I could make out the word "Amer-ee-cahn." Either they were coming around to deciding my presence was a mistake or talking about how to raise the ransom fee because of it.

We moved out and kept moving. I could sense the ride moving steadily south. We drove for hours, again with no explanation and without Jabreel anywhere in sight. All I could think about was, to the south lay the highly dangerous Al-Shabaab territory. Given the arguments over how much money we were worth, it began to look more and more as if the Chairman had decided to sell us off to them for a price closer to his liking, and let them use us either for ransom money or for torture toys. I knew rape would be the least of my worries in their hands.

Loud Somali pop music blared from the car stereos, driving the hyper mood higher among all the men with green slime running out of the corners of their mouths. They regarded us the way people look at cows in a 4-H Club competition. I knew about panic attacks from personal experience and felt a doozy coming over me then: the tight constriction of the chest that felt like suffocation, the need to break free into clear air. I was painfully aware that in the past these groups have been quite keen on selling off their captives to other groups when negotiations didn't go well. Ours were apparently going so badly the men were beating each other up and spending a lot of time arguing about their "Amer-ee-cahn" captive.

Poul and I had already agreed: *Whenever we can, we'll try to stick with the devil we know,* meaning it was better to stay with this group, crazy and dysfunctional as they seemed, than to take a chance on the mental stability of the next group's leader. We were, at least, alive so far. Poul had not been badly beaten and I hadn't been raped. It was hard to imagine better treatment from some other group. If we left this one there was no place to go but down.

They stopped the cars. There was no way of telling why. Someone pulled the doors open, and they ordered Poul and me to get out. With my anxiety mounting I saw them wave Poul back to the last of the four cars.

They're separating us! Why?

I began to cry and beg them not to split us up. Poul pleaded with them to be human while I clung to his arm. Did they understand us? Probably not the words but certainly the intention. It did no good. They ripped me away from him and escorted him out of there. He looked back and called to me to "be strong," and then they were gone with him.

The sense of time slows down and there is the actual, physical feeling of my stomach dropping like a bowling ball down an endless well. I'm keeping vomit choked back because it will surely trigger their outrage, giving them an excuse to explode. They all appear to be burning with an urgency so deep that it would be a relief to them to fall into slaughter mode and feed us their choice of knives or bullets.

So they've separated us now. They spent the evening talking about the "Amer-ee-cahn" and glaring at me. My God—Jabreel has disappeared. Poul is off with others, for some reason. I think he's back there now in the last of the four cars. We don't know if we'll see each other again.

I focus on my breathing and teeter on the edge of a drowning panic.

And because I pray, I call out to God in my heart, please make them kill me quickly. Whatever they are going to do, have mercy on me and make them kill me first.

On top of losing my only companion in this grotesque experience, I instantly felt the loss of his point of view on things. Poul had so many years in the region, his study of the intricate clan structure gave him insights into their status structure, their volatility, their possible reactions to the stress of bargaining in a hostage situation like this one.

Plus, he was one of us. On the most basic level, he was a companion, no matter what other attributes he had. His overall worldview was vital in helping me retain my own. When there is a genuine "us," countless tiny references back and forth are instantly understood, confirming dual membership in some meaningful slice of humanity. With Poul gone there was no "us" left. Now it was only them, and they were many, all with the eyes of the heavy *khat* users that seem dead and angry at the same time. It reduced their behavior to insistent monologues with nobody in particular, cackling and flashing their green teeth, then later crashing and flopping down to sleep in any spot at all.

People say the threat of immediate death concentrates the mind. I found it worked too well for me. A jerky freeze-frame of bizarre and terrifying moments ran past in a strobe. Each one landed a punch. Sneering faces. Screamed orders. Gun barrels waving.

Before long the agreement I had made with Poul about not allowing despair to take control of us began to feel starry-eyed to me, foolish. I couldn't help but look at our situation and think, *Oh, I am so screwed. We're in this way too far.*

To them I was a compliant captive who tried to do nothing to provoke them. But in truth I was more like a human radio beacon. I beamed out to the universe, out to any source in this world, in the next world, to please stop this. Somehow, put a stop to all this.

I struggled for some evidence of logic or clear reasoning in their behavior, for anything that would bolster me in rejecting the prospect of my destruction on these ridiculous terms. But I discovered how hard it is to think coherent thoughts when fear seizes you. The best I could come up with was the notion that if unimaginably bad things can strike against all odds, then the chance of some sort of miraculous escape must also exist. I had to find ways to live long enough for one to appear.

When it came to petitioning the universe, I learned I can scream bloody murder without making a sound. Without moving a muscle, really.

CHAPTER THIRTEEN

FBI Agent Matt Espenshade made arrangements for a special crisis counselor to meet with Erik. She began the conversation by letting him know she had previously met Jessica through their work and thought highly of her. The fact that she was an admirer of Jessica's was a bonus for Erik. While they talked, he felt reassured by her quick mind and evident compassion. He had already quit one therapist who just didn't resonate with the situation in a way that was helpful, but this time he sensed someone who could help him work through the acid drip of his outrage over the situation.

He explained to her that he was tormented by feelings of guilt for not fighting harder to keep Jessica at home. First there was his concern for what she was going through at that moment, but just behind that was his fear of alienation from her when she made it back home again. Would she feel somehow betrayed by his failure to stop her from taking the trip? Would she think he had abandoned her by not going after her, once everything went bad?

The therapist's manner was consoling. She offered assurances, but they were much like those expressed to him by friends and loved ones, all of them good to hear, but somehow ineffective against the gnawing sense of failure that just wouldn't leave him alone. He agreed to check back with her again in a couple of days to let her know how he was feeling then, but couldn't imagine how things could be much different then unless he got word Jess was safe and on her way home.

◆ ◆ ◆

Jessica:

After they separated me from Poul and took him to the rear car in the caravan, the engines all started up again, and we pulled away. We moved along the bumpy ruts of a road and I used the way the car threw our bodies around to sneak glances back and see if Poul's car was following us. I couldn't get a solid look, though. At this point my first full-blown anxiety attack hit me with a vengeance.

I called to Abdi to have the driver stop the car, gesturing to them I was going to be sick. I didn't expect them to care, but I hoped they didn't want to ride with vomit on the floor. They let me out long enough to run to the nearest bush, fall to my knees, and empty my guts out. The fear and my sense of outrage combined to eject what little food I had in my system. After that came the dry heaves while the emotions twisted through me. When my body calmed down a little bit, Abdi appeared with a diesel can and told me to hold out my hands. He splashed diesel-tainted water over my skin to replace the smell of vomit with the smell of petrol. It was an improvement. What can I say.

An odd air of compassion came over Abdi, unexpected and unreliable but no less welcome. He understood separating me from Poul had caused my panic, and quietly assured me the car holding my colleague was right behind us. Then he surprised me by asking if I wanted milk or meat to make me feel better. It was the first real food I'd been offered by these goons, but I was still too sick to have an appetite. I asked if there were any soft drinks around to help settle my stomach; he shook his head. But I'd seen others with them. Either they didn't have any more or I had reached the limit of his empathy.

Abdi tried to calm me down by asking if I had any children, which seemed a bit out of place under the circumstances. But something perked up in me; his questions contained an opportunity. I seized it and began to lie. Because Abdi's culture places a far higher value on mothers than upon more "disposable" single women, I spoke my first lie to him and replied yes, I have a one-year-old son. He asked my "son's" name and I was about to make one up when I realized they might make mention of my "son" in the negotiation phone calls. They could easily discover the ruse.

So instead I gave the name "Smulan," our dog. I'd pulled Smulan out from under a parked car, starving and crusted with dirt. He was now a loving member of our household, and I figured if there was any mention of my "son, Smulan," instead of my "son, Erik Junior," or some other name while they were on the phone, Erik was likely to play along. He has a fine ear for nuances of conversation, sharpened by years of ferreting out the truth in testy negotiations. I felt sure he would recognize this as a signal from me and wouldn't contradict me.

When we rescued Smulan in Hargeisa the year before, he was filthy, hungry, afraid—oddly enough a mirror image of my present condition—and now the thought of Smulan's gratitude for his new home and for the love he found there made me smile in spite of myself. That smile seemed to do the trick to convince Abdi I was smiling at the memory of my "son." In an odd way, Smulan brought me some welcome payback for his new home with us in that moment. I could take some degree of hope in having convinced Abdi I really was the mother of a little boy and that it might help me avoid rape. These circumstances offered little enough hope to any captive female, unless special considerations could be invoked. There was just so much drugged-out male energy everywhere. Otherwise the worst seemed inevitable, a matter of time and circumstance.

Abdi loosened up at the story of my "son" and confided his own situation as a father of four. I looked into his face—the bloodshot eyes, the green drool on his chin—and I could not repress a wave of real pity for those four kids. Here was Daddy at work.

We got back into the car, and the caravan started up again, proceeding out into the middle of the desert and more or less following an old camel track. There was no reliable sense of distance.

Just as the bump-along journey threatened to become boring, the first car in the convoy broke down and stalled the whole line. Several men swarmed the smoking car to begin makeshift repairs and scream at one another about the best way to do them.

Abdi shrugged and pulled out the sleeping mat, then went to the rear vehicle and pulled Poul out. It was good to see he was still with us. I was grateful for visible proof that I wasn't completely alone out there. Rationally, I realized there was nothing Poul could do to help me against these people, but he represented companionship. When he looked at me he saw me, Jessica, not an offensive piece of meat from a rich country who owed each and every one of them a millionaire's riches in compensation for their hardscrabble lives.

Abdi tossed the sleeping mat on the ground and placed Poul next to me. "Sleep!"

I could have hugged Poul and told him I was grateful they hadn't separated us. I didn't. He could have spoken to me about whatever greater fears he was able to discern from key words in their conversation during his solo ride. But the silence was already beginning. One meeting of my hot and swollen eyes with those of my fellow captive was all either one of us got.

For me, it was enough. The sense of aloneness disappeared with it. Aloneness is where despair begins, and we were still pledged to fight against that feeling.

But we both seemed to be in that strange place where you are so tired you can't make yourself sleep. After about an hour the squabbling, jabbering men, who didn't appear competent at much of anything, turned out, after all, to be competent. In my eerie state of unsleep I was physically weak and certainly confused, so I had to wonder how these men managed automobile maintenance under such heavy narcotic influence.

What explained their mechanical success, muscle memory? Maybe the guy who actually fixed the problem had done enough mechanic's work in his time that he could still pick up the right tools and twist the proper bolts even after chewing khat until his eyes popped.

At that moment I saw Jabreel come reeling by, still with us after all. Either his threats to leave were bluffs, or somebody was keeping him around. He looked as tired as I felt, and he was so blitzed on khat he couldn't walk straight. I couldn't tell whether his presence in this mess would make any genuine difference, but the sight of him was consoling.

Such was the state of things. He could speak with us when he was coherent and he had insisted several times that he realized the prices being quoted for us were madness. Perhaps he could somehow inject a little sanity into this squad of jabbering addicts, if he got some sleep and sobered up a little.

Abdi piled us back into our respective cars and the caravan started up again. After another fairly short drive they all stopped one more time, at a large man-made watering hole that had gone completely dry. The image crystallized our environment. The dry hole was surrounded by towering termite stacks six and seven feet in height. They were intact, although the insects who once benefited from the water there were probably gone. The fact that the stacks were still standing turned out to be the point of our stop here, not the dry watering hole. Jabreel clambered up onto the miniature hill and got a cell phone call through to Mohammed, the man claiming to speak for our NGO and our families, but whose identity we couldn't confirm.

This was our second proof-of-life call, supposedly made to our NGO's communicator. No one was telling us anything about that, however. What I knew for certain was I could hear the loud crackle of static and a male voice broken into bits by the shaky connection. There was nothing to do but play it out for real. Poul and I were each allowed to speak to the man calling himself Mohammed. I didn't bother quizzing him about his identity. If he was a fake he was probably prepared. *It can't hurt to send a message,* I thought. *The worst that will happen is it just won't go through. No harm done.*

"This is Jessica."

"This is Mohammed speaking, and I have authority to speak for the families and the employers. Do you have a message I can pass along to your people?"

"Yes, I have a message. Tell my family I love them. Ask them all to pray for us."

"Your family, yes."

"And my husband. Erik. His name is Erik. Tell him I love him."

"Tell your husband you love him."

"No, Erik. His name is Erik!"

"I understand. His name is Erik."

"Tell Erik I love him. And we will see each other again. It's important to tell him that. We will see each other again. *Tell him that!*"

"Yes, yes. Rest assured I will tell Erik. Now let me talk to Jabreel."

CHAPTER FOURTEEN

Erik got the call from Dan Hardy in the late afternoon, informing him the Crisis Management Team communicator had just spoken directly to Jess. They could confirm she was alive, but the captors were making insane demands. Like so many phone calls since his wife was taken, this one ended with another question mark. He hung up relieved over the proof of life, but frustrated by the risk that still surrounded her.

There was nothing else to do but sit down again and write to her. He hadn't missed a day yet, so he began another of the letters he hoped one day to give her to read.

Jess, I'm back on the tightrope. It's already becoming familiar, and I'm certain others who love you in their own way feel their own version of this. I balance gratitude and elation you're still alive with my outrage that we should have to wait here for little sips of news, for whatever they permit you to say. It doesn't seem unreasonable to pray anymore, and I pray for your safety most of all. I try to project the idea of a bubble of safety around you. From this foxhole, prayer is a logical alternative to the random cruelty that seems to be driving these people.

In the evening of that same day Dan Hardy called again with more details about what Jess said. They were dribbling out information to him in little spurts, each one screened by the Crisis Management Team. Dan had needed to get official clearance to release this information about her before he could elaborate beyond what he'd told Erik that afternoon. There was official concern over how much Erik was permitted to know, because of the CMT's concern that he might try to go get her.

Hardy didn't need to elaborate. Erik felt a wash of gratitude for the sense of release Jessica's few words gave him. For him, the next best piece of news after hearing of her survival was her assurance of love, after his worst fears and self-recriminations held him responsible for letting her make the trip. Her gift in those words was to reveal that the guilt was coming from within himself, not from her. She revealed the heavy sense of burden to be nothing worse than the question of how much guilt he was going to carry.

He only knew his fears couldn't be allowed to dominate his thinking or he would be lost. He kept busy by remaining in constant contact with their family on the phone, and locally with a few trusted friends. Secrecy was still basic to the family's plan. The people holding Jessica obviously had at least one cell phone, therefore they could somehow get online. He was certain they had internet access in the nearby town of Adado.

How sophisticated were they about electronic information? Would they force passwords from her and pull some sort of online identity scam? He had battened down the hatches by shutting down social sites and adjusting banking information, but if they were persistent they would try to find records of any purchase Jessica might have made online and take home addresses, phone numbers, private email addresses, any form of contact. A leak could be anywhere. Electronic "water" will find the weakest point.

He tried to unwind with a few forceful workouts at the gym. They did a lot to keep him from just grinding his teeth and pacing the floor. The physical effects of sustained anxiety had put sharp knots in his muscles, so the ability to throw his emotions into the workout loads helped to more or less slap him together and cast off a lot of the terrible energy for another few hours. He had also begun starting the mornings with long walks around their neighborhood, just trying to keep his head straight.

In the meantime he went off to oversee his work each day, determined to keep his routine as normal as possible. He thought about arranging to cancel his workload or get a replacement—but of course that would leave him there inside the long silence with nothing to do but think. That, he knew for certain, would not be good.

He could see how someone could be tempted, deeply tempted, to turn to alcohol or pills in a time like this. There is something basic to the survival instinct that wants to avoid deep, persistent pain. All animals avoid it when they can. Sleep doesn't do it; sleep is no protection from the subconscious mind.

With alcohol as a refuge, a person could start out the day mildly drunk in an attempt to escape dark thoughts, but quickly become completely intoxicated. Short of a blow to the head, the only thing completely effective at shutting off the tormented thinking and worst imagining is the oblivion delivered by drugs or alcohol. If he could have seen any way a drink or pill could help get Jessica back, he would have already been facedown on the floor.

Most professionals can keep up a certain persona regardless of other things going on in their lives. Erik was also able to fall into familiar behavior each day while in important business situations, but living with two such different versions of life was bizarre in the extreme. Everything around him felt fractured and segmented, as if life had been transformed into something by Picasso.

CHAPTER FIFTEEN

Jessica:

The days began to dissolve into one another, daylight hours dragging by while they held us under the cover of the trees, followed by nights of fitful half-sleep out in the chill of the open desert. Whatever dopey ideas they had about security from overhead surveillance, they never missed a day of hiding us from above, or a night of sending us into the desert to hide under an open sky.

Makes perfect sense, guys, I think to myself. Put us out in the open at night because surveillance planes or satellites could never spot us. After all, it's dark.

I've always found stupid people scarier than smart ones. Stupid evil people scare me more than smart evil people because a stupid man will gladly surrender his judgment to someone else. This makes him substantially more dangerous. If I had to choose between being held captive by a smart criminal and a dumb one, I would take the smart guy every time. At least I'd be dealing with someone who's got the capacity to understand his own situation— and perhaps be open to improving it.

Meanwhile, they continued to keep my medicine away from me, for reasons nobody would explain, and I got recurrent bladder infections. Maybe they were just acting on an order and didn't know why. My impression was there was no real justification for this, just the repressed resentment of somebody who would lift himself up by denying me something I needed. I could feel my internal balance already going off center, and within days of being taken I had felt a urinary tract infection and a rough stomach bug setting up shop together.

As for stomach troubles, no doubt a major factor had to be the disgusting fact that we had only two bowls and two spoons, a few cooking pots, and four cups for the *entire* camp to use. Thus any microbe hosted by any one of them was quickly shared with the rest of us.

Result? *Hey everybody, let's all take turns eating out of the same bowl with our bare hands. How could that be a problem?*

You can fight ignorance with education and you can ease poverty with financial opportunity, but as we've all heard it said, stupidity isn't fixable. Boy, was that ever playing out in front of me. A few dollars worth of cooking and eating utensils would have benefited the health of everyone there, but for that you might have to forgo a few mouthfuls of *khat*, and that would be asking too much.

I couldn't find any compassion in myself for these men, and that was unusual for me. But their conduct wasn't just the result of poverty; it was sheer idiocy to force a large group of people to eat from what amounted to a common bowl. It would have been astounding not to be sick.

There was no way to judge how the others felt. Their *khat* use numbed them to their true condition. It also seemed to numb them to everything that didn't have to do with guzzling soft drinks, chain-smoking cigarettes, and babbling hyperventilated monologues at one another while nobody seemed to listen. It's a strange drug. Give a man enough *khat* to chew and he can go completely paranoid over what your motives may be or what you "meant" by what you just said—all the while remaining unconcerned about bleeding from a wound.

The other assault on our health was the dismaying fact that Poul and I had to make do with scraps of cookie wrappers or bits of cloth for toilet tissue. The indigenous plants out there don't provide paperlike leaves, so their method of cleaning up after defecation was that method mentioned earlier, using a combination of water and their bare fingers. If they washed afterward at all, I didn't see them, and it would have been with the tainted diesel water anyway.

Strange, Jessica, you've got a bad tummyache . . .

Poul wasn't on any medication when we were taken, and so far he was doing a bit better, but we'd both been subjected to the same foul conditions. His body was objecting as well.

I heard a commotion over near the vehicles and saw about ten of the guards standing helplessly around. After a few moments I realized the friction was over keys being locked inside the car. Poul lifted his head off the sleeping mat and asked me what was going on.

"They've locked their keys inside the car." I sniffed. "It's official. We've been kidnapped by the world's dumbest pirates." The joke wasn't funny, but we laughed about it for a long time just because of the subtle defiance in it and because it felt so good to have an emotion that didn't involve concealing terror or swallowing outrage.

But then, as if one moment of levity magnetically attracted its opposite, Abdi started getting repeated calls on his cell phone, and each call left him more upset than the last. Abdi's ring tone itself was no help, being a recording of a Somali news report. Amid the words we didn't know there was always one we did: "Kalishnikov," a more formal name for the AK-47. We were surrounded by the weapons, and the terrible guns were to be seen everywhere in Somalia. I suppose anybody in that country would recognize the word.

We knew it wasn't good for Abdi to get upset because any time he did, somebody had to pay. Jabreel made himself scarce while Abdi cooed reassurance into the phone, then hung up and found somebody to scream at, only to be interrupted when another call came in and the process repeated.

Kalishnikov. Down Africa way, you might say we've all got a little Russian in us, when it comes to the daily awareness of this particular killing weapon. Aficionados the world over appreciate its ability to deliver massive killing force, something that is especially nice when the forces of individual liberty are beset by forces of tyranny. The darker reality is criminals love them for their power to transform anyone—even a child—into a true force of doom.

All of this and more springs to mind for anyone who's been down there long enough to notice that the scenery might change a dozen ways, but yet another AK-47 was never far away. And there was seldom only one.

We could tell by Abdi's level of deference it was the Chairman calling each time—Abdi was never obsequious unless he was high enough to feel benevolent and had plenty of *khat* left over for later, or when he was talking to his boss.

Suddenly I didn't feel the need to figure out what every word Abdi was speaking might mean. It was probably better not to know the details. We'd already heard enough to get the gist; the calls were not good and the repeated ring tone was pulling the other men out of their stupor. They took interest and started milling around, pseudocasual in movement. They weren't surrounding us, necessarily, but suddenly there were a lot more of them, and they felt too close.

Abdi's protests grew more frantic. He repeatedly screamed out "sagaal!" which means nine in Somali.

Nine million? They're still trying to get nine million?

Wasn't Jabreel able to talk any more sense into them than that? If he was their guy, and he was convinced we weren't a million-dollar ransom, how could they be stuck on numbers so high? If they truly didn't trust him, why was he still doing his job?

Nothing else we overheard clarified any of it. Apparently the boss kept on making those annoying, "and one more thing" calls. Each one whisked Abdi into turmoil so hot I knew the topic had to be money. I wondered how the Chairman could possibly understand the speech of a man in Abdi's condition. His naturally guttural speech had become even more distorted by the combination of drugs and emotion. Maybe that was why the Chairman had to keep calling back. And of course with each new call, the ring tone jabbered the same Somali newscast, indecipherable except for that word, "Kalishnikov."

And the kidnappers were still demanding $9 million for two broke-ass humanitarian aid workers. Under these circumstances, we each had the life expectancy of a soap bubble.

◆ ◆ ◆

With the passing of days and weeks, Erik had come to the point where he could think things through in a more rational way, even though his rage at the people holding Jessica was still very much present. His strongest desire was to be a bridge between her family and all the people working on the case. Besides keeping up the pressure on her employers to negotiate aggressively for her, he hounded the Crisis Management Team for as much information as possible.

The Crisis Management Team knew Erik was valuable for validating information on her or on her kidnappers as it came in, because of his experience in the region. Though some felt strongly that he and the entire family ought to be kept out of the negotiations as a form of information control, they were overruled.

It gave the families comfort to see that he was able to put some degree of influence to work when needed. In the unfamiliar position of being the one who must stand back instead of the one who is charged with fixing things, it was torturous for Erik to give away responsibility for Jess to strangers. But he knew Jessica's father, sister, and brother were in an even more disturbing condition. Sitting on another continent without knowing the people working on the case, they had no useful knowledge about the environment Jess was in.

A deep bond was shaped between them, growing stronger with each phone call, and they continued to talk over the phone every day. They came to the collective decision that all three of them would come down to Africa in the coming week if nothing new happened.

Erik knew they still wouldn't be told much, either, and that simply coming down to Africa wasn't going to change that. The taboo about sharing information with the kidnap victim's family would still be in place.

He understood the FBI reasoning on that, but it felt cold as steel. *Yes of course, perfectly reasonable to keep me off the phone so I can't be forced to witness Jess's torment.*

The kidnappers already had his head in a vise, and they were giving the handle one twist after another. He ended the last CMT call of the day glad to be alone again with the memory of the prior night's dream.

He wrote to Jessica about it right away. Finally, something good came from sleep: one of those dreams so real you don't dream at all, but are transported with all of your senses.

I am sailing a small boat into a Cape Town slip to buy a great bottle of celebratory wine. Then the scene changes to Somalia, and I'm carrying my wine bottle along with me while I go straight to the location where they're holding you, and I smuggle you out from under their sleeping noses.

It's easy. We blink and are both returned to our apartment in Nairobi, standing together out on the balcony with candles burning and the city spread out below us. Smulan comes running over, behaving joyfully for the first time since you disappeared. We sit down and take our time to talk about this future we hold again in our hands, this miracle of a new beginning together.

The dream was so real it left a kind of hangover, but it was a sweet one, like a subtle perfume that hangs in the air of an empty room.

Erik met with Dan Hardy to discuss the idea of getting a doctor from Adado to go in and check out Jessica's and Poul's condition, maybe deliver some medication. Hardy agreed that the idea of a doctor was good, since a local doctor was far more likely to receive the kidnappers' trust.

After being warned about his "need-to-know" status, Erik could only hope there wasn't bad news about Jess's condition motivating them to intervene, while keeping him in the dark for their own strategic reasons. He knew she needed her thyroid medication, and there was no guarantee it hadn't been taken from her. If she didn't have it, then she'd been without it for long enough that adverse reactions would soon begin to trouble her.

But it could easily be that Dan Hardy and his colleagues were concealing worse news, to keep him from organizing his own rescue.

CHAPTER SIXTEEN

Jessica:

My imagination had begun to occupy more of my awareness than physical reality. As happens with anything practiced for hours every day over a period of months, I had developed visualization skills that made living either in memory or in fantasy a convincing experience. I spent a lot of my childhood in solitary activities, so I had a vivid imagination. I enjoyed that part of life almost as much as having a few good friends and participating in social activities.

Still, I've always been a social person who enjoyed the company of others. And I felt how deeply this kidnapping ordeal had amplified my natural desire for human closeness, far beyond anything I'd known before. On most nights, that meant a silent conversation with my mom. Her passing in July 2010 was quick; she fell ill on a Friday with a case of severe flu. Nothing went right for her, and she was gone by Monday. That fast.

I happened to be home at the time on my annual leave, and I witnessed my grieving father standing in the kitchen of their home and shuddering under the weight of the news that his childhood sweetheart and lifelong companion was gone. In that moment, both of us were emotionally broken. I watched him stand gripping the back of a chair, head hanging.

He prayed, "God, I don't understand this. I don't understand you ... but I choose to trust you." It's the reason we all played "I Don't Understand Your Ways" at her funeral, a statement of acceptance of the unacceptable, of a higher purpose than we can comprehend.

When I lay on that sleeping mat and recalled that moment in his life, the darkest cave he had ever been in, I realized his choice was pivotal in his recovery. Not by making it easy, but by making it possible.

Even as confused as I was on spiritual issues back then, I felt the sheer power of that statement as soon as he made it, because in his case I knew his faith in that moment wasn't about religion; it was the acknowledgment of his subjective experience of the spiritual aspect of his life. It was a conscious decision to trust that spiritual sense, whether or not he could explain it.

After that day, he remained alone in their family home for the first time and began quietly grieving. Eventually it had been time for me to leave him there and return to Erik and our work in Africa.

I had seen for myself that he didn't just say the words "I don't understand you, but I choose to trust you." He lived by them. He went on from that moment, hour to hour and day to day, conducting himself the way he knew my mom would want him to do. I had already drifted from a lot of my childhood religious thinking, questioning various things, but that didn't seem to have anything to do with this strength of spirit I saw revealed in that hour.

So during my time in the desert, at nights under the desert stars, I discovered that I took some of that strength from remembering my dad's steady conduct. I echoed his words and willed them to be true for me as well, "God, I don't understand this, but

I choose to trust you." Any degree of peace I was able to attain out there began and ended with that conviction. I planted my feet on it and put down roots.

◆ ◆ ◆

The scrub desert region seldom gets rain, but when it does it comes in a liquid avalanche. I spent an entire day shivering in the kidnap car of the one called Dahir, with my clothing already soaked and the downpour drenching the rest of the camp. By this point we had nicknamed Dahir "Helper," because once in a while he would extend a small favor—in this case, allowing me to sit in his car while the world washed away. The stomach bug passing through the camp was wringing me out. I had to keep leaping out of the vehicle and running to a nearby bush through the pouring rain while diarrhea twisted through me, alternating with bouts of vomiting. Each time I got back to the car I was weaker.

This was the first time despair hit me so hard nothing I did could push it away. Since the first day our condition had steadily degraded, and nobody in the camp seemed to have the clarity to pull things together. Dahir didn't even look at me, though I couldn't tell if he was avoiding my eyes out of shame or if he just found me disgusting in my reduced condition. For that I couldn't blame him.

We weren't without entertainment, though. One of the pirates downloaded a news video to his cell phone, a real Saturday afternoon at the movies. The clip showed Somali kidnappers standing behind two captive Spanish sailors who had already been held for three months to the north of us, off the coast of the Puntland region. They were interviewed by Somali journalists. The video showed the two men sitting under ragged orange tarps and looking beaten down and forlorn. Somebody off-camera asked them about their experience in captivity. The poor men just kept saying they'd been held for months without any word from their employer, nothing from their government. They added that on some days they weren't even permitted water.

Abdi gloated and chuckled and preened, mouthing a mix of broken English and making dramatic gestures so expressive he could have been a street mime. The gist was the two men in the video had just been successfully ransomed for $35 million!

The other men cheered at that like sports fanatics during the playoffs. No matter what words Abdi had actually spoken, the meaning they took was "success is inevitable!"

I'm sure my mouth was wide open, I was gobsmacked. *He can't believe that! Thirty-five million dollars?*

I could only stare into Abdi's opaque red eyes and conclude that on some level he actually believed his absurd fantasy. But I didn't see anything on that clip about the Spaniards' being released, let alone any news of $35 million, money supposedly paid out for two old fishermen and a dinky boat. It was so idiotic it made me want to scream. Frustration put a bitter taste in my mouth.

By the end of the day my fever began to spike. I felt my temperature rising and my overall condition heading for the tank. I asked the men over and over to get me a doctor, but couldn't get the words out without sobbing. They hated it when I cried, and usually reacted with anger, ordering me to shut up. This time nobody bothered to threaten me. But I honestly couldn't tell if I was crying in sickness and fear, or just from the humiliation of having to beg for things most people wouldn't deny to an animal.

Poul finally dared to go to Jabreel on my behalf and plead the case for getting a doctor for me. But Abdi was nursing a *khat* hangover and anxiously awaiting their next delivery of the stuff. He flipped into a rage at the "insult" of Poul's daring to take the initiative and do something so bold as to ask a favor of him. Abdi railed and shouted more angry threats, coherent only in manifesting his ill intent. I asked him if I could call the contact man calling himself

Mohammed, hoping that if Mohammed was really connected to my NGO he would arrange medical treatment. The request was dismissed.

I think I was saved by greed in that moment. At some point Abdi or Jabreel must have looked at me and realized they were closing in on having a dead American kidnap victim on their hands. I don't think there is enough *khat* in Somalia to medicate away the anxiety over that. The concern I had heard from these men on the first day, when they were parroting "Amer-ee-cahn" and throwing glances at me, now came full circle.

They worried that my very presence in the plan was an unforeseen risk. If not, they had no reason to throw troubled looks at me and talk about an "Amer-ee-cahn." And now, right at this point, I felt everything take a change of direction just as solidly as you feel a train hit a fork in the tracks and head off on a new bearing. The power of greed caught hold.

A few hours later a local doctor was brought in. Nobody told me where they got him or what he had been told about us. He may have been a freelancer, or he could have been part of their group. Their number seemed to grow larger all the time.

But there he was. He brought a little bag of tetracycline to fight the bug and some Buscopan tablets for the stomach cramps. His exam consisted of taking my blood pressure and tossing the bag of pills at me—not to me, at me. I guess he wanted to make it clear whose side he was on. With that, he went off to chew *khat* with Jabreel and the other men instead of returning to wherever he came from, saying he needed to remain close by for the night to "check" on me. He never came back. However, since ordinary sleep was out of the question, I was up often enough to observe him throughout the night, motor-mouthing his way through the *khat* supply. In the morning, I watched him leave after sticking around long enough for Jama, the supply guy, to show up with the group's daily ration of *khat*.

The degree of control exerted by the ultimate operator of this venture was apparent in the handling of the *khat* deliveries. Each day's ration came in an amount limited to what the men could use in a single day. The fact that *khat* has to be chewed fresh-picked meant nobody could build up enough of a personal stash to walk away. Yet the delivery brought plenty for all, leaving the true *khat* aficionado with the taste of what it was like to have all the *khat* he could chew while knowing the supply would stop the instant he strayed. The luxury of that steady supply was an impressive binding force. It struck me that these guys were prisoners just as much as I was, maybe more so. At least if I could get out of there, I would be free. Addicts pack their troubles along with them.

Once everybody had a good chew going with the new supply, Abdi assembled his "militia," or unemployed pirates, or random criminal kidnappers, or whatever name best suited them. The purpose of the meeting appeared serious. He and all the men were in a somber mood. Poul and I kept out of the way and quietly attempted to decipher their purpose.

My natural optimism had me hoping they were meeting to discuss accepting a ransom settlement. That thought didn't last.

Instead the very nightmare that first called me to the African continent played itself out in front of us, because Abdi's current manic swing had convinced him the "militia" men needed some early morning training. Many of them were boys. Teenagers. And yet most appeared to weigh something like a hundred pounds. They were nearly skeletal.

Abdi ordered them to assemble into marching lines, and there I saw it: child or teenaged soldiers, in the terrible flesh, alongside the other grown men. Most were still in their underwear and all looked badly strung out or hung over.

More information was conveyed to me in that instant than I could absorb for many days afterward; those boys-who-were-not-boys had come to this place to do this dark work because somebody promised them all the *khat* they could chew, and maybe some goat meat once a week with a little powdered milk. And if the ransom came through, there might be some share of the spoils.

I figured that each guard's share would be minuscule. As bargaining positions go, what could be offered by any one of those boys? Each one knew there were countless lost souls who would do the same thing he was doing for the same compensation and same hope of reward. His share, if he ever saw it, would certainly not be enough to change his life. It would not buy him a new home. It wouldn't get his family out of poverty or even feed them for long. If he brought home significant money and allowed it to be known in a region so desperately poor, the word would spread like radio waves until the entire family was besieged by demands from every quarter.

It was a desperation they, as the new "rich" folks, would be obliged to relieve by Somali customs, whether from the kindness of their hearts or simply out of knowing what was good for them. If a soldier boy lived alone, the simple fact that he had anything more than the rags on his back would reveal money to one and all. His friends would be as desperate as anyone else, perhaps even more inclined to use violence, and here again the boy would share, either out of kindness or because he wanted to stay alive. I had lived with this culture long enough to know that whether he was alone or was part of a family, that kidnapper's share of the ransom would be gone in days.

Now against the African desert backdrop I watched mirror images of the lost souls who had first called to me years before, when I first learned about child soldiers. I had strained to make myself believe such a thing truly existed—artificially created juvenile psychotics, "soldiers" turned into killing machines by enforced drug addiction and the resignation of those with bridges burned beyond repair. Right there in front of me was the grotesque irony of my own good intentions turned back upon themselves. I watched my vision of coming to Africa to combat this dreadful phenomenon morph into a badly told joke.

I saw it, then: the piece missing from my original inspiration to come and work with such young people. My mistake had been to picture myself working with a human presence who hears you, one who sees you, one who—at the very least—has a functional consciousness you can engage.

None of that was present here. The damage done to these dead-eyed souls was now physically affecting them, exposed by their attempts at close-order drill; they all seemed to have bad motor skills. Whether it was their drug use or just the effect of long-term malnutrition, something had seriously reduced their level of physical control.

The impression was that their bloodstreams, flooded with *khat*, had reacted to a head full of memories of crimes committed against their families, and that the power of the mixture converted each one into a living zombie. Now they stumbled along glassy-eyed in their stained underpants. I saw nothing to connect with in their eyes. Nobody was home. It was as if the termites from the colonies out there had mystic powers, and now occupied these bodies, wearing them like giant meat sweaters while they shuffled around fingering their high-powered weapons.

By this time we'd come to call the youngest boy, Abdilahi—the one who used his mine awareness class bracelet to fasten a bipod to a gun barrel—"Crack Baby." Jabreel had kindly made sure we knew that "Crack Baby" was said to have killed three people already in his young life. His unpredictable behavior was a frequent source of menace. The dead eyes told a story so compelling I felt the impact in my bones. Upon an order by the Chairman, or by Abdi, perhaps even by Jabreel, any one of these parading kids would kill us. They could do that as easily as asking about the weather.

But so far they had held back. Why? Something had stayed their hands from us, at least up to that point. After all, they only needed us "alive" to assure the ransom, and there are a lot of degrees of "alive" that fall far below "alive and well." Why were they not more physically abusive? Poul got slugged around, but he hadn't been seriously injured by anyone, at least not yet. And while I'd been roughed up somewhat, we could have easily been in much worse condition. Past abductions of Westerners in this region included routine beatings during which victims were pulverized for nothing more than their captors' amusement. Some were tortured with thirst in more extreme versions of what was done to us; others had seen their families contacted directly by the kidnappers and emotionally tortured, thus raising the stakes for negotiators.

And yet something was preventing them from doing that degree of harm to us, even though they clearly had the capacity for it. Moreover, they acted amused by the prospect and had displayed their humor in fake-shooting us and continually pointing loaded weapons at us. Their abuse took the form of passive aggression instead of overt torture, denying us nearly everything we needed to survive and then grudgingly giving out little bits of it—but always only a little, nothing you could store up for a breakout.

Anyone keeping a score card of the ironies piling up would have made another entry, noting that the kidnappers' determination to make certain we never had more than we needed to survive that day was, in fact, the same strategy they lived under with the *khat* supply. We were all just prisoners there, not of our own device, as the Eagles song goes, but rather the devices of the Chairman, and perhaps someone else, if the Chairman was using an investor's money.

Irony functions poorly in the absence of an appreciative audience. The men didn't show any signs to indicate that anything about our common captivity humanized me in their eyes. Naturally, in such company the term "humanized" would be literal. As a woman and a foreigner, full human status was not mine to claim.

Poul could occasionally get a bit of conversation going with one of the men, but I would occupy the same social stratum as one of the termite stacks out there, if not for the ransom potential attached to me. At least the termite stacks had a clear function in helping provide better cell reception.

I searched in vain for signs of guilt in the eyes of anyone who looked at me. Sometimes they averted their gaze, but instead of shame what I saw there seemed more like a complete lack of interest. Some of the men obviously took personal amusement in my illness. When they looked at me it was clear they saw a spoiled American who deserved her fate. Nothing in any of that explained what element of restraint was operating here on my behalf, or whether that restraint would hold. Whatever was controlling their violence up to that point, the force of that invisible thing was keeping us alive.

It wasn't any form of affection. I didn't bother to attempt to position myself as one who had earned any special consideration from them because of my work, to let them see I was in this place to help their people regain a functional society. Here, those goals sounded like crap. *You've been in our country doing what? Really? And why is that?*

My mouth tasted of the bad diesel water we used for washing when we were lucky enough to get it. My lower torso throbbed with nausea while I got lost in silent arguments with myself: *I didn't put myself here.* But I did. *I didn't put myself here.* But I had. *I didn't put myself here.* But there I was anyway, stuck amid the jabbering of green-lipped zombies.

Surely one of the circles of Hell is where they make you wait for you know not what, and you are given no sign when it will end.

CHAPTER SEVENTEEN

Now that the Crisis Management Team had a line to the kidnappers, one of the essential challenges was to handle the delicate negotiations in such a way that the kidnappers wouldn't give up and sell their "property" rather than continue talking. The kidnappers' spokesman, Jabreel, repeatedly cried out, "Pirates crazy!" and warned them the crazy pirates were threatening to sell Jessica and her colleague to the Al-Shabaab network because the drawn-out negotiations were costing them too much. It was a tiresome threat, repeatedly raised, but the prospect remained too real to ignore.

Erik had always carried a certain sense of pride in his ability to show patience when necessary. Many times in his work, the ability served him well while he threaded legal needles in delicate negotiations. From the day of Jessica's capture he began learning about levels of patience unknown to him. Until then, patience had been the capacity to hold his tongue when somebody got hot under the collar in a negotiating situation and went overboard on the tough talk and the threats. But the cost of that sort of patience was nothing, truly nothing, compared to the cost of silence now.

This torture only began with the idiots on the other end of the kidnappers' phone connection. The worst of it for Erik was self-inflicted when he agonized over being helpless to take some sort of bold and sweeping action, and force all of this to a conclusion.

Take the old-fashioned caveman approach, hunt down those men and fight them to the death.

Even if he had all the information in the world, there was nothing to be done with it. He was already connected to a huge network ranging from top politicians to guys on the ground in Somalia, as well as former Special Forces people from different countries, all of whom had offered their help. What kept him from accepting it was his pledge to do only what was in Jessica's best interest. At this point he knew a private attack wasn't an option, and even if an armed rescue plan went forward, the real professionals needed to do it. That didn't mean the temptation wasn't severe.

It gave him no pleasure to recognize this in himself. This is what he experienced as the power of raw frustration mixed with mortal fear for a loved one. By this time in the waiting period he had already witnessed, in John Buchanan, how it was possible to remain essentially calm and steadfast even amid such terrible anguish. He just wasn't quite that way himself. He would have loved to have taken it all like some star in an action movie, one of those guys who always knows exactly how far to push things in order to save the day. But the world of movies had nothing to tell him.

What did he actually know? (1) They had a Crisis Management Team (CMT), made up of professional hostage negotiators and selected members of Jessica's NGO. This team was linked to the families' communicator, who spoke on the phone to Jabreel and funneled any news to Erik and the families via Dan or the CMT's family liaison. (2) The U.S. government was involved via the FBI, which provided inside consultation on the negotiation strategy to the CMT. (3) The U.S. government knew the exact location where Jessica was being held.

Her father, brother, and sister knew they couldn't do anything for her in Nairobi, any more than Erik could, but he understood how badly they needed to be there. They arrived from the United

States by way of London, all three sick from travel and stress, but after getting back to the apartment in Nairobi and talking things through, they decided to accompany him to Matt's house for an overview on the case and to hear of the Bureau's approval of the work being done by the CMT.

Erik could tell John appreciated Matt's low-key sincerity and his intense devotion to his job. Erik and John agreed that if you have to go through something as terrible as this, you are lucky to have someone on point as responsive as Matt had been.

It was good for Erik to get back to the apartment, cramped as it was, and have a long talk. They all prayed for Jess together, and he felt no conflict at all in openly engaging in prayer. Strangely, while he still had no idea what he really believed about the nature of existence, Jessica's example had taught him to separate spirituality from the dictates of organized religion.

They all agreed they didn't feel like doing the touristy types of things that they would have been doing if everyone was there together, but they also felt that they'd go crazy if they just stayed home and hoped for a phone call. Later, when they did have formal meetings with the CMT or Jessica's employers, Erik pushed them and repeatedly asked how they could have put their staff in danger like this if there was a threat to expats in Galkayo, strongly indicating to them it would be foolish to do anything less than their utmost to remedy this.

He demanded to know what medical and psychological arrangements they had prepared for Jess if she made it out. If she made it out tomorrow, what were their plans for her? They offered no answers that were good enough, and left him smashing his fists on the table. He consulted with them about doing whatever they could at that late hour, organizing community support such as local demonstrations and meetings with elders from the communities near the spot where they knew the hostages were being held. But nothing seemed to help.

Jessica's family decided to stay close to Erik and Jessica's apartment while only venturing out once in a while. Erik was glad to do a little sightseeing with them when he could, to at least give them a feel for some of the things that had made Jessica fall in love with the idea of living in Africa in the first place. It seemed important to communicate that her life there was much different from the madness confronting them. Jessica had known sunlight and happiness on this continent. She had earned the respect and in some cases even the love of people she knew and worked with. While she spent much of her personal time with Erik, she had spent her working life there giving the best of herself to the young minds of that emerging society.

He told anyone who would listen about her love for teaching, how she reveled in the successes of her students. Some of her students were impossible to reach, as they are at nearly any school. She hated that and took each loss personally. But Jessica had also seen the best of the young minds she encountered grasping the lifelines she threw them. She witnessed their own self-motivated climb, up and away into the future of those who have been awakened to their own potential. She knew students on that path might learn to reason their way through a complex world to find, somewhere within that world, a place they could fairly call their own. This was what Erik's wife had brought to Nairobi, and in Somalia she trained teaching staff and then observed them in the classroom, all to help give them a better chance in life. If only, he thought, there was some way to make these people understand that about her.

You can't let them take her from us. That night he prayed without any sense of what the listener might look like. Surely, he thought, the loved ones of kidnap victims all offer the same prayer, if they pray, hoping their cause somehow makes them more worthy of cosmic favor than mere gamblers praying for a happy roll of the dice.

◆ ◆ ◆

Jessica:

About two weeks into the kidnapping, Jabreel sidled over to me one evening and announced we would be talking to Mohammed that night. I had already started to fall asleep and didn't relish jumping into an SUV and bouncing across the desert to wherever they felt was a good strategic location for a call.

"Planes. Spies," Jabreel said, pointing overhead. "Amer-ee-cahn. We go far for call."

I rolled my eyes at that. Really, I couldn't help myself. The idea of magical American spy planes buzzing around overhead because of Poul and me was just another absurd image in this broken landscape.

"No planes, Jabreel. I'm not an important American." I pointed at him. "You. Too much *khat!*" I pretended to chew.

He looked up when something caught his eye, and we both turned to see a couple of cars pull up. Dahir and a few other familiar faces jumped out looking pleased with themselves. They presented Poul and me with a two-inch foam mattress for each of us, plus one pillow apiece and a *hijab* for me, to cover my head.

Jabreel beamed at me as if this was all his personal accomplishment while the men brought over a large bag of bananas and grapefruit. As hungry as we were for fresh food of any kind, my heart sank at the sight of this. These guys were hunkering down for the long haul and instructing us to do the same. Sure, I welcomed the idea of getting something soft between me and the ground. And a pillow? I hadn't even thought to ask for one. But still, I couldn't raise any enthusiasm for the specter of an extended stay.

Jabreel clearly wanted some sign of gratitude. The best I could offer was a politely vague response, so he quit and walked away.

Eventually some mysterious person decided it was too late to journey into the wilderness for a phone call that night. There was no way to know for certain whether my words or my attitude toward Jabreel actually had anything to do with the decision not to go, or if he was the one who made it. Being left in the dark about decisions was standard procedure for us.

Instead they walked us back out into the open for some sleep-or-we-shoot-you. We toted along our new mattresses and pillows, and as soon as we reached the selected spot we set up our beds right away, moving swiftly to make it unnecessary for anyone to yell, "Sleep!"

Repetition and habit were teaching us to move half a step ahead of the enforcers, doing everything possible to stay in rhythm with them and avoid triggering anyone's paranoia. I lay down like a good doggie who didn't need to be ordered to sleep. After that there was only the open sky and a veil of darkness that I hoped would be unfaithful to them.

A few more days blurred together into a single piece. They were more about frustrated boredom and smoldering resentment than the moments of terror we had before then. Poul and I agreed neither of us felt any sense of "Stockholm Syndrome" in terms of mentally joining these fools. But it was impossible not to feel attached to the rare individuals who seemed to look at us and see human beings, even for an instant.

When Dahir, the guy we nicknamed "Helper," had to take a car in for shop work or leave to pick up supplies, I felt insecure in his absence because at least he spoke some English. For that reason we didn't like to see him get too far away.

"Helper" often helped without realizing it; we could mark the passing of time by his punctual prayer sessions, repeated five times a day. He also carried a small radio around, which none of the others had, and we could sometimes overhear Somali BBC newscasts.

The most bizarre twist arrived when I heard my name and the name of our NGO within the indecipherable Somali commentary. But there was some comfort in simply hearing signs of life in the outside world, when our own world had shrunk down to this one small and unhappy camp.

I found myself late one morning sitting under a torn orange tarp and taking wry note of the fact that the tarp could have been taken from that pirate video showing those two captive Spanish sailors, the ones who complained of being held for months with no word on negotiations.

At least our people are talking, I thought. Maybe that thought activated Murphy's Law—Abdi walked in from the outskirts of the camp, where he had been pacing and screaming into his phone. He was in such a foul temper that when Poul asked to "use the toilet" (walk to a nearby bush), Abdi pointed to a large, heavy blanket and demanded Poul use it to cover up while doing his business. It was a ridiculous demand in the heavy heat of the day, good for nothing more than yet another petty humiliation. I suppose part of his screaming phone conversations regarded their growing fear that we were being monitored from airplanes. Couldn't these guys understand how much a search mission like that would cost? The planes? The pilots? The fuel?

To hell with it, I thought. I was tired of trying to argue away Abdi's paranoia.

Poul grudgingly did as he was told, but while he was gone Abdi picked up a large stick and began chopping at bushes with it, knocking down branches and banging it on the ground as if testing it for strength. He did it with more grace than a primate posturing for an adversary, but for the same reason and effect.

When Poul returned, Abdi's intentions became clear when he lifted the stick and attacked Poul with it, beating him to the ground. I felt my terror level spike.

"Where is big money?" Abdi shouted, swinging the stick like a bat. "Where is big money?" Smack. "Where is big money?" Smack. "Where is big money?"

"It's not our fault!" Poul cried, uselessly trying to reason with a stoned, raging speed freak. "We don't control Mohammed!"

"F**k Mohammed! He lie! Small money! Small money!"

He swung the stick against Poul's outstretched arms and hands. Poul cried out for him to stop, and I sobbed in frustration and outrage. Abdi noticed my distress, but as usual, my tears generated no sympathy and only provoked him further. He stomped over to me waving the stick.

"You up! Up! Up! *Hijab!* Walk!"

This amounted to an order from Abdi to stand up, cover my head with the *hijab*, and start walking out into the open desert. I started off without giving him any trouble, but even so Poul got whacked into following along with us. Abdi was in such a rage he couldn't seem to stop himself from continuing to assail Poul. His rage moved past any attempt to persuade Poul of anything and simply became therapy for Abdi's personal turmoil.

The instant lesson for me was that the specter of violent execution never gets better. We can adjust and inure ourselves to many hardships and challenges in this world, but the prospect of being murdered by a hateful enemy does not mellow over time. I had no clever lines to toss out, no movie-star cool to sneer at my captor, and I felt no sense of magical protection.

I knew there were centuries of human history packed with tales of faithful people who were killed in the midst of praying for release, and who found release only in death. Something told me not to bother to pray for cosmic magic. I just focused on praying for my own strength. I didn't doubt that if I allowed fear to overcome me, Abdi's rage would go over the tipping point. It was plain to me that when he looked at me now, he was starting to see red ink where dollar signs used to be.

We walked along with Abdi screaming into my face like a particularly energetic drill sergeant. "I am guerilla warrior! You f**k with me? You f**k with me? Where is big money?"

I forced my voice into a dead calm. "We don't control the money, Abdi. We don't even know Mohammed."

"F**k Mohammed! He give small money! Small money!"

"I'm sorry about that, Abdi, but—"

"Where is big money?"

"I don't know! You have to listen to me, Abdi! I don't know! Poul doesn't know! You hit us, we still don't know!"

He stopped us and forced us to the ground under a large bush, then squatted in front of me close enough to bathe me in his body odor and halitosis. He glared into my eyes and then used his fingertip to slowly and deliberately write the number 18 in the sand.

"I get eighteen million in seven days—*seven* days, Jesses—or I cut off your head!"

There are times when frustration is more painful than terror. With any form of fear, the message running through the body is simple: run or fight. Frustration occurs when you can't run, can't fight, and can't stop the torment. It not only fills you with the pain of an intense fight-or-flight adrenaline dose, it forces the muscles themselves to strain against the brain's demands to act, act, act.

If I had allowed myself to scream I wouldn't have been able to stop. I had no power to keep the tears out of my eyes or prevent them from running down my face, but I refused to openly cry. The only source of dignity left in that hour was to deny this man the satisfaction of goading me into some sort of hysterical response.

I glanced over at Poul and saw him crying, too. I think even the biggest and strongest man could be reduced to childhood emotions when sustained evil is done to him and he is powerless to fight back. I had seen interviews with war heroes who claimed anyone can be broken in captivity, no matter how strong he is, how well trained, how macho and defiant. They talked about how we all have the tiny and frightened child we once were still residing somewhere inside us. These guys had found ours with a few simple phrases.

"You die here!" and "I send Mohammed *your head!*"

Part Three

———

DANCE OF THE
GREEN-TEETH ZOMBIES

CHAPTER EIGHTEEN

From the first FBI phone call with Agent Matt Espenshade, Erik was informed that the situation would be monitored "at the highest level" of the U.S. government, and that if any military action came down in the form of a secret raid on foreign soil, the order had to originate from the Oval Office itself. It was helpful to have the chain of command explained to him, but there was no way to determine how much conviction stood behind the words. Was that explanation only a way to tell him the U.S. government was either too distracted or too uncommitted to help?

Everyone on the Crisis Management Team assured him the international diplomatic implications were disastrous for the United States if Jessica died before they got her out, or if any mission to save her and her colleague failed. Still, the list of obstacles facing any potential rescue team offered little chance of success. The same victims whose rescue was intended could easily become casualties amid the chaos of battle with a panicked band of drug-fueled fighters, most of whom had nowhere else to go and little to lose.

In the daily briefings, whether with Matt and the FBI or Dan and the CMT, Erik always made it a point to have questions ready, aimed at getting the others to consider things they might not have thought about yet. He repeatedly raised the question of risk to potential rescuers, the ones who would actually go into harm's way if there was no other choice. He spent days running around to the pharmacies and doctors to get her necessary medications to send to Jessica's captors. But the results were discouraging. He was able to be fairly certain the packages were getting as far as the town of Adado, near the kidnappers' camp, but at that point he had no way to know that the kidnappers were convinced there were tracking devices hidden inside the medicine packs, and therefore refused to let any of it near her, no matter how sick she became.

In the meantime he also used his knowledge of the Somali gossip line to deliberately spread rumors, especially when he was on a work trip in Somaliland, saying negotiations were going on but that the family had no idea where she was. He sent out another rumor saying both families were selling off private possessions to raise money, struggling for every dollar to raise the ransom money. The intent was to encourage overconfidence in the kidnappers and tempt them into relaxing their guard. He sent word via the local clan grapevines: There was no reason to panic or do anything rash; the kidnappers' plan was working so far—the families had no idea what to do and were raising money as fast as possible. It was a blind effort, blowing a fog of confusion toward the enemy, but he knew the landscape and trusted it to function.

Erik also worked to discourage Jess's family and friends from losing patience and expressing their frustration to the media or anyone outside their circle. Everything about this situation forced him to consider how the smallest slip of electronic information between two private people could be hijacked for use by distant criminals. His experience with local politics made him leery of discussing the case with anyone who might use it for personal promotion without regard to Jessica's welfare.

So far, no one could be certain the Somalis had any intention of selling off the hostages, so this meant that condition number one for mounting a rescue attempt (if Jess was known to be in immediate lethal danger) had not been met. And while Jessica's health had to have been badly affected by this entire experience, there was no specific information on that. Up to now, the kidnappers' communicator, Jabreel, hadn't allowed her to talk long enough to describe her physical state, so condition number two (that Jess's health was failing) had not been met either.

Condition number three (that negotiations had stalled) was drawing closer. Longer periods between calls were being enforced by the captors. Negotiations weren't going well at all. Even though Erik and the family were kept out of the dollar negotiations, they had to be told the ransom demands were far out of range in order to allow them to participate in strategy discussions.

This Jabreel character seemed to go into a rage every few seconds. More than his interest in communicating on behalf of the kidnappers, he constantly changed the topic to insist he was not one of "these pirates," and that he ran "a local NGO" and was "a respected citizen." He insisted he'd been brought in especially to give weight to the negotiations. Any comment made to Jabreel indicating he might be anything less was met with another emotional outburst from him, wasting valuable bits of communication time.

Erik's years of experience in the Somali political scene gave him certain insights into the reasons for the kidnappers' irrational demands, beyond what he was officially allowed to know as the husband of the American hostage. He had a good idea of what the American agencies in the area might be capable of doing in gathering intelligence. Having followed current events in Somalia over the years, he could imagine some of the surveillance methods used by Matt and his colleagues. It was public knowledge throughout the media that American drones were used in the region, and he had a few guesses about what other methods were employed.

He had knowledge of many of the local people who could

tap into the region's gossip network, and for all of technology's advancement, this network remained blind to the latest spy machinery. In this manner the old ways returned, back from the time before these dazzling things. This was the safest way for Erik to get messages to the kidnappers that they would not realize originated with him, hints of misinformation to help keep the kidnappers off-balance. On the verbal gossip network, communication was done quietly, one person to another, along a chain of speakers known to one another. Each one is responsible for whatever he speaks into that network. Liars wake up to groups of angry people crowded at their door. The fear of vengeance from one's neighbors keeps the network safe from loose lips. But it does not keep the network safe from outside information, clandestinely fed into the arteries of the community.

On the ground in Somalia, the kidnappers were plagued by ignorance of the capabilities of their opponents, but they used what they knew to put up their best defense. They kept the hostages covered under scrub tree branches during the daylight hours, which effectively concealed them from overhead observation. But their nighttime procedures failed them, when they consistently moved the hostages into the open for sleeping.

The raging paranoia of the kidnappers—their long trips into the desert to disguise their location with the cell signal, the days spent holding the hostages under tree cover—had a firm basis in reality, as far as it went. Although they held the upper hand through the blunt-force tactic of surrounding their hostages with armed fighters, their dominance ended with that one cold fact.

The Americans knew exactly where they were.

The Crisis Management Team was also gathering as much intelligence as possible on the daily life in the camp and what resources were consumed there. It was logical that the town of Adado was where they received daily shipments of everything they needed. Jabreel and several others stayed in or near Adado when they weren't out in the bush with the rest.

At this point the CMT knew which subclans were involved and even which of the clan elders and local political leaders could be trusted. Most important, they knew the local authorities were either too corrupt or too compromised to offer meaningful intervention. Uniformed authorities could not be counted on to participate in any part of a rescue, because in the planning stage there would be no way to seal the flow of information in advance of the attack. They could never rely on an air strike or a proxy attack by local authorities. Options began to crumble away.

CHAPTER NINETEEN

Jessica:

I don't think a person gets used to being forced to live in filthy conditions, but I found for the sake of my sanity that I had to give in to the idea of it, at least: using the "toilet" behind bushes, with men wandering in all directions, furtive body washing using a small bottle of water while huddled in a depression in the ground behind anything that could obscure the view. We had to use the same water for bathing they used for making tea or soup, and it all tasted as if they'd actually filled the cans without bothering to rinse out the traces of diesel fuel already in them. Eventually they must have realized diesel fuel can kill you, and began supplying us with bottled water for drinking, but the diesel water remained standard for any washing. The toughest part was trying to avoid the feeling that I was descending into an animal existence I would never escape.

To raise my spirits and give me something to do, I capitalized on the fact that the men were getting too lazy to bake bread, so I persuaded them to let me do it. My fledgling efforts amused them no end, but I soon got the hang of it. What a relief to prepare food that might have some sand in it but was at least free of the communal bacteria line.

I mixed several handfuls of flour with water and used my hands (washed as clean as possible) to knead the dough over and over again, then divided it into pieces about the size of a baseball. I pounded each "baseball" out into a disk shape, almost as flat as a pancake.

Poul and I found an excuse to spend a few minutes together each time I did it because he volunteered to gather armloads of thin, burnable sticks for firewood. Even though they kept us apart most of the time, we were able to manipulate them somewhat by playing on their laziness.

But what little conversation we could manage consisted mostly of mutual complaints, and yes, I believe the scale leaned hard toward my side. These angry thugs had managed to smear so many aspects of my dignity, of my sense of myself as a person. Somehow it felt as though I would have been cooperating with them by remaining silent and not complaining when I could.

We could absolutely agree on a few things: Most of these guys were drugged-up morons. We made small exchanges of passing remarks, and I found that I needed this conversation. The topics were all shallow enough, but that didn't matter at all. The power in it lay in simply having a few moments to speak with someone from your own world, all the while surrounded by so much that was not merely foreign, but also twisted and malignant.

On some mornings they would allow me to walk in circles with Poul around our tree, stretching our legs and doing a little deep breathing. We couldn't make noise or sing out loud for fear of drawing attention and causing somebody to get irritated, so while we shuffled along in those monotonous circles I sang under my breath, usually the same music we played at my mom's funeral. The version I knew was done by the singer Rita Springer. "*I don't understand your ways, but I will give you my song . . .*"

The familiarity of it put me in close touch with my mother, made me sense her energy. I always thought of her and Erik at the same time. The combined sense of each one's love for me formed a joyful wave. I felt it lifting me to its highest point every time I came to the lyric, "*I'm desperately seeking, in faith still believing, the sight of your face is all that I'm needing. And I will say to you—it's gonna be worth it, it's gonna be worth it, it's gonna be worth it all.*"

More than any other piece of music, this song was my sound-track to those monotonous circular walks. I'm sure there are many other ways for someone to deal with this particular form of tedium and danger. I sang my way through it. I freely admit to using the uplift from that lyric as a load-bearing wall for my morale and for the connection it represented to powerful forces in my life.

With the morning constitutional done, I made the bread dough for "Jessica's Captive Campfire Sand Rolls" while Poul built a roaring fire, then let it burn down to coals. We threw the pancake-shaped pieces of dough on top of the coals for a minute on each side, using a stick to turn them. No matter how long I spent pounding the dough, there was always sand left in it. But you go with what you've got.

Once they were a bit done on the outside and firm enough to gently handle, the inside still had to be cooked, but direct contact with the fire gave them too much heat. They would burn before they cooked through. The trick was to use a stick to make a hole in the sand, then place the bread in the hole, bury it under more hot sand, and then pile hot coals on top of the protective sand layer. About five minutes later, after using the ground for an oven, I used the stick to dig up a hot piece of something resembling bread. As for the final yield, you may wonder: Was the earth-oven roll tasty? Oh, yes—if you were one of those kids who ate paste in grade school, you'd love this stuff. What Dahir the "Helper" showed me how to do, to create what became my regular breakfast when we could have it, was to rip the bread into pieces and pour hot sweet tea over it. No, it wasn't a breakfast pastry, but the combination of bread and sugar brought that to mind.

To battle for survival among so many hostile males, I instinctively took to behavior I suppose I shared with female captives as far back in time as you'd care to go. I did everything I could to avoid provoking what might be called an "enthusiastic male response." The precautions included letting my appearance completely go except for basic cleanliness, such as that was. I also apparently guessed right in advertising my status as a "mother." As far as I could tell this was keeping the men at bay. Fortunately, Poul and I were kept so isolated that even though the men were in the camp area, there wasn't much occasion for any of them to interact directly with us.

This, as you can imagine, was more than fine with me. But Jabreel was another matter. Unlike everyone else except Abdi, Jabreel's job made it necessary for him to interact with us a great deal, now that the negotiations were underway. Jabreel seemed to be feeling the heady rush of being the contact point for the ransom they all anticipated. And like men down through the ages who suddenly find themselves in a key position of power, he was feeling frisky.

He fancied himself an artful molester. He made weak excuses to justify sitting next to me, maybe placing a reassuring hand on my shoulder, my arm, my thigh. He always acted with the thinnest possible cover, just "passing by" and passing too close, "guiding" me in one direction or another by physically handling me instead of just pointing. He might offer a sympathetic pat of "encouragement" or some piece of flattery about my light hair while he stroked his filthy hands over it.

At first he reacted playfully to me when I removed his hand, but it never discouraged him for long. While the days and nights progressed, the excuses for the touching became ugly satires of affection and kindness.

"Jesses, I come to America (stroke, stroke, pat, pat). Stay with you."

"No, Jabreel. No. I'm married."

"I am your good friend (stroke, rub, pat). You're my good friend?"

"I am your married friend, Jabreel."

"Erik?"

"Yes, Erik. I love Erik."

"I come to live with you and Erik! We are happy! (pat, pat, pat). I will sleep on floor. By your bed."

"By my . . . God."

"What you say?"

"I said I'm *married*, Jabreel. So are you."

"You are beautiful" (stroke, stroke, pat, pat, pat).

He had not become a rapist, quite. He was more like those memories so many women have: that one especially awful back-seat wrestling match with some seriously wasted horndog, pawing you like a St. Bernard and smelling of flop sweat.

Poul saw it, but there was nothing he could do. By now, I'm sure he knew as well as I did that another ticking clock had just appeared. Now, within that larger time pressure of the money negotiations was a secondary timer. It was measuring out Jabreel's dwindling sense of personal restraint.

He seemed to need secrecy to make his advances toward me. That was good in that it sharply reduced his times of opportunity. The brain of every Western woman working in the region, including mine, was imprinted with images from news footage of the bodies of female abductees, recovered long after a vicious gang rape and a final, merciful gunshot.

I made it a point to twist away from him as discreetly as possible. With a man as volatile as this, I had no doubt it would be suicidal to add public humiliation to the rejection of his poisonously childish advances.

On the night we recorded our first video message, he paused in his drunken frat boy behavior while he frowned and got to his feet. Our people, he said, were not cooperating, and their offers were much too small: less than three hundred thousand dollars. An insult. He sniffed at me when he said it, leaving me to wonder which insult he had in mind.

I understood the delicate situation, but I was just as perplexed by all the protracted negotiations as any of these kidnappers. I also couldn't help but wonder—*What is going on with the negotiators back home?* As with so much else about the experience, there was only silence for an answer.

Before long, we were rousted and thrust back into the kidnap cars and driven for hours out into the desert. The striking thing about each of these trips was that they were so long, apparently aimless, but determined in their length. We rolled out into the desert and pulled far off the track into the low brush to another anonymous location that looked like any other to me. Nevertheless, more men were waiting there, with Jabreel among them.

As soon as I saw him I asked what was going on. He responded, "Not good. They are fighting me because your people are not cooperating."

He then explained that we were going to make a video to see if that would speed up negotiations. Before showtime, Jabreel decided to play the happy salesman and brought us each a can of soda, a rare treat—warming us up for the camera, I guess. He walked us over to a nearby tree where several other men joined us. Jabreel pointed in their direction while they approached.

"Journalists!" he announced. The "journalists" brought one tiny video camera that they proceeded to mount on a huge tripod, creating a contraption that looked as if it belonged in an animated cartoon. There was no time to find any humor in it.

Jabreel told me in a grim voice, "You say this message. Say what I tell you."

They focused the camera against the brush in the background. Two guards, the "Colonel" and Mohammed (another Mohammed), wrapped their sleeping sheets around their heads and faces. The pastel sheet around one guy's head might have looked like a ridiculous excuse for a scary mask, if not for the belt of ammunition over his shoulders and the assault rifle pointed at me.

They took up menacing positions behind us, holding their weapons at the ready. All the elements of a viral death video.

My brain spun out desperate optimism: *At least this is only a video message. They're not going to kill us. Even if they put the words in our mouths, it's just a message. It's a proof-of-life type of thing—that's all.*

On the bright side this could have been, but apparently was not, our night to star in an execution video. Plenty of others already had. According to Abdi, we had yet one week before it came to that.

At first it seemed as if only Poul would be allowed to speak on camera. They put him on, and he began the speech they required of him, telling the camera we were "both okay," and stressing "there must be no attack by American military forces or any other forces acting on their behalf."

I expected that much, I guess, but then Poul went on to add a part I hadn't heard them tell him to say, imploring our families to get more directly involved and tap their own personal wealth on the ransom efforts. That gave me a real shock, though I was confident our families would see the video and realize we were being coached; there wasn't any "wealth" for them to tap, and they knew that I knew it. My head immediately filled with the pictures of Erik and of my family seeing this in the international media, whether that meant the internet, Al Jazeera, or the BBC. The desired effect was obviously to scare the hell out of them, and I doubted the Chairman understood how well that was going to work.

I certainly didn't want them to resort to mortgaging their homes, since it seemed to me that the people at my company needed to be the ones to make this work. Otherwise any money they came up with had to be from whatever my personal insurance policy would cover. There wasn't any vast reserve being held back out of sight. I knew the amount they offered had to be at the ceiling of what they could raise, and even that much would financially destroy them. It really took the shine off the thought of getting out of there via ransom and release.

My turn came to speak my forced spiel for the camera. Oddly enough, Abdi didn't seem to want us to repeat their announcement that we would lose our heads in a week if the money situation didn't improve. I was happy to forget that one as well. However, the message he wanted me to give was, essentially, "We know you have more money than this. Get serious."

He made a gruff poking gesture at me, his way of calling "Action!" I'd been placed in front of a giant scrub tree, and I knew the masked men with guns were directly behind us on either side. It went off like the world's weirdest screen test. I went passive on them, forgetting my lines over and over, thinking I was blowing my big moment. But eventually they seemed to get enough to satisfy them. Poul chimed in again to take up the slack.

With the video done, that was it. Finished for the night. No phone calls, no negotiations. Making the video was all they wanted and all they would allow.

While they drove us back, Jabreel went off with some of the other guys. It kept his hands away from me for the rest of the night. But I spent the long ride back to their camp with the sinking sensation that this video was about to pop up on the Al Jazeera network and go viral on the internet. What would it look like to outsiders? They had deliberately made it as menacing as possible. I had no doubt our poor families would be convinced we were in the hands of terrorists and doomed.

As of that day, that night, I'd sunk down from taking one day at a time to taking one little piece of a day at a time—just what I could carry—and those little pieces of the day kept getting smaller.

The men drove us for hours, this time. My back ached from bouncing over the terrain, my neck was on fire with muscle tension, and deep inside my body I was getting all sorts of little signals that things were not holding up well.

They had my medicine in their possession but kept finding excuses to "punish" me by withholding it. There was no discernible logic to any of it. They allowed me to keep my thyroid medication but withheld medicine for the infections that plagued me in that filthy camp. I could feel my state of general weakness growing each day.

The journey back to their camp was so long they stopped for the night in the middle of the dirt track, and in spite of our attempt to cooperate with the surprise video shoot, they took away our sleeping mattresses and pillows as "punishment" for the insulting amounts of money our people had been offering so far. It didn't seem to matter that they were responsible for the fact that there had been no fresh communication that night and no chance to improve things. It was punishment time, and they seemed convinced we needed it.

We lay still and managed to sleep a little bit, there in the roadway. Fortunately it was already late when we stopped, and sunrise seemed to come early. I awoke ready to rise and shine and get the hell out of there. Funny, but spending the night on the road—literally on the road—made going back to the wilderness camp seem like an improvement. While we climbed back into the cars, Poul got close enough to whisper, "This is going to take months."

No despair allowed. I didn't say what I couldn't help thinking: *Except Abdi just told us we only have a week.*

◆ ◆ ◆

Abdi's way of dealing with the one-week deadline was to ignore it when the week passed. I tried to be thankful for the reprieve, but it felt dangerous to assume we were out of the woods. When Thanksgiving approached, it was nearly a month since we were taken. At some recent point I suppose Abdi was either persuaded by Jabreel or had come to his own realization that if he killed us, all promise of money vanished. It was much better for him, he now realized and frequently assured us, to get far more money than this measly ransom offer by going to Al-Shabaab. They would pay well for us, and at least these poor guys could turn some measure of profit from all their hard work.

"I sell you Al-Shabaab! Five million!" He strutted around the camp glaring at us as if we had personally stolen his fortune. Abdi no longer believed our spokesman Mohammed was telling him the truth. And while he couldn't quite figure out how the "conspiracy" worked, he was committed to the suspicion that Mohammed was playing him off with the small offers because he intended to keep the bulk of the "millions" in ransom for himself.

Have you ever tried to convince someone you don't have money when he is convinced you do? Very hard to do, if it's possible at all.

It was about this time that word came down to Jabreel that he would no longer be allowed to speak with Mohammed until Jabreel got either my husband or Poul's wife on the phone and negotiated directly with one of them. He was to get them to personally confirm that Mohammed was truly speaking for us, for our families, and for our employers.

Jabreel had the phone number for the director of the Danish Refugee Council for the Horn of Africa. It was on an emergency card they found in our belongings, which they still kept away from us as punishment for the fact that we were failing to make them millionaires.

Poul had a longer relationship with the NGO staff, so he made the call to the director's number and gave his instructed lines, which in this case happened to be true. He revealed the kidnappers or pirates or whatever they ought to be called had demands about verifying Mohammed and added they were furious over the low amounts offered for our ransom.

I could faintly hear the director's voice. Then first thing I noticed was his attitude; he sounded engaged and concerned. His tone made me glad somebody was awake at the wheel on the other end. He assured Poul he would have Erik personally call Jabreel the following morning to confirm Mohammed's validity. It was all good to hear, and a few weeks earlier I would have been jumping out of my skin at the news. But I had already learned not to put faith in mere hopes.

Instead I spent the night and the following morning on pins and needles. Even though Poul is more reserved than I am, I didn't doubt he felt the same way. Finally the hour arrived. We made the ridiculous precall preparations, traveling out into the scrub for miles, then stopped and waited for Erik's call.

Somebody decided to allow me to answer the phone this time. Maybe they wanted to see me break down at the sound of my husband's voice, but the opportunity was too precious to waste like that. I resolved to keep my voice and emotions steady, no matter what I heard, no matter what happened, during every second of time that the phone connection was live.

For now, there was nothing as important as resetting the relationship between our captors and our NGO or the FBI or whoever was controlling Mohammed. And I would be damned if I would allow anybody in that place to make me scream or cry out in any way as long as Erik could hear me. I couldn't begin to imagine the torment he was suffering, in its own way as bad as mine, and I'd die before inflicting those sounds on him and then leaving him with a dead phone connection to contemplate.

CHAPTER TWENTY

Dear Jess—

I had a dream last night about my early days on the job. It seemed to concentrate this toxic frustration down to its essence. The details were different but the frustration was very much the same. My response was exactly what I'm dying to do today.

I'm at the doors of Galkayo Prison, scheduled to make a visit to check the conditions there to see if the prison qualifies for my NGO's help. I have an appointment, but nobody is coming to open the door. I stand with my small team feeling too angry at this neglect to simply walk away. It's early during my career in this country and I still have something of a cowboy mentality toward my job.

I stand beating on the door until my hands begin to bleed. Finally, in a dark imitation of the entry scene for The Wizard of Oz, a guard opens the door, pretending not to have known we were there all that time. We are admitted inside.

Before long, I'm almost sorry we got in. This isn't a prison; it's a dungeon, and in all the worst implications of that word. The men receive no fresh air or sunlight, and I already know some of them have been there for years without being brought to trial or even formally charged with a crime.

185

I notice they are chained together in groups of about ten men apiece, and I ask the purpose of this. They tell me the policy helps prevent escapes by making it hard for the men to move. But why, I ask, are so many men chained in a single group? And how can they use the toilet that way?

The guard just grins and points at a hole in the floor over in the corner. "All go together, every time!" He laughs. They live in the stench of one another's filth. As a group, each man in this chain watches one of the others defecate in close proximity at least ten times a day. That's only if nobody has diarrhea, which seems unlikely with the garbage I see them being fed. I try to imagine living in a tiny room that smells like the worst public restroom anyone has ever seen, with at least fifty other men, all chained in groups of eight to ten. The stench is like nothing I've encountered before. It's the odor of a poorly tended zoo.

Nobody would stay inside that toxic cloud by choice. I stare at these forlorn creatures and wonder if they somehow get used to the crowding and the filth, or if their senses are reoffended every time they wake up to find themselves in that place again.

And the men's medical condition—dreadful, even to the untrained eye. The inmates I see are all black African males, but most are literally ash gray in color. There is no natural human skin color like that. The question hits me, How long does a black man have to be held without sunlight for his skin to go so strangely gray?

Faces loom at me from the shadows of their cells, with shades of death stretched across their faces. My only purpose there is to help them. I have to find a way, but I don't even know where to start.

I ask a guard if the men ever go out into the courtyard. He laughs and points out at the courtyard's surface, covered in stones. "Too many rocks! The men get rocks and kill us!"

I tell him if he ever expects to get any help from my

organization maybe they should go out to the courtyard and remove the rocks so there's no longer a "security problem" lying around on the ground. Is it too much to ask, I want to know, to put in a little physical labor and clear the ground?

I am stunned with disbelief, not just by the primitive conditions but also by the laughing cruelty of the guards. The question of who would want a job like this is answered by their casual inhumanity. They appear to like their jobs for all the wrong reasons.

Finally, one of them begins tormenting an inmate by jabbing him through the bars with the barrel of his gun. He grins at me while he does it, as if fully expecting me to laugh along with him and encourage his behavior. Instead, my temper gets the best of me and I snap. I grab him by the front of his shirt, lift him several inches off the ground, and slam him back against the wall.

"What the hell do you think you're doing?" I demand. "You bastard! You bastard! Are you out of your mind?"

The answer comes not from him but from behind me. It is a fast series of metallic clicks. I turn to see AK-47 barrels all around me. Every one of them is pointed directly at my head.

All right, perhaps not the best tactic. I lower the man back to the ground . . .

Erik woke up then, but couldn't shake off the dream, which was all true, down to every haunted face. The question lingered—had he worked to release some of the men from that prison, only to return them to a life of crime—say, kidnapping for ransom? Could one of them be among the men holding Jess now?

His life was saved that day when the lazy prison commander showed up to calm the guards and escorted him out of the prison in one piece. Luck was with him; they won concessions from the prison to alter its restraint policy and went on to get releases for a number of the men being illegally held there. Those men escaped that hellhole with whatever health they had left. He could only imagine their joy and relief when they were shown the door and told to go, after giving themselves up for dead.

But while he lay in the dark and tried to sort his thoughts, bad ideas formed: Should he go appeal to the kidnappers on that basis? Let them know he had worked to free them, and if not them, then their brothers? Would they show Jess mercy in return?

It was only another extreme idea, based on nothing more than the frustrated desire to do something, do anything other than simply watch the clock. It echoed his wishful thinking for a time like that day at the prison when he was able to take effective action with no thought about risk to anyone but himself.

It was Thanksgiving morning when Erik's dream was interrupted by a call from Dan Hardy saying another proof-of-life call was scheduled with the kidnappers. In a quiet voice Dan asked if Erik would be willing to reverse the strategy and speak directly with the kidnapper and possibly with Jess as well. The CMT's hostage negotiation consultant chimed in and made it clear to Erik that every word he spoke would count. The slightest misstep could ruin everything, and therefore he didn't dare indulge in the sort of anger-based response he had used in that prison.

He would have to make the call alongside their communicator, Mohammed, along with the professional negotiator, with the FBI and CMT members standing in the next room and listening in. Jess would be surrounded by those kidnappers. Still, if they agreed to put her on the line, Erik would actually hear her voice for the first time since this all began. He was cautioned not to express any emotion to the kidnappers, and to remain calm and steady. The CMT's position was going to be that the Somalis had to advance the negotiations by coming down on their demands.

Beyond that, the Crisis Management Team was running out of options.

CHAPTER TWENTY-ONE

Jessica:

The phone rings. Jabreel is there to chaperone, but Abdi and the Colonel are sleeping, and this time Jabreel actually lets me hold the phone myself instead of having him hold it next to my ear. I answer on the first ring, with the speaker off. The line is full of static and the connection is iffy, so I jump right in.

"This is Jessica," I begin, holding my breath.

"Hey! . . . Uh, Jess, it's Erik."

And there it is. Now I get it.

Right there, in that first moment of hearing Erik's voice, I suddenly grasp the reason why we were warned in our training that we would probably not be allowed to speak with loved ones if we were ever taken for ransom. The rule always sounded excessive to me. *Okay,* I thought. *I get it now. I do.*

Because I know Erik too well and I can hear, even in those few opening words, his pain and his fear for me. At the same time I know others won't pick it up because he is so good at self-control under stress. I'd give anything to spare him this razor wire he's trying to walk, and I'm already glad I pulled my determination together before we started. I can only maintain equilibrium in this moment by lapsing into my best business mode. We could lose the connection at any second, and we have to get this right.

"Hi," I say.

"Hey—Hey. How *are* you?" he begins, and somehow manages to communicate all his concern for me in those few words.

"Okay. Um, we're okay."

People in the background are milling around now, disturbing my concentration. Word must be out that we have a connection. Everybody knows its all about money.

"Jess, I cannot hear you . . ."

I hold the phone closer and continue with the business at hand. I'm acutely aware of those parts of me that could easily dissolve into panic and blow this whole thing unless I stay strong. "I need you to verify that Mohammed is the one appointed for negotiation for the family."

"I can do that," Erik instantly replies. He keeps his voice cool. "Mohammed is our family's communicator, and he is our representative. For both families."

"Yeah, don't say anything about the organization, just say family."

"Yes. And it's just for our families," he replies right on top of the question.

"Yes." I turn to Helper and say, "Can you go get Abdi?" Helper hesitates because Abdi is sleeping off a *khat* high and nobody wants to be the one to wake him. I know Abdi's ways so I understand the hesitation. Too bad.

I raise my voice and look him in the eyes. Doing that is risky, but necessary. This has to work.

"Go get Abdi!" I say, as if to imply that if he fails, this deal could be ruined. "Can you go get Abdi?" I add, trying to look as if it would be his fault if the deal fails. He still looks as if he wants to sit back down. I point right at him.

"No, no," I tell him. "I want Abdi to hear!" He moves away on his mission.

But Poul snatches the phone away from me. He launches into a speech that comes from a dialogue he and I have shared over the past month, but it was also a conversation I didn't expect him to have with Erik unless I was prevented from coming to the phone.

Poul begins in a determined voice. "Um, two things: Jessica has not been touched. She has not been harmed."

"Good." Erik says it quietly. His voice is grim.

"She is, ah, stronger than you, you may think."

It's nice of Poul to say this, but he hasn't identified himself. I have to wonder if Erik realizes it's Poul, through all the distortion.

Erik says, "I'm very happy to hear that and of course I'm very worried. And I'm here with Mohammed now, I'm sitting next to him, and I want to confirm that Mohammed is our representative."

"Yes, from the family," Poul prompts him. "Don't mention any organization."

But now I can tell Erik thinks Poul is one of the kidnappers. He's not talking to Poul as if he knows him.

"Well, there's no organization to mention." Erik changes course so smoothly, even I barely notice. "It's just our families."

"That's fine. That's fine," Poul says. "I just wanted to tell you those two things."

"I'm very happy to hear that, and I hope that this will continue and that we can get Jessica out as quick as possible."

"Yes."

"Because we need to have her back . . . *okay?*"

"We need to have both back, I hope," Poul responds, sounding hurt. I don't think he realizes he's never identified himself.

"Yeah, of course! Is it Poul I'm talking with?"

"Yes."

"I didn't hear it was you, Poul. But of course we want both of you back!"

"Okay, but I am telling you these two things. She is stronger than you may think. And two, nobody has touched her. Nobody has harmed her."

"Very good, Poul. And you have to keep on being as strong as her."

"Yes."

"And you can be assured that we are doing everything we—"

"Oh, I'm out. I'm out," Poul says, just before I pull the phone from his hands.

"Erik?" I begin.

"Yes."

"Okay. The leader of the militia is coming."

"Okay . . ."

"So that he can hear what you're saying."

"Yeah . . ."

"Um, before he comes, I just want you to know I love you."

That one nearly gets him. I hear a heavy catch in his voice. "I love you, too."

"And I will get through this."

"Good, Jess," he says, but his voice is flat. He's obviously in a room full of people.

"You know . . ." he continues. "You know . . . before you say anything else, I just want you to know I am doing okay. Your family, they're all doing okay. We're all doing okay. We're just trying to solve this in the quickest manner we can. We're doing everything we can. Everything."

"Okay."

"So you just have to believe me when I'm saying to keep faith. And we, the whole family, we're praying, nonstop. We're doing everything we can."

My lifelong spiritual skeptic husband is praying right along with my family. Wonder of wonders. "Okay," I softly tell him.

". . . To get you out."

"Okay. Um, is the family there, any of them?"

". . . No. No. But we are in contact. And they're doing just fine, Jess. They're all together, where they are."

What did he just say? *They're all together, where they are?* My dad now lives in Virginia, my sister in Pennsylvania, and my brother in Tennessee. Erik's family lives in Sweden. What's he trying to say?

"Okay then."

Erik's voice takes on his negotiating tone. "But no one will be able to get in touch with us, any of the family, Jess . . ."

"I know," I tell him. And I do know, now. As of about two minutes ago, I completely get it about not talking to loved ones on these calls. It's a form of psychological torture that I'm certain would eventually break anybody who's got a working set of emotions. But Erik's warning is clear. There'll be no more family calls; we have to win at this.

"But, Erik," I add, "they need to understand, the leader here— he's insane."

"Oh, yeah. We understand that. But, ah, is the communicator for your side around? Jabreel? Or someone?"

"Yes, the leader is coming. Here he comes now. They're going to put you on speaker phone."

Abdi stumbles over to us still half asleep, face hanging forward, eyes puffy and nearly shut, chewing one of last night's leftover *khat* stems. He chews and drools and listens while Jabreel steps close to me and I put the phone in speaker mode.

◆ ◆ ◆

Erik made the call to Jessica while painfully aware it might be the last time they ever spoke. Still, there was nothing to do but try to exchange a few pieces of vital information as quickly as possible. Now while the kidnappers' leader came to listen in, there were no good choices. The only option was to stall while justifying that stalling to the kidnappers, hoping to get them to come back to earth with their ransom demands before the victims' health was broken.

The sound of Jessica's voice made him want to pour out his heart to her, but there was the extremely sticky job at hand of confirming to these fearful drug-addled thugs that the NGO's official communicator, Mohammed, was actually speaking for their side with Erik's full support. This process would never get anywhere if the kidnappers didn't believe in whoever they communicated with on their ransom calls. Erik had to confirm Mohammed's validity, show no fear to the kidnappers, and also make it clear to them that from now on neither Erik nor anyone else on their side would speak, *except* Mohammed. The kidnappers could not be allowed to begin worming their communications into the family structure. It felt like working on a bomb squad. He was certain of nothing except that he couldn't allow the bizarre nature of the conversation to get to him.

The kidnappers' phone was still in the speaker mode. Erik heard footsteps approach in the background and then the sounds of someone taking the phone.

"Allo?" From the first word, Jabreel's gruff voice was inflected with a thick version of the Somali accent Erik knew so well.

"Yes, hello?" Erik prompted him, without introducing himself.

"All of the others are—they are—the leader of the militia only wants to know you. This is the reason for calling you."

"Okay. Well, if he needs to hear it again, I can verify that Mohammed is our families' communicator. He is the only one with information, the only one you will gain anything from."

"Okay. So now we, the militia, can verify the family, you are family, can communicate this one time, just for now, with Moham-med. So is okay now, we will be finish with negotiation."

"Okay. And if this is Jabreel, I hope that you are taking good care of Jessica and Poul. Because we're doing *everything* that we can to get them back. So, we cannot do more on our side, and you now have to do all *you* can on your side."

"Okay, okay, I must tell you I am not one of them. Very difficult to reason with them. I must do as I am told. But if I have got the certification now, everything it will be soon. And they will come home to you as soon as possible."

"Okay, that is very good, Jabreel, and I'm happy to hear that, because we need for Jessica and Poul to come back. We need to have them back here at home with us. Do you understand me? They came to your country to help your people. So now you must use your manners in the Somali custom and treat them as guests. Be nice to them, Jabreel."

Through his foot-thick guttural accent and the crackling of a remote connection, Erik heard: "Yes I must be careful because I was just the NGO working that's why they want me here helping. And anyway, to thank you for your calling, and to listen to all par-ties. Now everything it will be easy to come home to you for your wife."

"Okay, I'm very happy about that. And now, I think, Jabreel, [after this verification] you can again talk with Mohammed here."

Erik knew this was all he was supposed to say. Make the veri-fication to them and get off the line before they can engage in any conversation. He found he couldn't go along with the restriction.

"And Jessica!" he called out. "If you're hearing this, know that we're praying for you and doing everything we can to get you and Poul back! And I'm ... we're all so happy to hear directly from both you and Poul today. But ... but this ... will be the last time, Jessica. Until you come out."

He couldn't look at anyone while he spoke the words or his throat would have seized. He had to trust that she would understand that this hard stance was purely a negotiating tactic.

He had already lied to her during this call by saying her family wasn't around, when in truth they were all right there in Nairobi, waiting with their lives on hold. And of course they wanted Jessica to know they were there for her, after coming all that distance. They wanted very much to communicate any sense of strength to her they could. But if he told her that, he had to assume someone else would hear it. And those men had made it plain they would try to put her family in play if they could.

Erik pitched his voice at a stronger level. "Mohammed will call you back in ten minutes! I'm now leaving the phone. I will not be on the phone again. So, Jabreel, please take care of my wife, and please take care of Poul."

"Okay, but I am very, very, important. I must be careful. I must be careful. For the importance of my work, I must—"

"Yes, yes," Erik cut him off. "Very good. Mohammed will call you back in ten minutes. So I'll say good-bye now. I love you, Jessica, if you can hear this. Take care, both you and Poul."

"Okay, I am listen to you. See? You love her, I must take care of her. Yes? Thank you very much."

Jabreel hung up and it was done. Erik knew Abdi had been listening in the background and had heard the confirmation. Most important, Erik had been assured by Jessica herself, not some third party, that she wasn't being harmed.

But to make their efforts effective and keep things from getting worse, he had to lie to her at a time when he knew without a doubt it would have given her real comfort to think of her sister, her brother, and her dad keeping the vigil for her, from right there in Nairobi. If something happened to her and this was the last conversation they had, he couldn't see how he could live with the knowledge that he lied about something so important to her. Even if they got her back without a hitch, he had to hope she would understand when he tried to explain the deceit.

She sounded good to him, though. He could live another day on the sound of her voice alone. It nearly made him laugh out loud to think of the stern tone she took with her kidnappers, demanding they go wake up their leader to listen over the speaker phone while Jessica made sure Mohammed got verified and negotiations reopened.

And as strange and unexpected as it was for Poul to jump on the line with his reassurances about Jessica, Erik was grateful to hear she wasn't being harmed. Nobody had touched her.

CHAPTER TWENTY-TWO

Jessica:

I was getting better at turning off my instinct to scream. There's nothing subtle to the technique. You know how to squeeze a tight fist? Just do it with your whole body.

When I stood there and listened to Poul on the phone assuring Erik "she hasn't been touched," the sensation was like being half encased in ice with the other half covered in flames. Because it was true I wanted Erik to hear that. I wanted to give him the mental picture of me in a reasonable state of safety. At the same time, it wasn't completely true, and my abuser was standing right there beside me, nodding along: *no, no, she hasn't been touched . . .*

Even someone who lives a nonviolent life, as I have always done, has to practice the art of remaining both passive and silent in moments like this. I must restrain the urge to claw at someone's eyes. I must ignore the desire to let him go right ahead and kill me, if he chooses, so long as I can take his eyeballs, first—and his other balls, second.

I didn't need to stand there and smile, but I knew to keep my face neutral. These kidnappers made it plain how they hated the tears. Crying caused them to poke at me with the barrels of their loaded guns. The first time one of them surprised me by shooting into the air a few inches from my head it practically knocked me out of my skin while it drilled home the ease with which any one of those things would spew death. And with the possibility of accidental discharge, it was a massive risk to do anything that would cause one of these goons to turn toward you with his weapon.

I had to learn to repress even the most basic of human urges, which would be to run from these brutal men, from their weapons, from their contaminated bare hands, from their shit-stained food bowls. My leg muscles were perpetually tight, as if waiting for me to fall asleep so they could propel me out of there before I realized what they were doing.

I hadn't been raped yet, but I could see it was now a matter of limited time. It was like the sound of a large incoming wave rolling toward a beach at night. But in the dark there would be no way of telling when the wave would break. Even so, it was coming, as evidenced by a noticeable decay of Jabreel's respect for my personal space. I had to avoid alienating the only English-speaking communicator here. He knew that, too. He traded on it. His unwanted attentions were more insistent every day, creating that old feeling of being slowly squeezed in the giant vise of someone else's sexual pressure. I think this is something a lot of women understand.

After that one call with Erik, they chose to punish us by separating Poul and me completely. That went on for two weeks, and during that time I saw no sign of anyone besides the *khat* zombies. But Abdi, it turned out, was also circling me. He began to sleep next to me on my mat. I felt certain he was inching closer each night. He was a shark sizing up its prey. I knew him well enough by then to be certain he would kill me in a fit of rage if I humiliated him in front of the others by screaming at him and fighting him off.

But Jabreel, the lesser physical threat, was the one I actually feared more. I felt there was no choice but to allow him to take advantage of me, up to a point, for the singular purpose of getting us out of there. The art of the dance was in maintaining a line that was not to be crossed.

Jabreel sort of played along. Once I woke up to find him sitting next to me. His hand was reaching under my blanket and touching my legs. I pulled away, "turning in my sleep," and he faded off—for the moment.

So we found ourselves in a twisted and lethal version of a game: the casual avoidance of the sort of unwanted sexual advances that continue long past the point where the abuser might credibly claim a "misunderstanding." Nobody was misunderstanding anything in my little corner of our makeshift camp.

His erratic behavior and level of drug use had long since convinced me he was capable of destroying half of this group's investment of money and labor, namely me, over sex. I could tell something was holding him back from cracking open in a full-out sexual attack, but short of that, he behaved like a Billy goat crossed with a whiney adolescent.

Whenever Jabreel was in our company and had no opportunity to misbehave, he liked to draw attention by spinning tales of his important NGO work, expounding on the vast difference between himself and "these pirates." But even in those obvious situations where I was a hands-off commodity, he tended to simper around me in childish intoxication. He was developing "hungry eyes," staring at me while he stretched a toothless smile across his face and aimed it at me. It was like staring into a gaping wound.

"Jesses. I come America live with you."

"No, Jabreel. I keep telling you, I'm married."

"I live with you and Erik . . . you hear me, Jesses? You hear me?"

"Yes. I hear you, Jabreel. I'm still married. I love my husband."

"But I love Jesses. When Colonel talk to me about you, we call you 'lei,' you know that? In Somali is 'golden.' I marry to you, all these men wish to be me!"

"Jabreel, think. Think! If you come to America, how will you get your *khat?*"

Blank face. Good. That shut him up while he mulled it over. The silence wouldn't last, but out there we were taking what we could get.

◆ ◆ ◆

After that quick phone call, we spent the next several days camping at that same nowhere site. We maintained the usual routine of being forced to hide under tree foliage by day and then force-walked out into the open at night, there to sort-of-sleep while I kept one eye open for Jabreel. When he came slithering around, the only control I could exert was to ignore his advances as much as possible, and then when ignoring him didn't work, resist him with a gut-wrenching show of false humility.

"No, no." I was careful to speak in a soothing tone. "I'm married, Jabreel. So are you."

When he began to shrug at the mention of his wife, I switched to a religious appeal. "What does your religion tell you, Jabreel?" I hoped to engage him as a man of faith, since he did, after all, pray five times a day.

Now on the heels of seeing my hopes of having a baby vanish, I was dodging impregnation by a man with a strict prayer schedule—or any of these other men. To me, the cruel irony of a forced pregnancy from this would be too foul to endure.

It was about at that point when it struck me that I still had one big choice available. I could, if I so chose, die fighting the bastard off. Before I allowed him to torture me into giving in, I could force him to copulate with a corpse. Leave him to pay for his perversity with the outrage of the others, once they realized their hope for ransom was dead. If I dared, I could do that to him.

It's never been in my nature to think such thoughts. I tend to avoid confrontation. But in that narrow list of choices left to me, there was nothing left besides how I chose to die. Rather, it was down to whether I chose to die on my own terms, or if I was prepared to allow them to decide my fate according to their whims and the quality of their *khat* supply.

I didn't expect Jabreel's fear of the other men to stop him from attacking me for much longer. So there it was: the brick wall—can't get over it, can't get under it, and there was no way we were going in through the door. I'd kept my sanity up to that point by giving in to the experience in every way I could, trying to avoid being in a state of friction all the time. But my limits of acceptance stopped at the wall. There was no acceptance for anything beyond it.

In the face of my alternatives, the grim choice of bringing on my death by attacking him before he got to me actually sounded better than all the other available options. After all, we were still on the other side of the looking glass, where you step up to go down, and step down to go up.

◆   ◆   ◆

Erik couldn't believe it was a coincidence when he came downstairs one morning to discover their car had been stolen. Because of the security at their compound, it was almost certainly an inside job involving the night guards.

Later in the day he learned that another car identical to theirs was also stolen in the neighborhood. It would seem the word was out on that particular make and model, possibly from a local chop shop, and somebody had paid off the guards. If so, this confirmed his growing suspicion that for people with a little cash to throw around, any form of live security protection could be penetrated.

The paranoia that had become a constant companion forced

him to wonder if the Somalis who were negotiating on behalf of the kidnappers were somehow behind the car thefts. Had he been targeted for additional "ransom" money he didn't even know he was paying?

He filed the useless paperwork on the missing car, hoping it was a random event and not the first ransom payment. In a separate story, there was now word that a $6 million ransom payment had just been made to Somali pirates holding a hijacked oil tanker. The kidnapping industry appeared to be booming, right at the time when they were trying to convince Jessica's captors their demands were completely unrealistic. He now feared that to Jess's captors, the $6 million just paid to those others sounded tantalizingly close to the $9 million they'd last demanded for Jessica and Poul. The clear message these kidnapping successes sent was that all Jessica's kidnappers had to do was to be brutal enough and hold out long enough—and magical millions of U.S. dollars would soon be coming to them, too.

Jessica's family couldn't stay in Africa any longer, and Erik sadly drove her father, brother, and sister back to the airport. With no end in sight, they had to face the reality of their own lives. He knew he would especially miss having John there. His steadfast belief that this would actually all work out had been a great influence to have around, and Erik hated to do without it.

He dropped them off thinking that being there had been good for them in spite of their having to leave frustrated, at least in allowing them to feel they were doing what they could to support her. The heartbreak lay in having to go back without being able to let her know they were there for her.

Erik's day ended with a depressing call from Matt, who told him to prepare for the possibility these negotiations could take longer than they hoped—maybe months. As hard as it was to hear that, his knowledge of the region had already told him that was so. He felt a certain relief that his own view was confirmed, since his world revolved around the absolute need to make the right choices in this.

He also heard the unspoken message in that call. It told Erik that Jessica's health wasn't going to hold out that long, and unless they found a way to get medicine through to her, she was unlikely to survive.

CHAPTER TWENTY-THREE

Jessica:

After weeks in the wild, the apparent identity of the true leader of the operation began to emerge. It wasn't the Chairman, whom we never saw anymore, nor was it Abdi, even though he was still a ranking officer. No, the one who made the others tremble was the one called Bashir, a chubby fellow of thirty-five or so, with extremely dark skin and a complexion troubled by acne. He walked hunched over a heavy paunch and drove a silver Land Cruiser with delicate pinstriping.

Bashir was the closest thing to an operational commander we were able to identify. Maybe he was also the money man and maybe not, but he was certainly the top dog, and he had emerged as the one with the iron fist. In recent days, Bashir had begun to display a much greater level of impatience over the stalled ransom negotiations, far more than any of the other men. When he flew into a rage, everyone ducked out of his way, including Jabreel and Abdi.

After one fruitless ransom call, Bashir got into a heated discussion with his lackey, a fat and disgusting guy we nicknamed the Turd, because he made it a habit to loudly pass gas at every opportunity. The Turd might have been answering questions. I could tell

Abdi was upset about money, about the pitiful ransom offers they were getting from our side. Even after demanding that the families' communicator Mohammed be replaced, this time by a female named Lisa, they were more unhappy with every passing hour.

Finally Bashir broke from the group and stormed over to the spot where Poul was being held under a tree. "Big money!" he screamed at Poul. "Where is big money?" Poul just looked at him and held up his hands in a gesture of surrender, trying to placate him.

Bashir stomped over to me. "We *kill* you! No big money, we *kill* you!" He rushed at Poul with his AK-47 pointed at him. "You stand up! Stand up now!" He pointed the barrel at Poul's long-sleeved shirt, lying on the ground.

"Put that on! Now! Now!"

Poul just held out his arms in a gesture of no-contest and quietly asked, "Bashir, why are you doing this?" He added some simple pantomime to reinforce his question, "What did I ever do to you?"

Bashir just glared at him for a charged moment, then screamed, "You come now! I sell you now! I get five million for you from Al-Shabaab!"

Poul glanced at me with deep worry on his face. "Bashir," he began, "please don't—"

"Walk!" Bashir screamed. "You walk!" They headed away toward the cars. I began to cry uncontrollably, forgetting all about their repugnance for displays of emotion from women. If they were splitting us up, it meant they were giving up on the negotiation process. It meant everything was over. I didn't even bother trying to hide my fearful crying. They knew I had good reason. They all knew.

Bashir vanished with Poul. Jabreel came over and knelt to me to offer "comfort." He made sure to put a consoling hand on my upper back, rubbing it in little circles.

"These men crazy (rub, rub, pat, pat). Pirates! You cannot talk to them for anything (stroke, stroke). They no believe me for the money. Bashir say he want me to leave."

I sighed, knowing what he wanted to hear. Even fleeing for his own safety, the same games applied with Jabreel. I was still crying, but now the tears were of frustration and personal humiliation.

"Jabreel . . . We need you here . . . We need you to speak for us . . . We need you to speak on the phone. Please. Make them let you stay."

The hypocrisy of my request, made to a man I had come to hate, left a foul taste in my mouth. If I hadn't already been sick from the microbes in the food, my own words would have been enough to turn my stomach.

At that moment Bashir returned alone, noticed me crying, and came over to roughly shove his gun barrel into my shoulder. "Shut up!" he bellowed into my face. Then he pulled out a Nokia cell phone and ordered Jabreel to call our NGO one more time.

"You tell them we now sell the man to Al-Shabaab!"

Jabreel dialed the number for our contact, and our director got on the line. When he handed the phone to me I couldn't help but fall into hysterics while I told the director they had just disappeared with Poul and had announced they were tired of the game and they intended to sell Poul to Al-Shabaab.

"Please!" I begged between sobs. "You know what that group will do to Poul! You have to stop this somehow. You have to do something!"

Our NGO's director had the impossible job of trying to assure me they were "doing everything" they could while I shouted back that it sure didn't look like anybody at all was doing "everything they could." Now Poul was gone, and I was getting sicker by the day, alone in a camp full of angry-looking males who were all stoned out of their minds.

"You have to get us out now! You have to get us out now!" I cried out to our director without listening to his spluttered replies.

I was openly in hysterics at that point and didn't care. This time nobody among the kidnappers put up an objection. My emotions played into their plan by turning up the pressure on the people on the other end of the line. I saw what was being done, but there was no way to stop it. I was grateful they never got any working personal phone numbers from me, or they would be calling our loved ones and letting them listen to me scream.

All I could think about was getting the man on the other end of the line to understand that we were living on the surface of a soap bubble here. The bubble couldn't last.

Bashir ordered Jabreel to give his phone back to him, and Jabreel promptly snatched it away from me. Just that quickly, the plea-for-ransom call was over. That was fine with me, odd as it may sound. Begging a stranger is a disgusting thing to have to do, and it was hardly more tolerable because it was forced on me.

Still, in spite of the fact that I knew the NGO's policy was not to pay ransom to criminal forces, I still believed they would do anything in their power to get us out. I reminded myself we were their employees, captured while doing their work. I knew the situation wasn't easy for anybody on the other end of that call, but I prayed they would take any gamble necessary to get us out. My most heartfelt desire was to have the chance at freedom, even just the chance of it, knowing any form of escape or delivery could go entirely wrong right at the point of exchange but desiring the chance to make a go of it anyway. These drugged-up speed freaks were as likely as not to find something to set off their paranoia, and end up opening fire on all of us. As far as I was concerned, any chance at all to make a break for it was better than this endless stalemate.

I wondered if Bashir was going to punish me now for my distasteful emotional display during the call. But this time, instead of registering any objection over my emotions, he just stared at me with a mixture of amusement and contempt. Apparently, I had performed just right for him, putting my fears and tears to work for the kidnappers in their quest to raise the price on us. *So be it, then*, I thought. *I'll help them if it helps us.*

Even knowing I'd played right into their hands and delivered what they wanted, I was glad for the chance to speak to the director myself. If I was going to die out there because of their inaction, I wanted him to have to hear straight from me before the end came. And who could tell, perhaps it would increase his sense of us as individuals and get something going while there was time. If there was time.

After the call, everybody else found an excuse to drift away and put distance between themselves and Bashir. That left just me. I was so filled with outrage and resentment that I found it easy to get my tears under control in his presence.

That flipped some kind of switch. The Turd lunged for me, pointing his AK-47 and screaming at the top of his voice, "You f**king shut up! F**king arms! Up! Shut! Up!"

In that instant I was too angry and disgusted to feel my natural fear of him. I deliberately glared right at him, boring a hole through him with my eyes, daring him to react. A typical Somali man is unaccustomed to seeing any women glare at him, unless she's his mother or his wife. It made these men ill at ease to be presented with defiance from someone expected to grovel.

I was too angry to care. After having watched him beat Poul for no reason and then take him away to whatever he had in store for him, I had reached the point where I needed to defy Bashir more than I needed to live. He looked surprised by my stiff reaction to his intimidation. For a second, he didn't appear to know what to do. Then he shook his gun in my face and marched away.

It was terrible to know after this I would be alone in that camp with those men. But at least Bashir's leaving and letting quiet return was some improvement. I needed to think. There was no safety or satisfaction to be had anywhere around me; the only place I would find any was within my imagination. A few hours of peace and quiet were what I needed most of all to put up my best memories and walk around inside them for a while. It felt as necessary as leaning my face out of a burning building in order to breathe clear air.

Lately it was taking me longer to get the images to zoom in and focus. My imagination was active, perhaps too much so, but I was having a harder time controlling what I'd see. In the beginning I'd been able to call up my store of beautiful memories practically on demand. All I needed to do was center my breathing to relax out from under the fear; better images and feelings would follow. In my current state it was getting much harder to concentrate. My physical weakness matched my sense of failing mental strength while these jackals gradually drained the life force out of us.

It was some measure of consolation that my brain appeared to be less and less interested in focusing on the kidnappers and more concerned with calling up memories of life as I once knew it. We had ended the second month. The daily routine hadn't varied much, but it was less and less a part of my conscious experience. I had earned enough trust that I was allowed to fix our food regularly. I could sometimes cut up potatoes and fry them in oil and salt. It gave me back a little control over food sanitation. While Poul was still with us, both of us felt sick most of the time with GI tract troubles. The other men didn't seem bothered by microbes nearly as much, even though most of them looked malnourished. Apparently a life of exposure to viciously infectious agents had tempered their immune systems, in spite of their poor nutrition.

❖ ❖ ❖

Before Jessica's family left Nairobi, Matt Espenshade and his wife invited them all to their home for dinner with their small children. Over the meal he made it clear that he understood that the effect of the kidnappings would be felt not just by Jessica and Erik, and their families, but by everyone who cared for her. Such crimes represented an ominous threat to the future of anyone daring to enter the region. This couldn't be tolerated, because the Horn of Africa had sunk into such economic and political chaos that to date nobody had found any way to recover without outside help and intervention. If this was to be the fate of those who brought that help, intervention and change for the better would be a long time coming.

He repeatedly assured Erik, "Once the FBI is on a case we never give up. There are dozens of people working on this. The FBI is dedicated to getting Jessica out. We won't rest until we do. I have the privilege of dealing with you and the family every day, but there are dozens of others, and I tell you, they're working tirelessly on this. These are people you'll probably never meet."

He added, "We'll get Jessica back alive." Erik was glad to hear it, but he had to wonder how Matt could know that.

"I've got eight years in the army," Matt told the family, "seventeen with the FBI. And I've never seen so many people working to retrieve one American citizen."

"Well, there's Poul, of course."

"Yes, but our mandate is to act on behalf of the American citizen. We have to hope Poul will benefit from that."

"So you're saying if you have to get kidnapped, try to be American."

"If you want American military help, it's the only way we can offer it. Now Jessica has that going for her, and it's no small consideration. Here's the thing: There are two potential outcomes here. One is that we can get them to agree to a ransom somebody can actually pay."

"The other one?"

"The other one is the armed rescue that we've already discussed. You know the dangers."

"Let's be positive for a minute here. Suppose they stage the raid and get both Jessica and Poul out?"

"Then the first leg of your journey is over and the next one begins. It could be just as rough in its own way."

"I don't like the sound of that."

"I wouldn't be helping you if I sat here and told you pretty lies."

Erik recognized the truth of that and felt grateful for someone who actually spoke straight to him. Matt showed compassion while staying away from false hope. By an expert associated with the Crisis Management Team, he was told, "The first concern is short-term medical, and that will be taken care of according to her initial evaluation, as soon as they pick her up."

"Good so far."

"So far. Then after short-term medical care comes the possibility of long-term medical care."

"What are you talking about?"

"Beyond any specific injuries, you have to consider post-traumatic stress disorder. The torment inside a person's mind can be much worse than anything the physical world can throw at you."

"But it can be treated, too?"

"Sometimes. We've had discussions with the Department of Defense, and they run a program aimed at rehabilitating returned war captives. It could also work for Jessica. The point is, you have to think about how she is going to pick up the reins of her life. This program acknowledges that it's not reasonable to expect anyone under these circumstances to just go back home and return to living as if they've been out on vacation."

"So it involves a stay in a hospital."

"It's whatever that person needs."

"In that case, I'd like to have a program like that available for her if she's willing."

"That's good. Are you certain about it?"

"Oh, yeah. Oh, yeah. If she's doing it, it means she's back here again."

"Africa Jess."

Erik Landemalm.

Married on
Tiwi Beach,
Mombasa,
Kenya.

Jessica and Erik at work with local Somalis.

Jess and a colleague meeting with local beneficiaries.

Somali girls are often denied
any education.

Jessica with a
Kenyan boy.

Erik in negotiations with
local authorities.

A Somali village outside Galkayo.

Erik at work in the field.

A generation of mine victims.

Jessica on site during a demolition.

"Sign language" on the entrance wall of the Somaliland Parliament warning not to bring these items inside.

"Technicals" are heavy guns mounted on small trucks. The dominant power in southern Somalia, many are owned by various warlords who answer to no one.

Captive Jessica's scrub desert road to nowhere.

Photo taken from Jessica's "proof of life" video.

President Obama calling John Buchanan with the news that Jessica had been rescued alive. (*Official White House Photo by Pete Souza*)

Jessica reunited with her sister, Amy.

Jessica reunited with
her brother, Stephen.

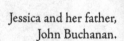

Jessica and her father,
John Buchanan.

After the rescue, with FBI
agent Matt Espenshade.

(Unless otherwise specified, all photos are courtesy of the authors.)

CHAPTER TWENTY-FOUR

Jessica:

There's no point in talking about Christmas. We spent Christmas at gunpoint in a scrub desert surrounded by the same essential collection of stooges who had cackled their way through Thanksgiving. The fact that some breezed into camp more frequently than others indicated the command structure almost as well their personal attitudes did. By now my waking hours were mostly spent firmly in the zone of an inner world. The ace up my sleeve was its invisibility, or they would have surely taken that away from me as well.

After December 27 I never saw Abdi again, which was nothing but a relief, but before he left he made sure to stamp his cruelty onto us. I became so numb to the constant threat level that I simply could not keep my moment-to-moment survival at the front of my mind every second. And even when I went about whatever little mundane activity I was permitted, somebody always found a reason to scream at me about something.

We knew enough about our surroundings at this point to convince us that in spite of all the jumping around these guys did, we were still spending our time just about fifteen minutes outside

Adado. I clearly recalled the sign welcoming all to "The International City of Adado." When the weather was right, we could see the lights of the city, not so far away, not really. Maybe not close enough to run to, but close enough for walking.

I could dream or daydream about escaping, as each day became more like the other. I could drift into a fantasy of slipping away and finding help there in Adado, so temptingly close by. The problem, of course, was that we weren't prisoners held by chains or bars. The most effective jail for us was isolation. No matter how metropolitan that "International City" might be, we could expect that for many miles in every direction, there was no one to help us.

Even for the greatest desert survivalists, there would be no way to get around the fact that you were surrounded by people who would consider it their great and grand duty to turn you back over to your pursuers. So the days and nights blended. We sat beneath scrub trees until around five in the evening, then boarded Land Cruisers and were driven to the opposite side of the town to sleep under the stars for the night. They always drove us through town by passing quietly along side streets through the outskirts of town to avoid drawing attention to us or the campsite, protecting their assets from theft.

Their maddening mix of compulsive detail and lack of reason never waned. They proved that on the day they took us directly into town, instead of sticking to the back roads—perhaps when they knew the region was safe from competitors—and they not only made no attempt to hide us but actually left us in the open on public display.

It began when we had passed a tiny airport at the edge of town, little more than a short landing strip, but with a good-sized plane sitting on the runway. Poul was still with us then. The driver, by instruction from Abdi, turned into the airport road as if the plane was our destination.

But as we got closer to the plane, we didn't slow down, didn't stop. We rode right on by. Abdi turned around from the front passenger seat and directed a cruel grin at us. He lifted his hand and waved, saying in a sing-song voice, "Wave good-bye, Poul and Jesses! No big money, no Nairobi! Bye-bye airplane! Bye-bye!" and started laughing.

The rest of the guys followed suit while I fought back the hot tears stinging my eyes and did my best to deny them the satisfaction of seeing how deeply they were tormenting me. Apparently, I did the job too well and deprived Abdi of the pain he wanted to see in me. So just to be certain we got the idea there was no hope, he had the driver take us directly into town this time. I looked at him and saw nothing in his seat but a monster poorly disguised as a human being.

Later he had them drive us through the center of a bustling little downtown area in some nameless desert town. This vehicle had tinted windows, which helped keep us from public view as long as we were moving quickly enough, and as always I kept my *hijab* on while we were away from the camp, which also helped a little.

But once the car stopped, anybody who took more than a passing glance could see there were two white people inside. This is rare in that region. The kidnappers pulled to a stop in town, either to actually conduct business or simply to leave us in the street on display, and it didn't take long for the locals to realize there was a show to be had inside that vehicle: two white people, two Westerners, two kidnap victims being held for ransom—we didn't need to understand their words to grasp their thinking. Men of all ages and a few females as well surrounded the car and gawked at us. They seemed to regard our misery as some sort of triumph for them.

The oddest thing about such an experience wasn't just the menace of it, since we were surrounded by deadly threats all the time; it was the blank eyes of the people staring back at us. I learned what it is to be a freshly captured zoo animal, trapped inside a tiny cage with nothing left to do but watch the creatures staring in at you.

I saw no sense of recognition from anyone outside those windows that they were looking at a fellow human being. I merely saw the idle curiosity of unfeeling people scoping out an interesting pair of unusual animals.

This particular crowd didn't directly menace us; they probably feared the guns of our captors too much to do anything like that. They were merely indifferent to our situation and to whatever human commonality we shared with them. They didn't gawk at us necessarily as people they wanted to see dead, they just made it clear our survival was a matter of indifference. It was our only visit to that place and did nothing to make me want to return. The most important lesson that day was to never forget that the silent roadway stretching off into the distance was only an illusion of freedom. In fact it represented nothing more than an opportunity for everything to quickly get much worse.

♦ ♦ ♦

Abdi's disappearance had little impact on the amount of casual cruelty displayed in that unhappy camp. The duty just seemed to fall to the next guy in line. In this fashion we greeted the New Year. I rose early at sunrise that morning, grumpy over pick-your-reason but glad to have a chance to make bread again that day. My first item of business was to get water heated over the fire and make tea, which could have been the beginning of a passable morning if we actually got a chance to have tea with sugar and dip our campfire sand bread in it.

We did not. The camp was favored by a visit from Abdilahi, the same young boy I saw on that first stinking day of this ordeal, the one who used to wear one of our mine awareness graduation bracelets, the one rumored to have killed three people already. His erratic personality and vicious flashes of *khat*-fueled temper made me glad he was usually someplace else. Though our code name for him was "Crack Baby," it wasn't much of a code. If any of the other guys spoke English, they would have recognized exactly who the name Crack Baby referred to.

There was a genuine "chicken or egg" conundrum in this remnant of a departed child. I wondered how badly scrambled his brain had already been, through trauma, disease, or genetic glitches, when he discovered *khat* and managed to get in the way of a daily supply. Who could say how many bales of leaves had passed through this kid? I tried to recall, had anybody ever studied the long-terms effects of *khat* use on a brain so young? But philosophy didn't matter here for Abdilahi, our Crack Baby, the miniature trouble zombie. Everything appeared to have been burned out of his brain except for a surprising capacity for meanness and provocation. Crack Baby walked through life pecking at trouble the same way a bird pecks at the ground: randomly, relentlessly, and without a moment's thought.

This morning, sorry to say, our Crack Baby was right there among us, swaggering and talking at a pointlessly loud volume and glancing around to lock eyes with his next target. Maybe I did something to draw his attention, maybe I just won the backward lottery that day. He and another youngster with the common name of Hassan were the only other people stirring in the camp then, and I'd had plenty of opportunities to see how these two fed one another's meanness.

So with the two camp delinquents as my sole companions, I moved away from the fire with my tea and walked a few steps over by the parked Land Cruisers. I tried to quietly blend into whatever I was standing next to and immediately noticed it hadn't worked.

SsssSSSTTT! That sound. Instantly recognizable. The sharp noise of air blasted from a soundless whistle. I recognized Crack Baby's trademark combination call and taunt, like yelling "Hey!" with a smile while flipping the bird.

I ignored it, which might have bought me a few more seconds but essentially didn't work. He had just "summoned" me, after all, and my response was not to his liking. Now he had his excuse. Hassan ricocheted attitudes back and forth with Crack Baby while they approached me over near the cars. This time he flicked his hand at me and did his noise: *ssssSSSTTT!*

Man, I hated that noise.

SsssSSSTTT! Like something whizzing past your ear. I think, when primates in cages run out of feces to fling, they will stab at one another with that noise. *SsssSSSTTT! SsssSSSTTT!*

Finally he adds a word: "Move!"

I think, What? Move? I'm not obstructing anything. I try to ignore him, but the noise is back: *SsssSSSTTT! SsssSSSTTT!*

"Move!" he hollers again, pointing at the ground a few feet from where I'm standing. "There! There!"

But there was nothing over there, no reason for me to move those few feet except for Crack Baby, who apparently wanted to show off for Hassan and make me jump through a few hoops.

I am really not a confrontational person; he just caught me on a very low morning, alone in the camp, no food today, seasonal cold air, chilled and damp with morning dew. Not a set of circumstances to keep one reminded of how easily an annoying kidnap victim can get killed out there.

I didn't shout my defiant English retort in his face, but I said it loud enough for him to hear. He either understood the translation or read the tone of voice. It was plain he got the gist of it. His face went dark with fury and he grabbed for the camp's only butcher knife, the long blade used on goats. He charged the eight or ten feet separating us and put the blade to my neck.

"Move!" he screamed into my face. Of course I should have moved much earlier. I certainly should have moved just then. I was just so angry, offended, and despairing of all this. I badly needed to reacquire some measure of dignity. Toward that end I had defiance available as a tool, but that was about the extent of it. Defiance it was, then.

I stood unmoving in that moment, showing more defiance than I could have explained even if they understood, even if they cared. He pushed the blade toward me and radiated enough psychotic energy that I woke up to the fact that I was about to throw my life away for the privilege of defying a child demon.

I moved.

It was all of five feet, but *this* spot was perfectly suited to Crack Baby's whim of the moment. I could tell he still didn't feel that he had scared me enough, though, in my "too mad to care" outrage. So when I turned my back to him and commenced walking in those endless little circles around the tree for a morning constitutional, he went off to wake up the Colonel.

The little creep glared back at me with a leering grin while he instigated one of the Colonel's famous fits of anger over being awakened. Everybody in camp knew not to disturb the Colonel's sleep, or to be ready for the explosion if they did. Crack Baby's evil genius was a mixture of careful lying and timing of delivery. He had the advantage of being able to address the Colonel in front of me without my knowing the translation, but his tone of voice said a lot.

He was telling him that I had tried to wander off, to sneak away. No doubt it was a story claiming that if not for the quick wit and eternal vigilance of our Crack Baby, I would have slipped into the desert and made good my escape. Fortunately the Colonel was a lot smarter than this kid. He knew I had nowhere to run, and more important, he knew I realized that. I could see he was angry and puffy-eyed over being awakened, but his "punishment" for me showed he wasn't fooled by Crack Baby's fake escape story. All he did was order me to quit walking in little circles and instead sit down under the tree. This way he maintained his dignity as a leader by "dealing" with the complaint about me, but it in a manner that showed he didn't seriously regard it as a threat.

◆ ◆ ◆

After a few days of separation, somebody decided to bring Poul back to the camp. No explanation, of course, just one day there he was. We tried to catch up on what had been going on, but real conversation remained difficult around those guys. It was just another term of isolation served out here on the nothing farm where nothing is planted and nothing is grown. They kept us physically separated nearly all of the time, enough to prevent any conversation.

There was a buzzing sound, faint but noticeable, and it seemed to come from somewhere way up in the air, so far overhead there was nothing to see. Like somebody operating a gas engine generator right behind the nearest cloud. It made the Somalis nervous. They always jumped up and made certain we were covered by overhead branches when they noticed the buzzing sound. I stifled a bitter laugh to think these people actually believed two aid workers were going to draw surveillance from the U.S. military. But I was happy to see their fear; it helped quash a little of the arrogance they so often displayed.

I only half noticed the sound. There was the buzzing of desert insects, the playing of the breeze in scrub brush branches. Faint background sounds constantly blended into a low fog of soft noise. With Poul unceremoniously returned from his separation "punishment," the two of us were once again permitted to walk in circles around the tree for exercise. He also watched the sky for satellites at night and told me how he could tell the difference between them and stars. I could understand using any technique to mentally escape, and I never gave much thought to whatever these guys feared was up there, overhead.

All of that seemed too far away, too removed from us, to have any meaning. Instead, my days blended away inside my imagination. Since I didn't know if I would ever see my home again, I visited it in my mind and made it a point to visualize every detail I could, to deepen the experience and prolong the amount of time I might have away from my surroundings. In spite of the fact that it had become so difficult to concentrate, I pushed myself to focus.

I imagined being back in the apartment Erik and I shared in Nairobi, slowly walking in through the door and standing in the entranceway to look around the living room and take in every detail. I didn't picture Erik there, at first, because I needed to warm up to the idea so I wouldn't start crying and draw angry captors down on me or Poul.

I mentally moved through each room, pausing to look in every direction, remembering where every piece of furniture, every piece of artwork, every decoration would be. I checked under the sofa for dust bunnies and looked over the titles in the bookcase. I smelled the warm human scent of our bedroom in the mornings. I smelled our dog, Smulan, when he was fresh from the bath. And finally, when I was ready, I pictured Erik there waiting for me, and we took each other in our arms, and I smelled his body and felt his warmth. And for just a little while, I was free in spite of this rotten place and I was happy in spite of my mortal fear. Our tormentors had no way to touch me, just then.

I couldn't go so far in this fantasy as to picture us making love. I thought it would surely break my heart and leave me sobbing like a kid while screaming Somali faces blew their *khat* breath on me and called for silence. Instead I stayed inside the apartment with him and told him everything I would say if he were right there in front of me. Once I got myself in the groove, the force of memory was nearly hypnotic. I found I could pass hours that way.

The men still wouldn't give me the antibiotics Erik sent, and my urinary tract infection had become so severe the only way to get comfortable was to lie in the fetal position on my sleeping mat and take imaginary cruises through my past. At least the mental journeys didn't cause gravity to work against my troubled bladder.

I remained at my parking spot under the tree one day while Poul accepted a surprise invitation to chew *khat* with some of the men. I had no idea what an invitation like that from men like these was supposed to mean, but they seemed to find it amusing to watch a foreigner partake of their favorite drug, and they seemed to want to test Poul's response to the stuff. Naturally as a woman I wasn't included, which was a relief in this instance. I had no desire to join these guys in their bloodshot paradise.

And by this point I also had no illusions that this bought Poul any extra favor with them. They might have been willing to "entertain" him in this fashion, but they had no more feeling for him than that. One of them could just as easily have an attack of paranoia, decide Poul had insulted him in some way, and shoot him for his trouble.

By the time January 24 rolled around I was still sick. It had been eight days since our last proof-of-life phone call, and the Somalis merely handed me some antibiotics they got somewhere and which didn't seem to be right for my infection. I'd been through two rounds of them and was still weak and in pain, but at least it was a little easier to move around instead of spending all my time on the mat curled into a ball.

They were doing a pretty good job of "punishing" me and Poul for not providing their expected millions. I felt certain the only reason they gave me any medicine at all was that if they let me get any sicker I wouldn't be able to do the proof-of-life calls. That wouldn't play well for them. So there we were, at a standstill.

Over the past two weeks, Poul and I had been subjected to a second "punishment" of forced separation and virtual solitary confinement. So it was good news when Dahir the Helper took advantage of the fact that the Colonel and Jabreel were away and let the two hostages get together to have a meal.

I had long since been forced to abandon my vegetarian diet, because the men were convinced I was only getting sick because I wouldn't eat meat. They refused to allow me enough nonmeat items to survive on, and I was forced to begin ingesting whatever they let us have, just for the calorie value. I had already lost too much weight.

The men responsible for bringing in that day's *khat* supply also brought along a live goat. It caused a major stir in camp. For these men, this was a significant event.

Helab! Helab! (Meat! Meat!) the men cried with the joy of combat troops getting a visit from the Dallas Cheerleaders. My revulsion at the slaughter of animals was part of my reason for being a vegetarian in the first place, which made it hard to stand there while the animal was killed, and impossible not to notice that the few seconds needed to cut its throat and let it bleed to death were all it would take for them to do the same to us.

When one of them passed a severed goat leg to me and Poul, I knew better than to refuse the food; there might not be anything else. The knife Abdi had at my throat earlier was the only cooking knife in the camp, so we used it to cut the meat into pieces. We fried the goat bits in oil over Poul's cooking fire. My body was so starved for protein that the meat actually tasted very good, even though I wasn't used to eating it. But for the next few hours, my stomach felt as though I'd swallowed a big ball of dirt.

Although Dahir the Helper had brought a watermelon into the camp on the previous day and let us have some, there was no way to get enough calories from the few fruits, vegetables, or grains they provided to prevent us from starving. Our problem in that regard was that they didn't need for us to be healthy; they only needed us to be alive.

Meanwhile the others cut up the rest of the animal's carcass and threw it into a big pot to boil over the fire. As soon as it was cooked they all fell on it, sucking marrow from the bones, drinking the fat floating on the surface of the pot, and spitting bits of gristle into the fire. The camp went quiet except for the sounds of a dozen men engaged in a rhythm of eat, suck, smack, spit. Poul and I had to turn away.

We knew it wouldn't be long before they returned us to our isolation, so we tried to quietly talk while the men were occupied. After three months, there was nothing new to talk about, but any interaction bolstered our spirits by reminding us we weren't completely isolated there.

I think Helper was trying to make up for the fact that in December he had confided to us that we were to be released by January 1. When that date passed, he then came with the news that it would be done by January 15. Now, nine days afterward, it was obvious he was either lying, which would be odd for Dahir, given his normal behavior, or he had genuinely thought he possessed inside information. I told myself the date could have been changed without his input and without any notice, because of his low rank. Either way, I was touched that he even concerned himself enough to find the failure of his predictions embarrassing, instead of merely amusing himself with our disappointment.

As the sun went down, the big guy called "African" was in charge of the men while the Colonel was away. I didn't know what made African any more African than the others, but that's how he was known. He was dirt poor, wearing only a very old and tattered cotton shirt, the traditional Somali men's skirt, and nothing else, every day. He didn't seem to possess anything else, either. And yet for some reason the Colonel had decided to leave African in charge. I guess it was a simple matter of size.

We hadn't seen Jabreel for days; he wasn't spending as much time at the camp with the men so unhappy over his negotiation efforts. This was fine with me; it provided a little breathing room. Poul was permitted to come and help me move my sleeping mat and the foam mattress down to our sleep spot out under the open sky. I usually moved them myself every night, but it was getting hard to walk without stabbing lower pains from my bladder infection. I was glad for the help and a minute of company.

But when no one was paying attention, he muttered that he had information. I was so skeptical at this point, I didn't even react. He confided that Dahir had talked to Jabreel a few days ago and asked him when this was all going to be over. He claimed that Jabreel promised it would all be finished in two weeks. They said Bashir planned to accept whatever our people offered to them.

My problem with that idea was mostly that Dahir had been telling us pretty stories for over a month. I found this one hard to believe, but the cruelty of hope is such that I couldn't keep myself from igniting a little flame in my heart. It might have been idle gossip, but at least it was positive news, not another assurance that we would be killed or sold off if the price wasn't met. We bid each other goodnight, and Poul headed for the other side of the camp to go count the satellites.

I made my crude bed and lay down to wait for my mom to show up. I always gave her name to the first star to appear at night. Soon she emerged, and I could see her star, shining bright. I talked to her for a while, telling her about my day almost as if writing a verbal diary. I sometimes imagined what her answers would be. It was almost like hearing them.

Finally, a thin overcast engulfed the sky, and the stars were blotted out. I think I closed my eyes at that point, but the sky was so dark it was hard to tell. Sleep was elusive for awhile, so I began another mental walk through our apartment at home. I moved into our living room, slowly dragging my fingertips across the images of the keepsakes lying around the room, trying to actually feel them, the unique feel of each one, the texture and temperature. I traveled down the hall to our bedroom, felt the floor under my feet, my constantly bare feet. I climbed into our big Zanzibar bed, felt the mattress sink under my weight, just a little, not too much, the sheets, freshly laundered, crisp and clean against the skin.

The scene I played out there was always the same. It was the best I could imagine, and there was no need to change or improve it.

Erik appears and we sit together in the bed, holding our new baby, our first child, here at last. The scene becomes more real than the ground beneath my dirty foam mattress. Soon I hear Erik's voice, feel his touch and the strength of his arms, the stubble on his face, the scent of his skin.

And our baby—a boy, I think, but don't really know—I feel the impossibly smooth baby skin and smell the clean baby hair. Here nothing matters but that our child is with us and we are together and I can feel the whispery breeze of baby breath gentle against my lips.

That scene helped me keep going, much farther than I would have been able to do on my own, reminding me I had to survive this ordeal and allow the images to become reality. I prayed for strength and asked God to be with Erik and my dad on the coming day. I could feel that Erik was pounding down every door he could. For him, the sheer frustration of it had to be as corrosive as my sustained hunger and deteriorating medical condition. Knowing him and his need to put things right, I wondered if his torment was worse than mine.

I fall asleep in his arms, holding our baby, safe with my husband and our child in our great big bed at home.

Part Four

———

Night of the
Black Magic Sleep

CHAPTER TWENTY-FIVE

In the ninety-three days since the kidnappings, the FBI team had accumulated a trove of secret intelligence on the kidnappers. The U.S. clandestine service keeps up an active surveillance all around the Horn of Africa region because of its importance to international shipping and vulnerability to terrorism. When working an active case, observations from the ground and the air are supervised and coordinated by the FBI's Nairobi office, which shares the same responsibility with all foreign FBI offices representing American interests abroad. Most of the time this involves fighting complex structures of international crime, but it also applies to the protection of any individual citizen who falls victim to major crime abroad.

In both cases, the FBI works on the premise that its law enforcement efforts not only help American citizens but also help secure the region for local people. This aids in maintaining a collaborative atmosphere that proves vital during times when a little quid pro quo is needed and local intelligence is required.

In Jessica's case, the FBI traced the forces behind the kidnapping to a consortium of three local clans from southern Somalia. The Habr Gidir clan region stretches from the southern part of Galkayo down toward the capital of Mogadishu. Criminals belonging to three of the Habr Gidir subclans, Sa'ad, Suleiman, and Ayr, were believed to have cooperated in arming and manning the operation.

Unfortunately for the kidnappers' venture, by the time President Obama was ready to order a raid, the Americans knew exactly how many were on the Somali side: twenty-six grown men and teenaged soldiers, all rotating through the camp in shifts.

Information about whether an aerial surveillance drone was used in this rescue operation is classified, and there is a chance the distant engine that sounded like a generator, which Jessica, Poul, and the kidnappers sometimes heard in the distance, wasn't a drone, but an actual generator out there in the scrub desert.

If a drone was in fact employed, the capabilities of prevailing technology would have enabled it to circle at altitudes beyond visual range, and it would have been able to loiter over the site for hours at a time. If it was there, publicly available knowledge confirms it would have been able to transmit clear photos and video shots regardless of the lighting, day or night. When this data was combined with the information gleaned from the ground (if in fact it was), the Americans would have learned the specific kinds of weapons and ammunition available to the Somalis and the approximate level of skill and determination they were likely to display. The weaponry in the camp was that of quasimilitary militia, and the fighters had to be expected to put up stiff resistance if they had the chance.

The Americans also knew that each of the dozen times medicine was sent in to her, the kidnappers intercepted it and refused to pass it on. The Americans knew the "doctor" claiming to be kept on hand by the kidnappers to "guarantee the health of the hostages" was doing no such thing. They knew he had done nothing for either hostage beyond checking blood pressure on one occasion. He was described by Jabreel the negotiator as "available around the clock," but instead he spent most of his time unavailable in the nearby "International City of Adado," staying in the same guesthouse Jabreel was using. His cover story fooled no one, and the negotiator lied badly about his actions. Again the kidnappers failed to grasp the reality of modern surveillance.

The FBI knew Jess's NGO had paid more than $12,000 in "fees" to get a doctor in to see Jess, in a desperate attempt to get the life-saving medicine to her. And thanks to Erik's tireless updates on her condition, made possible by his ability to read between the lines of what she told them to hear what she wasn't permitted to say, the Bureau knew that internal infections from the filthy conditions had begun to wreck her kidney function. They advised the military to have the necessary medical supplies on hand at the moment of rescue.

The FBI knew, most of all, that this complete lack of medical assistance was being inflicted strictly for the purpose of increasing the tension for Jessica's family. The kidnappers hoped to raise the ransom level by forcing her family or friends or employers to hurry up and "save" her.

This, as it happens, was their greatest moment of fatal vision. Because it completed the third of the three necessary ingredients for triggering the order to make a military raid on foreign soil— that the kidnap hostage's survival is in immediate peril. Jessica was being gradually killed by her captors, and the process was picking up speed. Although there was no word indicating her male colleague was also in a medical crisis, the conditions inflicted on both of them would ruin anyone's health.

Prompted by the medical report provided by Erik from their consulting physician, the Bureau sent their simple analysis traveling on up the food chain. The problem caused by Jessica's continued lack of access to the medication to regulate her thyroid was compounded by the infection that began in her urinary tract but was guaranteed to spread, given her overall weakened state. If her weakened thyroid picked up the infection, her system could quickly fail. It was now clear that unless drastic measures were immediately taken, the American hostage would soon become a casualty.

There were compelling reasons to prevent her death, on top of the usual humanitarian concerns. Jessica was known to have been part of an organization involved in a demining project to help protect the local people. This nongovernment organization supplies direct relief to some 450,000 refugees in the border region of Somalia-Kenya. As a worker struggling to help save the local children, her death at her captors' hands couldn't be a worse tragedy at both the personal and the political levels. Her devastated family would be joined in their grieving by an outraged population.

Erik saw to it that everyone in the chain of command got the information that the tipping point had been reached; if they didn't get her out fast she would soon die. He also understood that upon Jessica's demise, the prognosis for her Danish colleague would be just as bad. At this point those authorities agreed with the need for a rescue attempt.

The conclusion was submitted to the secretary of defense: Immediate risk now exceeds the many dangers of a raid. The required response was now a studied act of extreme prejudice, forcing a decisive conclusion, and terminating any hostiles who got in the way.

President Obama received a briefing telling him the health of American Jessica Buchanan was rapidly failing. His decision had boiled down to the choices of sending in a rescue team or hoping she could somehow survive on her own. He ordered immediate planning for a raid by SEAL Team Six.

On the twenty-third of January, he met with his advisory team on the matter. The gist of their news for him was clear: Nothing's going well with the negotiations, the kidnappers continue to make irrational demands, and the American hostage is in failing health. There is, however, going to be a full dark of the moon in two days' time, during the early morning hours.

After hearing the latest assessment of the situation, the president ordered Secretary of Defense Leon Panetta to have the rescue mission go hot. Panetta conveyed the order directly to the SEAL team commander, keeping the circle of information tight to maximize secrecy.

The attack was set to launch from the military base in Djibouti, taking off in a specially equipped air force C-130 on the evening of the following day. The strike team would fly down through Somalia, then parachute from the plane at a high altitude, landing a safe distance from the camp to silently prepare the raid.

♦ ♦ ♦

Twenty-four Navy SEAL special operatives flying at a classified high altitude responded to the jump command like coiled springs, launching themselves into a brief free fall through the evening sky. As masters of the HAHO jump—High Altitude, High Opening—the elite SEAL team members confidently fell "dick in the dirt," thrusting hips and torso into the direction of the fall, with arms and legs splayed wide to stabilize them. In the pitch black of the new moon there was no way for ground forces to see their aircraft or pick out the men descending toward them as tiny grains of silent trouble. Within a few seconds of leaving the plane, the SEAL warriors deployed their wing-shaped air foils and quietly flew their canopies down to the landing zone. The high-altitude openings prevented the popping sounds of the deploying chutes from being detected on the ground.

From the air, each man scanned the ground below for potential trouble and listened for anything that would give warning of a hostile presence. The SEALs all landed safely in one of the flat zones between mounds of scrub brush and the scraggly acacia trees not far from "The International City of Adado," an oblong cluster of low-roofed buildings stretched about a mile in length and perhaps half that in width. Its sparse population was a definite asset to the SEAL team. Unlike urban missions, in this one there would be no hordes of local fighters to spill out of nearby houses and plague the rescue. On this night there were no sounds but the faint noises of the squad switching out of their birdman rigs and into overland travel mode.

The land was so dark at that hour that naked human eyes were useless beyond arm's length. To the extent that the men remained silent in the inkpad blackness, they were invisible. But for those with state-of-the-art optical equipment, each man was marked by an infrared beacon on his helmet. To one another they were brightly apparent and far less likely to draw friendly fire.

Within minutes, the two dozen SEAL warriors had stowed their gear and prepped for the silent hike to their target objective. They already knew they would be facing high-powered Kalishnikov assault rifles. Their sixty-pound vests included heavy ballistic plates for additional protection that could sometimes repel AK-47 rounds, under ideal circumstances. Because of them, pistol rounds, ricocheted rifle rounds, and even knife attacks were less of a threat.

But ballistic plates and Kevlar helmets offer scant protection against heavy-gauge rifle fire. Each of the SEAL operatives knew the enemy had been seen with heavy machine guns, and they knew the kidnappers were financed well enough to possess Russian-made RPG-7 rocket launchers. A single round could take out a large portion of the attack force and eliminate the hostages at the same time. These heavy weapons meant all of the captors had to be incapacitated with such speed there would be no time to put such things into play.

The SEAL attackers knew they were about to face such weapons because of detailed information gathered over the past three months. Each SEAL even wore desert camouflage matched to the local background. But these were the men you don't see coming. If they properly executed their careful plan there would be no need to hide. By the time daylight arrived they would have attacked unseen and disappeared in the same fashion.

Of all the SEAL team's weaponry, their best protection on this night was offered by their night vision capability. Better to see and avoid the enemy than have to deal with his bullets. In the most advanced available version, four infrared vision tubes instead of the usual two allowed for a better field of vision. They rendered depth perception superior to anything else in the field. They would clearly reveal the details of the photograph each man carried of their American quarry. The picture could identify her if she couldn't speak for herself.

The mission plan was to arrive at the site deep in the night, long after the new shift came on duty and the guards' nerves were relaxed, their senses dulled. This might offer only the smallest battle advantage, but the SEAL team worked with whatever they could get.

The challenge facing the SEAL warriors had been put to them by their commander-in-chief because of the enormous national prestige at stake, but they were expected to ignore political pressures in the execution of the mission. No matter what the political players might have to say about it, everyone involved knew the only definition of success for this mission was to annihilate the kidnappers before they could harm or kill the two hostages—and to do it without killing the hostages themselves.

Once they were given the mission and cut loose, it didn't matter who had sent them. The attack would be sudden, harsh, and unrelenting.

Any assault force can minimize the risk of stray rounds by cutting down the number of bullets fired. But while knife attacks from the SEAL team might guarantee the hostages weren't exposed to friendly fire, blades alone couldn't be trusted to get the job done quickly enough to prevent any cries of alarm.

Thus it was unlikely the SEAL team could thin the opposition by selecting the closest few guards and surprising them with blades to their throats while they slept. The potential silence-breaker would come from that one guy who didn't die on the first slice and managed to get his hand on a sidearm long enough to fire off a single shot. In seconds, random gunfire would be tearing through the campsite and be just as likely to kill the hostages as save them.

Still, when the SEAL team's GPS units indicated they were closing on the campsite, the faceless men from DEVGRU glided through the darkness knowing it was safe to exploit their enemy's most grievous tactical error.

There were no dogs.

Many people in that region have no affection for dogs, considering them unclean and good for nothing, one more mouth to feed. A more dog-friendly attitude would have greatly benefitted the kidnappers. If any had been out there, it would have severely complicated the infiltration effort. That simple precaution is often effective against sneak attacks because it can be so tricky to take out dogs in silence without alerting anybody.

The SEAL operators moving to their preattack locations shared the kidnappers' appreciation for a lack of dogs. The element of surprise lay at the heart of their attack plan.

Zero hour found each of the SEAL special operators at his pre-arranged location with the weaponry specific to his job. Grenades and all heavy weapons were left behind, too hot for a surgical job like this. However, the Heckler & Koch MP-7 was ideal for close-quarters fighting, compact even with the suppressor mounted. Likewise the smaller MP-5 machine pistol. The larger H&K 416 assault rifle, with its longer barrel, would be more effective if kill shots were necessary at a distance. Suppressed large-caliber handguns topped their close-quarter firearms list. And the long-bladed knife strapped to each man gave him the opportunity to perform a silent kill up close, or provided a last chance at survival if he got separated from his firearms.

They arrived already knowing the expected locations of Poul Thisted and Jessica Buchanan in the camp. They knew each one slept on the ground, ringed by guards. Their night vision systems allowed them to silently surround the camp and prepare to launch a coordinated attack under the welcome blanket of darkness.

But the appearance of the camp was all wrong. There were no fires for cooking. In spite of a chill in the night air there were no fires for warmth. The guards all appeared to be fast asleep—every one of them, even though guarding the prisoners was what they were there to do. And for some reason, the American female was moving around the camp by herself in the dark.

CHAPTER TWENTY-SIX

The paralyzing frustration had driven Erik into another nightmare, and he found himself clawing at Jessica's attackers. The dream captured his extreme frustration. In the dream, Erik fought with faceless bureaucrats standing in the way of a rescue mission and keeping him from Jessica. He struggled to get past them and past the dream attackers to reach her, tearing at them with every combat move he knew. There were always more coming, always more.

He woke up gasping and angry. The clock showed it was past midnight, now the 25th of January. There had been some talk of a possible rescue attempt on the 24th, but now there was another day come and gone with nothing, no call.

He lay back down, but was too awake to sleep again. Pretty soon he was back up and pacing around, trying to talk himself out from under the tension. The CMT expected a raid within six days of receiving Erik's certification on Jessica's condition. But the 24th was the sixth day, and something obviously caused them to pause in their timeline. There had to be a reason or reasons, but they existed behind the official barrier of secrecy. He could only hope their delay would be short before they launched the team. Jessica's entire system was under attack from infections her kidneys couldn't handle simply because those people hadn't allowed any of the medicine sent in to them to get to her.

Thoughts of murderous revenge kept interrupting his concentration. The idea of an entire group of men working together to inflict this slow suffering on an innocent woman left him with no desire for another wasted word of negotiation.

As far as he was concerned, the authorities would have to get the job done right away. He was so exhausted from holding back out of concern over doing more harm, even as their inaction harmed her anyway, that if they abandoned plans to go in for any reason, he knew where to get a team of experienced men who would help him make the attempt himself. Every one of the perfectly good reasons not to do that was growing smaller in his mind. There was nothing left but the hell of the ticking clock until the "go" command was given, with the window of opportunity quickly closing. Once it was shut, nobody's rescue attempt would do any good.

◆ ◆ ◆

Jessica:

I opened my eyes and looked up from my place on the sleeping mat, but the sky was still so black that things didn't look any different whether my eyelids were open or closed. There was no moon, and a heavy haze blotted out the starlight. This was the deepest pitch black I'd ever seen out there. The chill in the air was sharp and woke me up in spite of, or maybe because of, the thin blanket and the damp sleeping mat. I guessed it was well after midnight, probably around 2:00 a.m. Time for a trip to the bush.

Oh, I hated to get up. I had to force my shivering muscles to stand. But the damned urinary tract infections made it impossible for me to sleep through the night. It was my first time getting up since falling asleep, but I knew there'd be more.

The routine was always the same. I stood in place and quietly said, "Toilet." I had to get approval to move off the sleeping mat. To get off the mat without that permission would risk having someone think I was making an escape attempt. I called out softly enough to avoid waking everybody, but loudly enough so one of the nearby guards would hear me and, I hoped, give me permission to step away.

The problem was that nobody answered. I told myself they might be preoccupied or might not have heard me. So I repeated, still speaking softly but a little bit louder this time, "Toilet."

I stood still and held my breath to listen. There was no response from any of them.

What is this? The silence and stillness was so bizarre I felt my adrenaline spike, and I was instantly wide awake. There were nine guards surrounding us. I could hear our Helper, Dahir, snoring close by. Surely they weren't all asleep at the same time. No way. It never happened.

Poul ought to have been sleeping about twenty feet away, maybe more, though I couldn't see him. Each of us was forced to sleep surrounded by our own group of guards. It just didn't seem possible that not one of either group of guards was awake. Unbelievable. It was wrong in a huge way. I felt my hearbeat begin to speed up, although I couldn't have explained why, since there was no apparent danger. There was just this new and unbelievable situation.

I struggled to reason this thing through. They had spent the day loaded to the gills on *khat* and stuffed themselves with roasted goat for dinner. So maybe they had all crashed at the same time and didn't bother to set a guard? But that idea landed with a thud. All of them at once? These were paid mercenaries.

If Bashir caught his men doing this there would surely be bloodshed. The man who had been left in command, the big one called African, should absolutely have been awake and pushing the others to stay awake as well.

I raised my voice just a little louder. "Toilet! Come on, you guys! Dahir, you hear me? *Toilet,* okay?"

Not a peep. They either didn't hear me or didn't care. Must've been a great party.

The continual infliction of unnecessary difficulties was already a sore spot with me. Being stuck on that mat was at the top of the list. Right at the moment, I needed to go, and somebody had to respond. But when I squinted as hard as I could into the dark, everything was washed in black. My eyes hadn't been able to get used to the dark because there was just no light out there to take in. No firelight, no ambient light from any source. The overcast continued to block the stars. We might as well have been in a deep cavern.

I gritted my teeth and exhaled in exasperation. *Great. Here we go, fellas . . .*

I grabbed a little penlight that still had some battery power and used it to light the ground in front of me, just enough to walk without tripping over somebody. I made it to the nearest bush without raising an alarm from anyone, but the whole time I was out there I kept up a flashing pulse with the light, just to make it plain I wasn't trying to hide or run off.

Then I was alone out there in the bushes, and everything was peaceful and very quiet. I couldn't hear a thing but an occasional skittering leaf moving on a breeze. Small sounds, just here and there, barely enough to perceive at all. Maybe those sounds were out there all the time, and I just never noticed them before: nocturnal movements of tiny life forms in the tropical scrub desert. All were somehow closer on this night. I wondered, had this pitch blackness forced my ears to work harder, like those of a blind person?

The darkness itself felt protective, as if it was inviting me to slip away into it and disappear, bound for any destination far from this place. And then, perhaps because of the unusual factors of the sleeping guards and the dark moon and the overcast sky, I imagined making my way over to Poul and rousting him. *Come on, while they're all out cold!*

I suddenly felt convinced we could vanish together in darkness like this. *If I could just shake this fever. We could hoof it out of here. I could stand the pain. I'm ready to try, anyway.*

We might get lucky, if we just made a break for it and stayed away from people and made our way on foot. We could power though it and avoid people entirely and just keep going until we crossed the Green Line and could appeal to someone for help.

There were watering holes out there, once used for livestock back when there were herds. We might have to walk a hundred miles, maybe more, I thought. Could a person walk a hundred miles without food? Could I? Could I do that even if we found water along the way? Could I do it in my current condition, when just standing up felt like taking a stabbing? *Stick close to the bushes while we run. Hunt for small game, eat it raw.*

I was ready to believe we would be protected in the inky black. I told myself the plan could work. As long as sunrise never came and the inkjet darkness cloaked us, it could absolutely work. All we needed to do was freeze time for a few days while we effected a clean getaway.

With that, the images left me. I was glad for them to go. Entertaining fantasies about unreal escapes did nothing but sharpen all those jagged feelings of isolation.

There was some physical relief when I was finished, but the

pain stayed in my lower abdomen. *Escape? Oh, yeah. We might have made it a few hundred yards.*

I padded back to the sleeping mat, avoiding the inert guards. I got a glimpse of Dahir a few feet from the bottom of my mat. He was usually responsive to me when Jabreel wasn't around. He also tended to be far less in the grip of *khat* than the other men. It was hard to see him included in this goofy party.

Dahir was probably in his early forties, well-groomed, and a trusted driver for the group. His green Land Cruiser brought regular shipments of those humble supplies that were allowed to us. It was surreal that he had included himself in this first-ever group sleepover. I hated to see him get down on their level. Among that unhappy lineup of men, Dahir was a good man by comparison.

Dahir, the Helper, spoke a little English, and indicated he was married with eight, yes eight, children plus his own house, somewhere nearby. For some reason, Dahir was finding it difficult to support a household of at least ten people in a broken society. I suppose that's what put him there.

He always seemed to have a conscience about things and never mistreated me. If he was supposed to make me do something, he was respectful about it. I liked having his sympathetic presence around, and he seemed happy to remain right at my side whenever he was on duty.

Unlike Jabreel, Dahir was shy and restrained in his manners, and his behavior was never improper. He prayed five times a day, something Jabreel also did, though Helper appeared to be trying to live by his faith, as long as you set aside the little bits about kidnapping, sick prisoners, and withholding necessary medicine.

Dahir the Helper was what passed for a friend in this dark place, where it was so black at night and somehow just as dark with the sun shining. All he did was drive the car and deliver the supplies, so I suppose he mentally divorced himself from sharing guilt over the rest of it.

He was a living portrait of how a good-hearted man of peace conducts himself when carrying out terrible actions for an evil design. He tries to be nice about it.

I lay down on my side and curled into a ball for warmth, feeling like a bag of mud. I had lost fifteen or twenty pounds and my bony body couldn't seem to retain heat anymore. It would have been some consolation to be able to see my mom's star, but that was no option on this odd night when nothing was visible. So I conjured up images of her instead and projected them out into the solid black sky, using it as the world's largest movie screen.

Even though I couldn't see Mom's star, I sent her my deepest feelings, my longing for the depth of love I once felt from her. The yearning for it wasn't diminished after she was taken from us.

Mom, I just don't think I can make it through any more of this. Whatever the plan for all this may be, I don't think it includes my survival. I think this is what dying feels like. I'm so sorry, I know you would want me to stand strong. I know you would want me to believe Erik can find a way to make rescuers come, and I've tried to hold up in the face of this ordeal, but I don't know anymore. I would never agree to leave Erik behind, but I can feel this body dying. Mom, you felt the shadow of death coming over you, and now it's trying to tear me out of this world. Maybe that's why the desert seems so dark tonight.

I'm not asking to be saved from this anymore. If I can't survive this, please let me know I can somehow reach Erik with my love for him. It's going to devastate him if I never get home. He'll face such terrible loneliness, and it will be much worse than what I've been feeling, because he'll have no hope at all of getting our lives back again. I've lived on that hope for so long, but it's melting away now.

If there's no hope left for Erik and me as a couple, can you help me cross over? I think I could die without fear if I could sense you there with me.

Noises stopped me. My concentration up to then had been nearly hypnotic, but these irritating little noises broke it. Those faint animal sounds, insect sounds, whatever they were. The damned noises were nearly faint enough to ignore, but they hovered right at the edge of my hearing.

A tiny cracking of a thin twig, one dry branch of a bush scraping across another, a bouncing pebble. Like feathers tickling away at my ears, they refused to leave me to my thoughts.

"Aggghhh!" I said it out loud in spite of myself. This was really the end. A bunch of weirdly lethargic captors lay all around me, I couldn't see a thing under this thick darkness, and I couldn't even take advantage of the silence to reach out to my mother's spirit without having my attention tugged by whatever was out there.

I decided the unusually deep darkness was fitting. Here in the final stages of this long execution by starvation and medical neglect, there really wasn't anything to see anyway.

More little noises. *What's out there?* Frustration and anger made me bold enough to stand up on the mat and switch on the flashlight. I played the beam all around the camp, looking for the source of the noises. Nothing.

I wondered again, was I hearing anything new? Or had my mental state simply combined with the darkness to make me start hallucinating?

I directed the beam around in a full circle one more time: still nothing, only the inert forms of a bunch of desperate men sleeping off their drug stupor, men who only used the drugs to pad the harshness of their lives within their broken society, who were playing this deadly kidnapping game as their best attempt to feed their families. My heart would go out to them, except they were attempting to do this by slowly grinding me to death in a bizarre game of "chicken" with my family and employers, to see how much of my misery it might take to pull maximum money out of them.

Their main question at this point was nothing more than whether I could survive long enough to make their game pay off. It occurred to me then that the only satisfaction I might see in this thing could be my dying knowledge that my death itself would screw up their plans and leave them with nothing.

I snapped off the light and lay back down, but the "consolation" of thinking my death would cost them their gamble was cold comfort. The more rational thought of leaving Poul alone to their torments was enough to keep me from feeling any satisfaction at the thought of my own demise. There had been no offers of millions from the Danish side, as with the American side, and I knew there never would be. So once these desperados accepted the fact that I was gone and Poul's people weren't going to ride in with bags of cash, what would his life be worth? How much of their frustration and outrage would they take out on him? I had been forced to watch them beat him with branches for nothing more than showing them some resistance, some hesitation to snap to and follow their orders.

If I died, I feared they would sell him to Al-Shabaab. They'd have to. The only thing I felt certain of was that his death with that group would be worse than my death from illness, more terrifying and far more violent. I curled up in a ball again and lay with my back to the largest clump of sleeping men. It was a useless gesture, but it gave me the illusion of shutting them out in some way.

For the next minute or two I lay without moving, focusing on my breathing and trying to slow my thoughts. Each time I started to feel myself drifting there was another little noise. It sounded as if the giant beetles that populated the area were coming out of their nests for the night. The things were so large I sometimes heard them skittering across my sleeping mat, loud enough to wake me up.

But I'd already paused to listen, shined the light around, seen nothing, and that was all I could do about it. Now I just ignored the bugs while I heard them coming closer and I tried to find sleep again. Before long, I heard the little sounds right at the edge of the mat.

I didn't bother to move. There wasn't anything left to worry about. I had once been concerned about the possibility of poisonous bites from those insects, but what difference would that make now? It was over. *I'd rather get some stinking sleep.*

I think it's fair to say I was beaten, then. I curled up as tightly as I could. This was the deepest, darkest cave I'd ever been in, and I had nothing left by way of response. All my past promises about avoiding despair were smoke in the wind. There was nothing around me to come to my aid, and I had depleted my inner resources to the bone.

At that instant I heard someone, Dahir, I think, leap to his feet and give out an intense whisper, calling for his boss. I heard him cock his rifle. His voice was full of panic.

"*Afree-cahn!*"

Nothing. No sound of African or anyone else reacting to the alarm. Dahir kept his voice low but tried again.

"*Afree-cahn!*" There was a hanging pause, then sudden sounds of movement all around the camp, men jumping to their feet, weapons being cocked . . .

Then everything exploded. Instant Armageddon.

Gunfire broke out in every direction, and even the shock waves were terrible. All my pent-up fear and anxiety took over my thinking. I was aware of chaos but had no understanding of it. I'm sure I was screaming but couldn't hear myself above the din. I don't know if I was praying in silence or screaming out loud, but all I could think was the phrase, "Oh, God, Oh, God," repeating on a loop.

It had to be another clan coming to steal us, or even a raid by Al-Shabaab. I put my heart and my mind with my family. I sent out my love to Erik the same way I would have released a homing pigeon with a message, if I could have done it. *I swear to God, Erik, I would have been a good wife, I would have loved you, I would have given you children. We would have been so happy.*

Between the staccato gunshots, I heard the Somalis screaming useless orders to each other, then screaming with the impact of bullets, then screaming in their death throes. A flash lit up Dahir's face for just an instant. I saw a mask of pure fear. It was the face of a man who knew he would never see his children again.

Someone shouted, "Oh, no!" It might have been Dahir, but I couldn't be sure. I heard him gasp when the bullets hit him. Darkness hid his expression, so at least I didn't have to watch him die.

Strong hands grabbed at my blanket. I put up a fight to keep it. I don't know why it represented some primal security, but it did.

"Jessica!" a male voice called.

It stopped me like a slap to the face. *An American accent?*

I relaxed a bit in confusion, and somebody snatched away the blanket in that instant, tricky bastards. My face was no longer covered, but the black sky blended well with the black masks I could see in front of me. They were like ghosts with deadly weapons.

Something in my brain couldn't register that these people might be attempting to help me. I'd only heard my name—was I wrong about the American accent? Had I just been duped into confirming my identity? The magical effect of that American voice was gone. My brain couldn't accept it. The optimism well was dry.

The only thought I had for myself was if this turned out to be a takeover raid by Al-Shabaab forces, then the one thing in the world that could make things worse than they already were was happening at that moment. The survival drive is such a powerful engine; I struggled and screamed with all my strength. Even though I expected them to kill me soon enough, I fought back out of instinct. Then I heard it:

"Jessica! This is the American military. We've come to take you home. You're safe."

Not "Jesses" but *Jessica*. My American name spoken by an American voice.

The light went on for me. It finally registered. I got it, got it, got it.

And those words were more beautiful than any piece of music I'd ever heard. "Jessica, this is the American military. We've come to take you home. You're safe."

CHAPTER TWENTY-SEVEN

Beginning with the second week of the kidnapping, attempts were made to get care packages to Jessica via different couriers and different routes. A new one went out every few days. Each was a knapsack filled with toiletries, basic first aid, snacks, anything they thought she might need. They kept on sending them all through those three months—fifteen care packages in all.

One method was to send the package to Galkayo, where the NGO's staff then gave it to a taxi driver to transport down to "The International City of Adado," where people had been located who promised to deliver it, for a fee of course. Not one of the packages ever reached her. Information came in saying several of the care packages actually got through to the kidnappers, but they also knew from Jessica's remarks to the family communicator that the kidnappers refused to pass such sources of comfort along to her. All those efforts did no good at all, other than to confirm the level of inhumanity her captors were willing to display.

They also got a package through to the "doctor" in Adado who was supposed to carry it to her when he went to do a checkup on December 21, but even this "doctor" proved unable to convince the kidnappers of the importance of it, just as he couldn't find it in himself to do any actual doctoring. Thousands of dollars went into these repeated and maddening efforts simply because there was no way to know if they would work at all without trying again and again.

On the morning of January 25, Erik had finally managed to get back into a state vaguely resembling sleep after waking up too early and pacing the floor. But the sleep wasn't the kind that makes you feel rested. He found himself back in the land of tormented dreams.

He dreamed the phone rang and it was Matt calling to tell him there had been a rescue attempt and another one of those terrible disasters had taken place. He ran from the dream version of Matt and his terrible news by waking himself up, but the fearful impulse driving the dream followed him. As soon as he began to drift off again, the same dream repeated. Ring, ring, bad news calling. It was so realistic that he thought he was awake and answering his phone.

Again he heard Matt's voice on the other end. The sound of his pain at having to make this call was already telling Erik everything before a single detail came out. A clean rescue had been too much to hope for, after all. The unpredictability factor always rears its ugly head at the worst moment, and obviously this is what had happened with the rescue team.

The voice switched to Jessica. She sounded as clear as if she were calling from the building next door. There was no static, no background noise, nobody else talking over her. Every word she spoke was crystal clear while she screamed that Erik had failed to keep his promise. Instead of coming for her, he had listened to Matt and the Crisis Management Team and left the love of his life to the torments of those criminals. And as he feared, her voice revealed she had a mountain of rage and bitterness toward him for letting her down.

"Why did you listen to them?" she demanded. "Why didn't you ignore them and come for me? How could you leave me here?"

And with that question, the dream that seemed real gave way to a waking world that didn't. He sat on the edge of the bed in the early morning light and tried to think of a way to answer those questions if they ever got her back.

◆ ◆ ◆

Jessica:

The gunfire slowed. I noticed that I wasn't dead and felt astounded to be drawing breath. There was no time to see anything. It struck me none of the men seemed to need a flashlight. Still in pitch blackness, I felt myself picked up and thrown in a fireman carry position by a guy who took off running with me as if I were a student backpack. We were quickly away from the campsite. He put me down in a small clearing. The quiet was thick, pocked by isolated shots from that direction.

The same guy who carried me asked if I had shoes. "Uh, yes. But I can't remember where they are." Of course they had to be back by my sleeping mat, but my brain had no candlepower at all.

"Did you leave them at your blanket?"

"I must have. They're actually sandals, but at least they cover my—"

He was already up and running. I could hear his footsteps recede. In moments he returned with my sandals.

"Did you just go back for my—"

"Yes. Is there anything else you need?"

"What? From back *there*?"

"Yes. If there's anything, tell us now. We're getting out of here."

"My little black bag with my medicine in it is right there at the blanket, but don't risk going back again just for—"

His footsteps sprinted away and he was gone one more time. I lay back and tried to get my breathing under control. Someone handed me a bottle of water, I drank, then the bottle was gone again.

The soldier made it back quickly, and I noticed the gunfire had completely died out. I don't recall just when it stopped; it seemed to be over as suddenly as it had begun. But I felt amazed and grateful that a soldier would make two trips back into that place just to get my things for me. He had to do it without knowing whether somebody else was lying in wait for him, ready to shoot as soon as he got within range. And yet there he was, back with my things like a guy just returning from the store.

Even though one of them had specifically told me they were there to rescue us, my brain couldn't process the information. I'd lived in my head so much of the past few weeks that I was having trouble getting a fix on reality.

"You're Americans?" I asked. "Americans? You're Americans?" I must have sounded like a drunk.

"Just wait here," one told me.

Wait here? Why would he want me to wait there? Why weren't we running for our lives? We were still in grave danger. We had to be. Was it possible these guys didn't understand that? I knew the darkness could explode with rocket fire and blow us up at any second. Fear and shock made me shiver so hard my teeth chattered.

"No! Don't leave us here!" I tried to cry out, but my voice was tiny. "We have to get out of here! They'll be coming! Where's Poul? Did you get him?"

Someone took my hand and extended my arm. I touched Poul, who was already there next to me in the darkness. He was fine, but clearly just as stunned as I was. I moved close enough to see that at least he had managed to get out with his pants and shoes on. We couldn't talk there, but we had discussed a possible escape often enough that we both knew without talking about it: If our captors had the smallest ability to retaliate, they would certainly be doing it any second now.

While we huddled on the ground in the dark, some of the soldiers tried to comfort me with normal conversation. That may be something they do under such circumstances to help rescued people adjust, but at the time the ability to converse was way beyond me. My memory wasn't working well, either. I couldn't get anything to stick.

The soldier who went back for my things amid the gunfire did much more than just carry me out of that camp; he took me all the way back out through the looking glass. And now, just like that, here we were again on the normal side. After months in the company of captors whose sensibilities seemed to leave their humanity largely unused, right there was a knight in armor who made two trips back into a hot shooting zone, just to retrieve things I might need if we got out of there alive. After spending those months having to ask permission just to pee at night, the thought of someone assuming such risks simply to make me more comfortable or safe was astounding. It added itself to the list of things that were leaving me speechless.

Still, we couldn't get out of there fast enough as far as I was concerned. I'll bet the feeling is known to anyone who's ever had that nightmare of running through sand or deep water with a monster in hot pursuit. At last we began to move and the group quickly went into a brisk jog. Someone held me up and guided my steps.

There were lots of footstep noises around me. I had the sense of people running along right next to me, others a few yards away. It didn't sound like there were many of us out there, given what we were up against.

Poul and I had come to know the men of this criminal militia and we had seen their heavy weapons, the rocket launchers that could take out all of us with a couple of rounds. I didn't want to guess at their savagery in open combat if they had the chance to steal back their prize captives.

But even in that early hour, these SEAL warriors were already heroes just for getting me out, just for getting me this far. If we never made it all the way home, they had nevertheless given me a chance at least to die in the quest for freedom among my own people, after so long. From my standpoint, I was surrounded by magical heroes. They brought this terrible explosion of violence that popped the locks on our invisible prison. They reached in there and snatched us out alive—I couldn't see how, but I was impossibly alive—and there we were, getting the hell out of there.

Most of our captors would have killed us, if they could have, before allowing us to escape. And it had torn a piece out of me to see Dahir's terrified face in the flashes of the guns. I felt another piece of myself tear away when I heard him cry out. He alone among them had made a point of behaving with respect and without arrogance. There was no way for me not to feel pain on his behalf.

Still, I thought they had to be coming. We represented a major investment. I knew there had been nine guards on duty, at least—maybe more, if some had arrived while I was sleeping. In addition, the rest of the crew had to stay close enough to the camp during their off hours to be able to get back and forth when they took over their next shift. Surely some of those guys were coming for us, by this point. All anybody needed to do was get off a call to the Colonel or to the Chairman. Cell phones, walkie-talkies, ham radios, signal drums, the sound of distant gunfire, that was all it took. The fighters would rally. They would roll down over us with an avalanche of bad news.

We probably only ran for a couple of minutes, but they were the kind that each takes an hour. Then helicopters appeared out of nowhere. Three of them, I think, although the noise and downdrafts made it hard to tell. The soldiers started guiding me toward a specific chopper, but I sprinted the last few yards on my own and dove into the open hatch, then skittered across the fuselage and plastered my back against the side. Lights were muted inside the aircraft. I could only make out silhouettes. The soldiers all wore helmets and face masks with special goggles. It looked as if I'd been picked up by space aliens.

The strangeness of each coming moment surpassed the one before. I had no control over any of it. Nothing felt real, and it certainly didn't seem to be possible that both of us could actually be out of there alive after such a vicious firefight. But before I knew it Poul and the soldiers all piled in, and we took off. I tensed and waited for the explosions from the incoming Somali rockets or their heavy machine guns. Amazingly, nobody tried to shoot us down. We were quickly out of the neighborhood. Before much longer it was too late for them to try.

It was only in that moment that it hit me—I had stopped expecting to see this day. Whatever the outcome was to be, I had let go in my attempt to die with some measure of dignity. Instead, my fate had just spun on its heels one more time and delivered the very escape that had been withheld for so long.

CHAPTER TWENTY-EIGHT

By the time Erik's phone rang at 6:41 a.m. on January 25, he was seriously doubting whether he had really been reasonable in standing back and letting the authorities handle Jessica's rescue, instead of going after her himself. His early morning news feed that day told of a Vietnamese kidnap victim in Somalia, captured by pirates who decided to stimulate ransom money by chopping off one of his arms and sending it to his family. The story further agitated Erik's state of mind. He answered the phone after the first ring, but it was with real trepidation.

"Erik, it's Matt."

Cold fear shot through him. Who ever gets good news at that hour?

But this time the dreaded words didn't come. "She's free, Erik. We got her."

"What? Matt, we—we what?" He automatically gave himself a reality check. Was he dreaming? Was this real?

"We got her, Erik. Both of them. Unharmed."

"Matt! Matt, I . . . Are you *sure*?"

"I can tell you at this moment, Jess and Poul are at our base in Djibouti for debriefing and medical care. Jess is sick but her condition's been stabilized. The main thing is, you don't need to be worried anymore, Erik. She made it. You both made it."

The news smashed Erik open like a *piñata*. He screamed for joy at the top of his lungs, dancing around the room half naked, crying, shouting "Yes! Yes!" If anybody had video of that moment, it would have convinced them he was crazy, and of course he wouldn't have cared.

Jess was coming home. She would be back here in their home with him before too much longer. They might somehow have a chance at a future together, after all—if she still wanted him after the treatment she had endured.

It took him awhile to reach John Buchanan, who happened to be in Washington, D.C., with Jess's sister for a meeting with the FBI and Jess's organization. Erik kept trying until he got a decent connection. He thought he would be breaking this incredible news that she was out and safe. But when he finally got through, he heard a joyful and highly relieved father on the other end of the line, who already knew the whole escape story. Somebody had gotten to John ahead of Erik and stolen his thunder on delivering the big news.

At 10:32 p.m. in Washington, D.C., President Obama had called Jess's father to break the news himself. So John got the chance to personally convey his deep gratitude to the president for taking the political risk to send in SEAL Team Six after his daughter, in spite of the countless hazards.

Finally, Erik thought, it was a good day to be John Buchanan.

◆ ◆ ◆

Jessica:

It took us about thirty minutes to get to a drop point on the northern side of the Green Line. Throughout the flight, I kept trying to fight off the shock and clear my head, but my thoughts were slow and thick. I could barely understand the questions being put to me. I realized the soldiers were trying to be kind, and I certainly didn't feel threatened anymore, but only about half my brain power was working at the moment, and there didn't seem to be much I could do to speed it up. All I was certain about was my deep gratitude for this rescue, this second chance at life. I thanked the men and kept thanking them, over and over. They must have thought there was something wrong with me, and I suppose there was. But my mind was clear enough to know how much I had to be grateful for. It was either a bona fide miracle or something very close to one.

"Can we call my husband? I have to call my husband and let him know!"

"Not yet," one soldier shouted over the noise of the rotors. "But you can call him from the base."

On a more earthly level, I soon noticed that my need to urinate was strong and quickly growing worse, but there was no toilet on the helicopter. They asked if I could wait a few more minutes, and I told them there didn't seem to be much choice.

The men were heartbreakingly polite. They made special efforts to be kind, these athletic hunter-killers who had just taken out a camp full of armed men. They tried to engage me in conversation to determine how well I was processing my thoughts. The simple truth is that I was not thinking clearly at all, but they were kind enough not to mention it. Instead they just directed friendly one-liners to me, sort of open-ended in nature, the kind of thing you can either reply to or let pass by. They brought me up to speed on the Super Bowl game between the Giants and the Patriots, only eleven days away. They groused about the NBA strike.

I nodded from time to time to let them know I was taking it in, but I couldn't get much of a response to come out. A young medic who looked just like one of the muscular athletic department students I used to see around back in college knelt by me to take my vitals. With that, I experienced what may have been the very first blush of a reawakening of my identity as a person in the civilized world: a flash of embarrassment over my condition. I had been tall and thin back when this began; now I was just emaciated.

In terms of my self-image, the sudden embarrassment was condensed from the worst part of my youthful self-consciousness as a thirteen-year-old beanpole. Except now I was also deep down dirty, half starved, dressed in a filthy cotton *deera* that was ripped down the back. I was painfully aware that I had on no proper underwear, just the men's athletic shorts which were all I'd been given. I'd lost so much weight I no longer need to wear a bra. I just wore a faded and ripped tank top under the *deera*, while I walked in the same sandals I'd been wearing when we were taken and every day since. I was months away from anything resembling a real bath. Many captive animals, upon release after months in a cage, would probably step out with the same sensations of confusion and uncertainty I felt swimming around inside me.

I still couldn't conceive of how they had pulled off the attack. Because of the merciful darkness and the chaos of gunfire, I saw nothing of its inner workings except to say it was hard and fast. It was unbelievably hard and fast. I gained instant insight into why the SEAL teams are said to train with such intensity. The depth of violence in the attack hits you all the way down to the bones. It sets off deep instincts to either flee or dive for cover. It must take a special form of hardening of the nerves to be able to remain calm and do your job in the midst of so much heavy gunfire. I had learned firsthand that morning that in such moments our untrained, non-SEAL survival instinct wants nothing but to hide or flee.

As soon as the chopper put down on the airstrip in Galkayo, I told them I really had to relieve myself now. I asked if there would be a toilet on the plane that we were supposed to board next. They regretfully informed me I would have to pee on the tarmac next to the plane. They looked as if they expected me to balk at that. Who, me? Me, in my gross condition? Surrounded by hostile men for ninety-three days? It would take a lot more than that to shame me. I could pee anywhere.

Still, a couple of the men gallantly stepped out onto the tarmac with blankets and held them up to form a little booth so I could relieve myself with some privacy, since by this point it was going to happen no matter where I was. But even through the fog of my confusion then, I was struck by the civility and the casual decency of these men. Without their masks, some were my contemporaries, some were even younger. And they were nothing whatsoever like those images of jeering, sneering young manhood permeating our media-driven culture.

I was Alice, back on the good side of the looking glass, but it was still surreal to see how these compassionate gentlemen each bristled with deadly weapons that were just now cooling down after the battle. It occurred to me then that they must have killed all the Somalis. How else could we have gotten out of there like that?

It might have been possible for one or two of the kidnappers to run away, but considering the night vision goggles the SEAL team used, it was hard to believe any glowing green human figures were going to skulk off into the flat scrub desert without being spotted. I knew all too well, after thinking about it so often, that there was nowhere to hide out there.

From the rendezvous airstrip we boarded an air force C-130 for the flight up to Djibouti, the small country on Somalia's northern border. During the flight a few of the men tried to be social once again and do some simple joking around with me, but I still felt completely locked up. Simple conversational responses felt foreign. I was surprised to discover how difficult it was to think and speak my way through an ordinary conversation. It felt as awkward and unnatural as writing with the wrong hand. The feeling persisted even after my adrenaline burned itself out. They gave me some privacy for a while by simply leaving me in peace, a luxury in itself. A form of relaxation settled in that was mainly composed of fatigue, but it slowed me down enough that I could set about trying to swallow what had just happened.

Okay, we're out, Poul's out, too. We're both uninjured. Their medic even says none of the SEALs got hurt. As for the Somalis, they're probably all dead—the ones in the camp, anyway. As for the rest . . .

The trouble was that the country is known as a nerve center for social gossip. No doubt the word was already traveling about the ambush, the dead guards, the escaped hostages, the lost opportunity.

Somebody out there—whether it was Bashir, the Colonel, the Chairman, or some unknown Galmudug clan leader—somebody had just lost a ton of investment on us. Somebody was not only furious, but might feel the need to seek retribution to regain status in the eyes of his fellows.

It struck me to wonder how hard would it be to dispatch a couple of *khat*-loaded killers to Hargeisa or Nairobi to take revenge on Erik. He was known to many of the local people, and it would have been easy to find him. With retaliation as a distinct possibility, I pushed my sluggish brain to think of something, do something, fight back the drowsy feeling and let these SEAL team fighters know this thing might not be over.

I piped up over the engine noise, "We have to call Erik and tell him to get out of the house! To get away! By now the kidnappers could already be ordering someone to go after him!"

The man just gave a small, confident shake of his head. "Not likely." He didn't say why he thought that.

I nodded as if I understood, but only to hide that I had no idea what to say. I felt socially damaged, as if something had happened to me while I was out there but I was only now realizing the effect. One of the guys showed me the photo they carried for the purpose of recognizing me, if it came down to a question of identification, which I suppose meant identifying my body. The photo was a still shot taken from the proof-of-life video. It was taken weeks earlier, and I was already looking bad at the time, hollow-eyed and distant. That begged the question of what I must look like at the moment; I was too tired to go anywhere near it.

The rest of the flight went by in a state of melted consciousness between wakefulness and sleep. I had to let others take over and lead me around. One soldier handed me a Kashi granola bar, and I would have sworn then and there it was the most wonderful food on Earth. Actual nutrition—it seemed as if I could taste it with every cell in my body. Some other guy offered "chips and salsa," which got a laugh, through I'm not certain there was any on board.

We were still in the air when one of the SEAL warriors handed me a beautifully folded American flag. Simply said, I have never felt prouder to be an American.

One of the guys was the FBI Hostage Rescue Team member on the scene, and he pulled a unit insignia patch from his uniform and handed it to me, saying it was a custom to award one directly from the strike team to any successfully rescued hostage. I didn't know anything about such a custom, but it made no difference to me in that moment if it was a thousand years old or invented on the spot from one man's kindness. I did my best not to completely break down under a very humble sense of gratitude and relief. There was mixed success with that one.

It was so hard to respond, filled with indescribable emotions and completely overwhelmed. But once we were on the ground I was clearheaded enough to hurry to the cockpit and profusely thank the pilots for getting us out. I kept thanking each man on the team while I passed him in the aisle or he passed me. I think I thanked a few of them several times.

Sunrise came a little after six-thirty, and although we landed in early morning light we deplaned to a wave of heat so intense it nearly slapped me back inside. A whole new crowd of people were waiting for us at the plane's exit, and they quickly whisked us out of there. I looked back for the soldiers who rescued us, but they had already melted away.

CHAPTER TWENTY-NINE

Jessica:

My first contact on the ground was a psychiatrist named Dr. Ray, who worked with the Department of Defense. Their concern was the specific level of treatment we experienced. I didn't mind telling him whatever I could, but I doubt I was all that clear yet. We interviewed in his DOD van, and the air-conditioning was exquisite. While we talked he offered me the small supply of junk food they were able to pull from vending machines at that early hour. I was so starved for nutrition that these items were beyond delicious; I could actually feel my body soaking up the energy they provided.

I suppose he decided I was okay to pass on to the next stage of the debriefing process, pleased, perhaps, that I wasn't raving. We went next to the clinic for a more thorough medical exam. The experience was extraordinary; they were all so kind. Maybe it was the contrast of their civility with months of random insults, outbursts of violence, and medical neglect. I kept choking up at the sound of civil voices addressing me with gentleness and courtesy.

A young female doctor took me to a private room and asked if I had been raped. There would be a much different protocol if the threat of HIV/AIDS was involved. I explained that I didn't know why a full sexual attack never took place, given the callous attitudes of the men, but I was happy to report that unwanted pregnancy or STDs weren't going to be an issue.

This greatly simplified my treatment, leaving me yet another reason to be grateful the SEAL attackers arrived before Jabreel's inevitable attack, or Abdi's, or that of any of the men who arrived and departed on the breezes out there. The more I thought about the perfection of the raid's timing, right down to the dark of the moon and the careless guards, the more unreal it appeared. I had to get very small in my thinking and just take one moment after the next, to keep from being completely overloaded.

The nurse made a fresh pot of coffee and brought me a cup with sugar and cream. Until the moment I tasted the brew I hadn't realized the taste of coffee with sugar and cream was a basic sense-memory for me, fundamental to the lines of memory running through my life. It was a warm reminder that this was all real.

At last I was allowed the luxury of a long, hot shower. Oh, it was good, though it wasn't going to be too long, this time; since the FBI was eager to interview us and gain anything they could about the surviving kidnappers. I agreed to do whatever they asked, feeling no desire to argue with people who had just brought me back for one more chance at life, a surprise do-over after lengthy head-time spent considering how that life might best be employed, if it was somehow returned to me.

So I stood in that first shower washing away layers of dirt, noticing how bony I was to my own touch. I not only had a sense of being unreal within these surroundings, I felt unreal to myself. The dirt rinsed away well enough, but how dark were the stains on me going to be in the long run? I stood in the thick steam under the luxury of running water and safety and privacy, wondering who was under the hot spray.

I remembered who I had been, well enough. But I had no clear sense of who remained after this experience, or how I was to return to ordinary life, do ordinary things. All I felt certain about was that this experience had swept through my life with a wide broom, pushing away so much that seemed terribly important, right up until that first automatic rifle barrel was thrust into my face.

I soaped myself all over for maybe the fourth or fifth time and loved the sensations of shaving my legs. I know the ritual is considered pointless in some parts of the world, but it's a basic part of my picture of myself, and I was surprised by how good it felt. The ritual had power, voodoolike in its ability to act on me and restore some of the fundamental sensations of how it is supposed to feel to be myself, living in my body as I know it, and in my world as I choose to exist in it. Simple personal grooming restored some part of me in a genuine rush of strength and determination.

I was already resolved to make it the first thing I did in this new second chance at life to convince Erik our priorities had been shifted by this thing. We had to start avoiding such long work hours. We had to stop taking risks in the field and instead live like people who intended to have a full family life together and survive long enough to live it out. And of course that meant we would resume our efforts to get pregnant and not allow this thing to interrupt what had been so important to us before it all began.

Because the one thing that emerged stronger and clearer to me out of this experience was the certain knowledge that I wanted more than anything else to be a mother. That and my love for Erik were ultimately the strongest forces to keep my hopes for the future intact when illness and despair would have otherwise taken me away, perhaps long before rescuers had the chance to arrive.

It's funny how the act of getting nice and clean clears up your thinking. I stepped out of the shower convinced that even though I was still full of doubt over my impeded social abilities, I was now clearly focused on the next step for me in this life with Erik in Africa, or anywhere else we might live in the future. I dried with an actual bath towel, thick and freshly laundered, and then opened the toiletry kit some of the men had gallantly assembled for me. I noticed there were four sports bras in various sizes but no panties. Well-intentioned males: You've gotta love 'em.

I timidly asked a nurse about it. She gave an embarrassed laugh and had somebody bring me some underwear, but they turned out to be an extra-large pair of granny panties. Did I object? Are you kidding? They were actual underwear, clean, and meant for a woman.

I was getting anxious to see Erik, but one of the first things they got across to me in my initial psych interview was their official concern for how and when Erik and I were to be reunited. Nobody knew if I was going to go hysterical, blame him somehow, scream recriminations, slap and claw at him—I guess they'd seen a wide range of behavior from people held in captivity for long periods.

I felt no such anger or desire to cast blame on him, but I also had to privately admit I wouldn't really be able to judge the effect of all this until Erik and I were back together and in a situation where we could talk it out. I knew he'd been racked with worry, and it seemed obvious the best way to bring a halt to that was for us to reunite without delay. So while I was eager to cooperate with my rescuers, their concerns sounded a little dramatic to me.

They told me my initial phone calls to Erik and my father should be kept to a maximum of five minutes each. So I steeled myself for another couple of stilted, brief conversations that would at least be something, some small bit of direct contact.

My first attempt to get through to Erik failed, so I tried my dad's cell phone and got him on the first try. "Jess!" he cried out, and this man who was usually not an emotional guy sounded ecstatic. He called to my sister, who was right there with him, and she got on the line with us. We all cried together in sheer relief, and I apologized profusely for putting them through months of hell. Our call was short, but the effect on each of us was powerful.

Shortly afterward, one of the FBI agents walked in with his phone, saying Erik was on the line. As eager as I felt to take that call, from the moment we lurched into the conversation, I began to understand the reasons for restricting initial contact. The floodgates of emotion opened wide. We were both completely overcome, dissolving into tears. I felt nearly too stunned to speak. His voice sounded so good, just as I remembered it, sweet and loving. We could do little more than assure one another, over and over, that we still loved each other, no matter what.

"But, Erik," I told him just before the phone was taken away from me, "I need to tell you that we're going to have to have a long talk."

"Of course, Jess! Of course! We have so much to talk about, everything that happened—"

"No, Erik," I interrupted him. "I mean us. We have to do things differently from now on."

"We will! We will, Jess. Whatever you want. Your NGO is arranging to fly me to you as soon as possible. Jess, I can't wait to see you! Honey, I'm so sorry that all this happened, but we have the rest of our lives to figure things out. It will all be good."

"I can't go there now. We have to talk. We have to do better this time. For now, I just want you to please get out of Hargeisa and away from any revenge these guys might be planning. We have to think about their desire for retaliation."

"All right, I'm leaving for the airport soon. God, Jess, I can't wait to see you!"

We hung up a few moments later, each one assuring the other our love was alive and well. Still, as soon as the call ended I felt the full force of the wisdom behind the restricted time on first calls to loved ones. I was emotionally wrung out.

Somebody brought more coffee, and then somehow, running on adrenaline and repeated doses of caffeine, I sustained eight straight hours of interviews. We drew up a complete list of the kidnappers, including names, physical characteristics, personality traits, and personal strengths and weaknesses.

Once the FBI and the doctors were finally convinced they had learned everything they were going to get from me and the doctors had tested everything there was to test, they finally released me to go get some sleep. Poul and I ran into each other in the clinic hallway, and all I could do was put my head on his shoulder and weep. He just stood there and quietly hugged me back.

I got my first sleep on the plane, at last, twelve hours after arriving in Djibouti. I lay down wrapped in a thick sleeping bag and strapped into a canvas medical stretcher on the biggest cargo plane I've ever seen, this one bound for a U.S. military base in Italy. I was soon oblivious and slept soundly for most of the trip, unperturbed by the noise of the engines or the other people around me. It was my first safe sleep in months, and that narrow little stretcher was a beautiful luxury. The sense of peace and safety was so strong, a deep slumber held me in its grip throughout the flight.

CHAPTER THIRTY

Erik arrived in Italy to learn that the authorities wouldn't allow him to see Jessica yet and required him to wait until the following day. The psychologists with the hostage reintegration program had long experience in working with hostage returnees and believed even five minutes together might be too much for reunited loved ones. Their experience showed them how immersion back into one's life needs to be slow and careful, like climbing into a steaming hot tub.

Jessica remained in a private room with the first real bed she'd been on since her capture. The staff traded her ragged clothing for fresh, warm winter items and the first shoes she had felt in months. She was surprised by how strange it felt to have real shoes on her feet.

The next day she paced the floor in her room with the door cracked open a few inches while she waited for Erik to arrive for their first brief session together. She gasped when she saw his fingers reach around the edge of the door and pull it open. A moment later, there he was for her and there she was for him, and they fell into each other's arms, both of them openly sobbing.

"Jess," Erik struggled to speak, "before we say anything, I want you to know your family has been so strong—all of us are much closer because of this—and they feel the same as I do. We'll do anything we need to, in order to get you one hundred percent back to your life. I want you to know that whatever happened to you, Jess, I don't care. I love you. I'll always love you. If you need time away from me, just tell me. Please. I'll give you all the room you want."

"Stop," she quietly told him. "Stop. I don't need time alone and we aren't splitting up."

"Jess, as long as we're together, I can do anything. I want you to know I'll do whatever you need me to do. Anything you need."

"Listen," she whispered into his ear. "Listen to me. We're not splitting up. You aren't going anywhere. I'm not leaving you. Erik, I never thought I'd see you again. It was the thought of us together that kept me alive." She leaned back and looked into his eyes. "But we're going to have to do things differently, now."

"Okay."

"More time together. No more workaholic hours."

"Yes. Okay. Good."

She smiled at him. "And I want us to go right back to starting our family. I want a baby."

He threw his arms around her again and suddenly neither of them had much more to say except to assure each other that no damage to their love and devotion had taken place. They spent most of that first session holding each other and murmuring terms of endearment.

Before they knew it their scheduled hour was over. They made arrangements to meet for lunch the following day for a longer session under doctor's supervision, for more detailed conversation and the million questions each one had. By the time Erik left her there after that first encounter, not even her happiness and gratitude could escape the exhaustion gripping her.

They met the next day for a much longer session. The emotions were powerful, but by the time their second day's meeting was over, Jessica and Erik knew their relationship had survived. They went through the rest of their family reunions as a dedicated couple, amazed at their good fortune and determined not to waste this second chance at life.

For John Buchanan, as well as Jessica's brother and sister, the final payoff came when they all united in Portland, Oregon, to spend a week together and do nothing but work on reconnecting with one another. His steadfast patience and faith in the eventual outcome had brought him back to a full reunion with all three of his children.

◆ ◆ ◆

President Barack Obama addressed the press about the rescue in Somalia by SEAL Team Six on January 25, 2012, saying, "The United States will not tolerate the abduction of our people, and will spare no effort to secure the safety of our citizens and to bring their captors to justice."

Back in Somalia, at the ruined campsite outside "The International City of Adado," there was no room for doubt about the truth of the president's statement for the ones hauling away the bodies of the felled captors. The folly of attracting military attention by kidnapping innocent civilians will undoubtedly be discussed in the lairs of future kidnappers. One of them will undoubtedly be Jabreel himself.

Dan Hardy showed Erik a text message he sent to Jabreel's phone after the rescue. Though Jabreel was lucky enough to have been absent from the camp that night, he surely felt less fortunate when the message arrived. Nobody on the case was forgetting how Jabreel had toyed with them over long months of negotiations. Nor were they forgetting about his personal torments of Jessica throughout that time, which now were known by everyone involved. The message contained only three simple words, sent for him to consider while he looked back on the experience, as he would surely do.

"*You're next, motherf**ker.*"

Jabreel's cell phone account immediately went dead.

The statement was hardly mere bravado, as Jabreel and the surviving kidnappers now know from experience. Matt Espenshade confirmed that in spite of the deaths of so many of the kidnappers, many more are still at large, including their leaders. Those men might hope to be forgotten; they are not. The FBI has continued its investigative interest in those involved with the kidnapping. The leaders, especially, are of prime interest to the Bureau. And now the considerable unseen assets in that region are steadily feeding back information on these targeted individuals to learn their operational methods and their locations and hunt them down.

The surviving kidnappers and their colleagues are welcome to sneer at the danger. It may help them pass the time, just as it did for Bin Laden's henchmen to chuckle at the idea of payback. If the men nobody sees coming are dispatched to capture or kill them, the surviving kidnappers will find themselves dealing with a force of air, sea, and land fighters so obsessed with the work they do that they have trained themselves into the physical and mental toughness of world-class athletes. They will carry the latest in weapons, armor, visual systems, and communication devices. Whether they are Navy SEAL fighters, DEVGRU warriors, Army Delta Force soldiers, Green Berets, or any of the elite soldiers under United States Special Operations Command (SOCOM), they will share the elite warriors' determination to achieve success in their mission assignment.

The news that they are coming for you is the worst you could receive. But nobody gets advance warning from these men. They consider themselves born for this. They have fought like panthers to be part of their team. For most of them, there is a strong sense of pride in succeeding at missions nobody else can get done; in lethal challenges. They actually prefer levels of difficulty so high it seems only a sucker would seek them, the sorts of situations seen more and more often these days. Impossible odds.

Epilogue

Erik:

I was especially moved by prayer groups that steadfastly remained active on behalf of Jess and her colleague, Poul Thisted, because they did this without inquiring whether Jess or Poul held their beliefs. In today's divisive climate, how often is such acceptance shown?

Before anyone gets caught up in useless debates about religion, there is the simple question of whether one feels a sense of spirituality in the experience of being alive. Either we do or we don't. All dogma aside, it seems to me that the perception of a benevolent source of order to our existence is all that's necessary to truthfully claim a spiritual life.

And I can say no matter what forces kept Jess alive and protected from murder or rape by ideologues or by thugs, those forces worked magnificently well and beyond any practical explanation. She was somehow protected from the worst, in a time and place where the worst was very likely to occur.

Our family's love was the primary source of our endurance. It steadied me when the terrible time came to make sure the entire command chain knew when the three requirements were met for ordering an armed attack, but it also helped me stand firm against taking violent action if there was any chance at all for a peaceful resolution. They helped me shoulder the responsibility of instigating the military action that I knew might get Jess killed.

Those many expressions of love are what propelled our end of this miracle, really. I say this knowing it will cause a certain rolling of the eyes among some. Coming from my nonreligious background, I understand all the arguments behind the eye-rolling.

It's just that I was there, that's all. I saw the real-world effects of forces that cannot themselves be seen. I saw other people's spiritual sense—not their religion, not their church attendance—keep them afloat and hold them steady. I saw this shared sense binding people together in mutual reinforcement instead of driving them apart with disputes and recriminations, as terrible stress can do.

Never, throughout this ordeal, did I hear anyone's description of God. I didn't hear anyone's opinion of the validity of the Bible, the Koran, the Vedas. I still have no idea what those people visualize when they pray, or what they would tell me if I asked them why they pray at all.

And yet even though love itself is invisible, I saw the tracks of it everywhere along this bizarre journey, and they were just as real and clear as tracks along a safari trail. It finds a home in the common truth revealed by their shared actions, and that truth is profoundly simple: God is love.

Forget all the fine print. Forget the edicts, the authorities, the fear, the guilt. Forget all the shiny robes.

God is love. My acceptance of that simple but powerful idea is merely one of the jewels Jess has brought into my life. And the concept is part of what our son will hear from us when he grows older and it's time to tell him this story. If he asks where God was to be found during this ordeal, he will be pointed toward that invisible force. He will be able to follow the story and watch this force in action, moving all those people around to help his mom return home, so he could be born to us.

◆ ◆ ◆

Jessica:

No matter how many doubts I had about this new future of mine, of ours, I felt them all overpowered by my determination to tell this story to my children one day, and to have happy and healthy children to tell it to. It was apparent this could only happen if I truly moved on. Enough trauma already.

I had plenty of personal fears about my recovery, but they got trumped by a deep yearning, heavy as a falling rock. That yearning blew through obstacles, pulled along by the gravitational force of the ones who matter the most to us. This yearning was so strong I couldn't let myself buy into the official worries about whether I could handle the return. It just needed to be handled. It had to be handled.

The professionals around me were careful and kind, fortunately, but the need to get back to my life remained strong. I did my best to cooperate with all the interview and testing procedures in their hostage recovery program to keep things moving along and just kept smiling at everybody. Nothing wrong here, folks.

The official concern was that after having no control over any part of everyday life for so long, I wouldn't know how to function in an ordinary manner out there in general society. I could certainly agree with their question about whether I would get myself past all this, but there was never one moment of those ninety-three days when I doubted that I wanted to be back with Erik. For me, with the rescue behind us, the simplest way to get back together was to let it happen. Let us be together.

It was only in the aftermath that I found myself able to grasp the scope of the operation executed by SEAL Team Six, and the apparent size of their extensive command and support operations on the ground. It forces an uncomfortable question: Am I worth it? Is anyone?

Well, I can tell you that on top of my many points of gratitude for the way this story played out, I am grateful most of all for the will of the American people as expressed in the policy of the United States, and for *any other nation* that will assert that yes, we are worth it—all of us. For now, let me just say how wonderful it is to be back in sync with a reality that is precious to me, so warm and intimate that I dare to grow bored from time to time. But even the boredom is good, because it is my own, it is my chosen use of that enchanted moment of a life I was never favored to regain.

People ask what I intend to do with my renewed life, and I can tell you nothing has softened my conviction that one of the world's enduring obstacles to development is the issue of education for children. This basic right is accepted in the United States and Europe—but not always in Africa and the developing countries. I will continue working on the problem as best I can with caring and qualified people.

The overall effect of this experience has been to renew the spiritual sense in my life. I'd gone through a dark time after my mother's death and felt so alone without her. I'm afraid I needed something to shake me out of my anger over losing her so early. It was the months in captivity that brought me back to the same sentiment I saw my father express in the middle of his grief over losing Mom, "God, I don't understand you but I am choosing to trust you." In his pain on that day, he gave me a gift I didn't recognize until much later. I saw it out there while I was captive under the trees. I see it now.

When it came to the simple goals of rejoining Erik, finally having our baby together, and beginning our family life, the odds against us were impossible. Therefore we will raise this family with the knowledge that every day leading forward from this new beginning is truly a gift, a wonderful thing whose value cannot be measured.

Just over nine months after her rescue, Jessica and Erik greeted the arrival of their son, August.
© *Erik Esbjörnsson*

Afterword

Jessica:

As I sat day after day in captivity, struggling not to lose my sanity to boredom, frustration, and lack of control, I made a promise to myself that should I ever be fortunate enough to live something that even remotely resembled a life—or more important, *my life*— I would never again complain about mundane tasks.

Prior to the kidnapping, it had been our long-term plan to live in East Africa, to raise our family there, and continue to work in our respective sectors for as long as we could. I had always imagined my children running free in the African sun, barefoot and without a care in the world. But, when things in life go wrong, as they often do, new plans must be formed and dreams become just dreams, so I had to adjust those images to something else. My heart and mind felt sort of empty. Erik and I knew we had many loose ends that needed to be tied up, both professionally and personally, and so after time together with our families in the United States and Europe following my rescue, we decided it was time to go back and take care of them. We knew we could not let the pirates dictate our future; they had already decided too many things in our past. We had to take back control of our own lives and make it *our* decision to leave the continent that we had made a life in and loved so much. Those who understood us held us tightly, and then let us go. They watched as we boarded a plane bound for Nairobi, hand in hand, with little August in my belly.

We found a safe place to live and did our best to sort things out. We found comfort in being close to friends who were living and working in the area. Many of them had been there for Erik and my family during the course of the kidnapping and needed the closure of seeing me and us together in order to move on. After all, it wasn't just me, Erik, and our families who had been traumatized by this whole ordeal. Erik carried on working in and out of Somaliland and Somalia for short stints, spending most of his time with me in Nairobi. I worked on recovering, all the while pregnant, with much support from caring friends.

Shortly after August was born, it was surprisingly clear that it was time to decide whether or not to stay in Africa. As heartbreaking as it was to leave our dream, we finally concluded that it would be best for us to relocate to the United States in order to be closer to family and to start a new chapter—actually, a whole new life. So with that in our hearts, Erik and I decided to set out on a new adventure and begin life as a family (including our dog, Smulan) in Washington, D.C. This enabled us to be near to my dad and to carry on with development work. While we weren't *in* Africa, we were hopeful we could still work *with* Africa.

It had been almost seven years since I'd lived in the United States, but now I'd come back as a wife, a mother, and a survivor. I was completely overwhelmed with the options and opportunities that were being presented to me. People wanted to hear our story—of captivity and rescue—but they were also asking difficult questions. Did we still believe in the humanitarian world and the issues affecting the countries like Somalia? How had my kidnapping affected everyday life? Would we ever consider going back to Africa?

After some time and immersion into a culture that had changed so much since I last called it home, I decided that I still very much believed in making necessary changes *anywhere* in the world where men, women, and children don't have access to food, clean water, health care, and education. It doesn't just have to be Africa, it can be here in the United States. Africa will always be in my heart, along with its constant range of issues. However, I understand that there are many people right here who need help, and I hope to continue working to promote awareness and assistance in whatever capacity I can.

One of the greatest opportunities I have been afforded since relocating to the United States is to work closely with the Navy SEAL Foundation—a group that is tirelessly working to provide support to families of fallen SEALs. Having attended many events in which I've had the immense honor of meeting and being in the company of retired and active-duty SEALs, as well as their wives and children, has deepened my sense of gratitude in a way that is difficult to put into words. I will never be able to repay them for bringing me back to life, but with every speech I make, I feel a little more connected to them, as if we are all working together for the future, somehow, and for each other. And no, I haven't met "my" SEALs. I never will—but I've been assured they know how grateful I am.

Erik and I continue to share our lessons learned with a wide range of different groups around the United States and Europe. We've had the opportunity to meet with, as well as learn from, others who have had significant challenges of their own. One does not endure hardship and survive cruelty and keep it to one's self.

While I am still in the early stages of motherhood, I realize that it's been a second type of rescue that I did not expect, and have at times, resisted. Because I had very little choice in the matter, I decided early on to surrender to it in a slow and sleep-deprived way, and as I have learned throughout the last couple of years, I will not take on more than I can handle. Having August, feeling him grow in my belly and now being witness to this beautiful thriving being who is willful and loving and full of life, is a constant reminder that I must trust. It's a constant reminder that I *can* trust. I can trust my instincts and my intuition. Even though I once ignored their crucial importance in my life prior to the kidnapping, I have been given a second chance of sorts, and being a mother has shown me that they are not broken. Indeed, they are very alive, and I must rely on them heavily when everything else seems difficult and sometimes very confusing. August has been a healing balm to the deep wounds that otherwise could have become very infected by self-pity, anger and an inability to forgive. He teaches me grace and allows me to be easy on myself and to take my time. He is my greatest teacher and loves me unconditionally. He will forever be my hero.

There are still a litany of issues that I continue to work through both consciously and subconsciously. I suspect they will always be there—maybe moving more to my subconscious over time. Sharing my experience has certainly helped me process, and I believe there is more to discover as to how this will continue to shape my life.

I still wake up every morning with my father's prayer on my lips. Although I do not understand so many things, even still, I hope I will continue to trust that this has been a part of my path, my journey. I'm still young, there is a lot more to travel, and I'm reminded by that when I watch Erik and August running through the house, giggling and screaming, whiling away hours on a snowy afternoon. I don't have to go anywhere, be anyone, do anything. I am as free as free gets, and so I join in the giggling and the screaming.

The beauty of the prayer now is that Erik and August are snuggled up next to me every morning when my heart whispers those words. I'm not alone in the desert anymore, and so most days I feel okay in not understanding. I have a renewed strength to trust in this beautiful, abnormal yet normal thing called my life. It's not always easy, but again, anything worth having always takes a lot of work. The trick is to understand that the work didn't end with the rescue. But like I said at the beginning, all I wanted was to have something to *do*, no matter how mundane. Life may not be boring, but it's mine, and it's all that matters for the moment.

Selected References

1. Bahadur, Jay. *The Pirates of Somalia: Inside Their Hidden World* (New York: Dutton, 2011).
2. Wasdin, Howard E., and Templin, Stephen. *SEAL Team Six: Memoirs of an Elite Navy SEAL Sniper* (New York: St. Martin's Press, 2011).
3. Owen, Mark, with Lewis, Iowan M. *No Easy Day* (New York: Dutton, 2012).
4. Lewis, Iowan M. *Understanding Somalia and Somaliland: Culture, History, Society* (New York: Columbia/Hurst, 2011).
5. Harper, Mary Jane. *Getting Somalia Wrong? Faith, War and Hope in a Shattered State* (African Arguments) (London, ZED Books, 2012).
6. Biset, Blain, *"Reduce Poverty in Africa—Educate a Girl"* (allAfrica.com, face page, English Edition, October 11, 2012).

Acknowledgments

From Anthony:

I will always be grateful to Erik and Jessica for trusting me to write their story. They endured months of long Skype interviews and my endless questions across the time difference of many hours between Seattle and Nairobi, and did so with graceful patience.

Atria Books' Senior Editor Sarah Durand was indispensible to this project. She pursued this story with determination, acquired the book rights, and approved the unconventional narrative style I was convinced this story needed. She has been a creative and positive advocate for this book from the beginning, guiding it through the publication process with sensitivity and skill, along with her most capable assistant, Daniella Wexler.

Any book's fate rests with the talents and abilities of its publishing team. Judith Curr, Publisher at Atria Books, and Paul Olsewski, Atria's Vice President and Director of Publicity, put enough publishing muscle behind this book to see to it the world would come to know this story.

Ann Clark at Edelman Public Relations handled the initial media barrage following the kidnapping and aggressively maintained Jessica and Erik's privacy during their reunion.

And finally, Sharlene Martin of Martin Literary Management put her company's weight and personal acumen behind bringing this story to the world. The results of her efforts are here in every line.

From Erik:

To Jess: For being the magnificent person you are. Words cannot describe the love and admiration I feel for you. The courage and determination you showed during our horrible days apart as well as in the aftermath has cemented those feelings. Waking up by your side every day is a treasure, and we will now get to see and experience all those things we postponed, together. What an amazing gift, to share life with the person you love.

To John Buchanan: For believing in me when doubt and animosity could have been the easier ways out. When times were tough you remained faithful and determined that Jess would come back alive and you gave me the strength I needed. The endless hours we spent on the phone were of paramount importance to me. Your dedication is inspiring. I am proud to be part of your family and I am learning by your example.

To President Barack Obama: For your personal commitment in making it possible to rescue Jess. So many things could have gone wrong, but you made the tough decision that was needed, and for that reason Jess is alive today.

To Navy SEAL Team Six: I understand you did your jobs that dark night on January 25, 2012, but for me you did much more, risking yourselves to give life back to my family. I also want to extend a special acknowledgment to your families in the United States, for supporting and allowing you to do this vital work.

To the FBI (and "other agencies" involved): For the impressive work conducted during Jess's captivity, rescue, and postrelease, I will never understand the full extent of your work, but the dedication and devotion shown by the people I have had the pleasure of meeting speaks for itself.

To Matt Espenshade: For your professional and personal involvement in our struggle. You reached beyond what anyone could have asked for. Simply put, without you, Jess and I would most likely not have had the opportunity to tell our story.

To Ann Soucy, Dan Hardy, and the Crisis Management Team: For all the hard work you did during this ordeal and for listening when needed and reacting when needed even more.

To Leila Gupta, our Crisis Counselor: For being there at the right time for me, Jess, and her family; your professional advice and ability to listen were crucial for all of us.

To Poul: For having been there for Jess during the ninety-three days of captivity. I know how much you helped each other and found strength in each other's company.

To Amy and Stephen: For being the resourceful persons you are; you never stopped believing in your sister, and when times were tough you kept on reminding me how strong Jess is. You both had to endure so much during this time and yet you remained positive.

To Anthony and Sharlene: For taking such an interest in our lives and the story we have to tell. How nice it has been to work with both of you. Without you, none of this would have been possible.

To my parents, Johan and Lena: For having been the best parents I could wish for. Without your support and belief in me I would not have come to Africa and Somalia in the first place. Even though you were not always happy about it, you accepted it. You are both role models in your own unique ways and I hope to follow your example, providing your grandson with the unconditional love you have always shown to me.

To my sister, Linnea: For always loving and being there for me, in hard times and in good times, and for now being such a wonderful auntie to our son, August. I am so proud to have you as my sister.

To all you known and unknown friends around the world, believers of different faiths and nonbelievers alike, who gave strength to us during this ordeal with your thoughts and prayers, my deep and enduring thanks.

From Jessica:

To Erik: I never knew I could love someone so much until I found myself in the middle of that desert, wondering if I would ever see you again. I was always sure you were back at home beating down every door, shouting at anyone who would listen, and exhausting every option to ensure my freedom. Thank you for all you did then and for all you continue to do for me now. You are a gift of a husband, my best friend, confidant, and the love of my life.

To Daddy: Every morning I would call upon your strength and your faith, believing that your prayers for me were reaching high into the heavens. Thank you for your unwavering love, support, and wisdom throughout this whole ordeal. I couldn't have gotten through this without you.

To Mama: I missed you then and I miss you now. Thank you for holding me when I was so afraid, stroking my hair and keeping me safe, whispering reassurances to me that if I didn't make it, you were waiting for me on the other side. I'll see you when I get there . . .

To Amy and Stephen: What incredibly beautiful, strong, courageous siblings I have. You both are gifts that I treasure beyond measure. I continued to hope and believe, during those dark moments, that I would live to see you both have families and that we would all grow old together. What a privilege it is to know you both, and to witness all that you are accomplishing in your lives. Thank you for not giving up on me, and most of all, for understanding me.

To Matt, the FBI Team, and other government agencies: Thank you for your tireless efforts to find and rescue me. Because of your commitment to your jobs, I am alive today. Matt—not only did you put in far more than many others would, on a professional level, you also gave the extra measure of support Erik and my family so desperately needed to survive this ordeal. I know you didn't have to do that, and I am infinitely grateful to you and your family for the sacrifices you made to ensure my safe rescue.

To the CMT (Crisis Management Team): Thank you for all the efforts you made to ensure my release and safe return. I understand it was a horrific ninety-three days for you as well and am so very grateful for all you did to help get us through.

To Poul: "Still is still moving." Thank you for that beautiful meditative reminder, so helpful in keeping me strong out there. You protected my mind as well as kept me physically safe, and I will always admire you for the way you live out your beliefs through your work.

To President Obama and SEAL Team Six: Thank you will never be enough to express my gratitude for the difficult decisions you had to make, and the risks you had to take, so that I could have my life back. I have never been prouder to be an American and hope I can continue to live my life in a way that makes America proud to belong to me. To the heroic members of SEAL Team Six, thank you for risking your lives to save mine. I will never understand how you do what you do, but my respect for the service and sacrifice you each make continues to grow as I comprehend all you have done for me.

To Anthony and Sharlene: Thank you for finding our story worth telling, and for helping us tell it in a way that we can be proud to someday show our son. You were the first to hear the whole story and we will always hold you dear to our hearts.

To friends around the world: Thank you infinitely for your love, prayers, and thoughts. They lifted me up over and over during my captivity. I felt that energy giving me strength to get up and endure every morning, bringing me peace every afternoon. My heart is so grateful for the kindness you have shown to me and my family.

Index